# TAKING CHILDREN AND YOUNG PEOPLE SERIOUSLY

Children and young people are active agents with motives and intentions who can contribute to their social worlds. Taking children seriously involves both accessing their perspectives as they make sense of the world and working relationally with them to guide their motive orientations. In this book, Hedegaard and Edwards draw upon their own and others' research on children from birth to school leaving age to advocate for relational support for learners and to emphasize the caring aspects of this support. The authors provide a scholarly account of the cultural-historical underpinnings of their caring relational approach, while bringing these ideas to life through examples of practices in families and in more formal settings. Written for those who work with children and young people in varied capacities, this book reveals the knowledge and skills required for the subtle and reciprocal work of supporting the learning and development of children and young people.

MARIANE HEDEGAARD is Professor Emerita in the Department of Psychology at Copenhagen University, Denmark. She is also a senior research fellow in the Department of Education at the University of Oxford, UK and has an honorary degree from the University of Pablo de Olavide, Spain. The relations between children's motive orientation and institutional demands are central themes in her work. She has authored and edited several books, including *Motives in Children's Development* (2012) and *Learning, Play and Children's Development* (2013).

ANNE EDWARDS is Professor Emerita in the Department of Education at the University of Oxford, UK. She has honorary doctorates from the University of Helsinki, Finland and the University of Oslo, Norway for her work on cultural-historical approaches to learning across the lifespan. In 2022 her lifetime's contribution to the field was recognized by the Cultural-Historical Research Special Interest Group of the American Educational Research Association.

# TAKING CHILDREN AND YOUNG PEOPLE SERIOUSLY

*A Caring Relational Approach to Education*

MARIANE HEDEGAARD

*University of Copenhagen*

ANNE EDWARDS

*University of Oxford*

Shaftesbury Road, Cambridge CB2 8EA, United Kingdom

One Liberty Plaza, 20th Floor, New York, NY 10006, USA

477 Williamstown Road, Port Melbourne, VIC 3207, Australia

314–321, 3rd Floor, Plot 3, Splendor Forum, Jasola District Centre, New Delhi – 110025, India

103 Penang Road, #05–06/07, Visioncrest Commercial, Singapore 238467

Cambridge University Press is part of Cambridge University Press & Assessment, a department of the University of Cambridge.

We share the University's mission to contribute to society through the pursuit of education, learning and research at the highest international levels of excellence.

www.cambridge.org
Information on this title: www.cambridge.org/9781108833486

DOI: 10.1017/9781108980869

© Mariane Hedegaard and Anne Edwards 2023

This publication is in copyright. Subject to statutory exception and to the provisions of relevant collective licensing agreements, no reproduction of any part may take place without the written permission of Cambridge University Press & Assessment.

First published 2023

*A catalogue record for this publication is available from the British Library.*

*Library of Congress Cataloging-in-Publication Data*
NAMES: Hedegaard, Mariane, author. | Edwards, Anne, 1946- author.
TITLE: Taking children and young people seriously : a caring relational approach to education / Mariane Hedegaard, University of Copenhagen, Anne Edwards, University of Oxford.
DESCRIPTION: First edition. | New York : Cambridge University Press, 2023. | Includes bibliographical references and index.
IDENTIFIERS: LCCN 2022052981 (print) | LCCN 2022052982 (ebook) | ISBN 9781108833486 (hardback) | ISBN 9781108970518 (paperback) | ISBN 9781108980869 (epub)
SUBJECTS: LCSH: Learning, Psychology of. | Communication in education. | Child development. | Teacher-student relationships. | Children and adults.
CLASSIFICATION: LCC LB1060 .H394 2023 (print) | LCC LB1060 (ebook) | DDC 370.15–dc23/eng/20230210
LC record available at https://lccn.loc.gov/2022052981
LC ebook record available at https://lccn.loc.gov/2022052982

ISBN 978-1-108-83348-6 Hardback

Cambridge University Press & Assessment has no responsibility for the persistence or accuracy of URLs for external or third-party internet websites referred to in this publication and does not guarantee that any content on such websites is, or will remain, accurate or appropriate.

# Contents

| | |
|---|---|
| List of Figures | page ix |
| List of Tables | xi |

### 1 Taking Children and Young People Seriously: A Caring Relational Approach to Education — 1
- Introduction — 1
- The Cultural-Historical Theoretical Underpinnings of Understanding Children's Development — 4
- A Wholeness Approach — 7
- A Relational Approach to Education — 12
- Unfolding Agency for Social Inclusion — 15
- How the Book Is Organized — 16

### 2 A Cultural-Historical Approach to Children's Development and Childhood — 19
- Introduction — 19
- A Wholeness Approach — 19
- A Society Creates Conditions for Children's Development through Different Forms of Institutional Practices — 23
- Age Periods Framed by Leading Relations — 29
- Children's Emotional Crises Indicating Developmental Changes in Their Motive Orientation — 34
- The Zone of Proximal Development Seen from the Perspective of Different Age Periods Characterized by Different Learning Forms — 40
- Methodology: Age Periods and the Child's Social Situation of Development — 43
- Final Reflections — 46

### 3 Working Relationally with Other Professionals and Families — 48
- Introduction — 48
- The Three Relational Concepts in Work with Other Professionals and with Families — 49
- Relational Support for Children in Transitions — 53

| | | |
|---|---|---|
| | Working Relationally across Roles and Positions | 55 |
| | Building Common Knowledge in the Space of Reasons | 57 |
| | Working Relationally for Social Inclusion in and across Institutions | 62 |
| | Using the Relational Concepts to Assess and Develop Collaboration for the Support of Children | 65 |
| | Final Reflections | 67 |
| 4 | **Very Young Children: Taking a Double Perspective in Understanding Their Development** | **68** |
| | Introduction | 68 |
| | Communication as the Key to Young Children's Development | 70 |
| | The Changing Dynamic between Caregivers and Infants in Different Phases in Children's Development | 73 |
| | The Neonate's Social Situation of Development | 73 |
| | The Infant's Social Situation of Development | 76 |
| | A Nursery Child's Social Situation of Development | 83 |
| | The Interactive Observation Method | 84 |
| | Assessment of a Nursery Child's Social Situation of Development Using the Interactive Observation Method | 87 |
| | The Use of the Observation for a Critical Common-sense Interpretation | 90 |
| | Interpretation of Simon's Social Situation of Development | 92 |
| | Conclusion and Suggestions for Intervention in Simon's Everyday Nursery Activities | 93 |
| | Relational Expertise, Common Knowledge and Relational Agency: Supporting Families in Supporting Their Young Children | 94 |
| | Final Reflections | 99 |
| 5 | **Care and Education in Kindergarten with Play as the Core Activity** | **101** |
| | Introduction | 101 |
| | Ways of Learning in Kindergarten Practice | 103 |
| | Play as the Central Way to Learn in the Preschool Age | 105 |
| | Adults' Role in Children's Play | 105 |
| | Emotional Experiences and Feelings as Foundations for Children's Imagination in Play | 107 |
| | Emotional Tension in Children's Play | 111 |
| | Children's Lifeworlds and Adults' Creation of Play Worlds | 114 |
| | Assessing Children's Social Situation of Development Focusing on Activities | 118 |
| | The Design of UBUS 3 and UBUS 5 | 121 |
| | Case: Analysis of Five-Year-Old Inunaq's Development Situation | 123 |
| | Final Reflections | 125 |

| | | |
|---|---|---|
| 6 | **Engaging with Knowledge When Starting School** | 127 |
| | Introduction | 127 |
| | Transition to School | 128 |
| | Children's Development of a Motive Orientation toward School Activities | 131 |
| | Children's Learning of Word Meanings and Everyday Concepts | 133 |
| | Emotional Imagination and Motive Orientation in Play: Children's Formation of Everyday Concepts | 137 |
| | The Relation between Everyday and Scientific Concepts | 142 |
| | Final Reflections | 145 |
| 7 | **Caring Approaches to Pedagogy** | 147 |
| | Introduction | 147 |
| | Relational Work at Home | 150 |
| | Relational Work in Formal Educational Settings: Establishing Common Knowledge between Teachers and Learners | 151 |
| | A Sequence of Pedagogic Activities for Qualitative Changes in Children's Learning | 154 |
| | From Orientation to Mental Actions | 159 |
| | Developmental Teaching and Motives | 161 |
| | Working Relationally for School Inclusion | 164 |
| |     Using Common Knowledge and Relational Expertise in the Unfolding of Relational Agency | 166 |
| |     A Growth in Student Agency: A Shift in Responsibility from Teacher to Learner Over Time | 166 |
| | Final Reflections | 168 |
| 8 | **The Primary School Age: Enabling the Agentic Learner** | 170 |
| | Introduction | 170 |
| | New Demands in the Transition to School | 171 |
| | Agency, Learning and Development in the Primary School Phase | 174 |
| | Children's Development of New Motives and Concepts in Primary School | 176 |
| | Taking the Child's Perspective in Teaching | 179 |
| | Challenge and Support for Agentic Learners | 183 |
| | The Double Move and "Radical-Local Teaching and Learning" | 185 |
| | Creating Challenge and Reflective Awareness through Assessment for Learning | 187 |
| | Digital Resources and Agentic Learners | 190 |
| | Developing Self-Awareness in Primary Age Children | 196 |
| | Supporting Inclusion and Nurturing Resilience | 197 |
| | Final Reflections | 200 |

## Contents

9 **Developmental Teaching as a Double Move between Subject Knowledge and Children's Appropriation of Personal Knowledge** — 202
- Introduction — 202
- Different Collective Knowledge Forms in School Teaching — 203
- The Appropriation of Personal Knowledge in School — 208
- The Double Move Approach: Using Germ-Cell Models — 211
  - The Germ-Cell Model of the Evolution of Species Guiding the Teaching Activity — 213
  - How to Create a Motive for Engagement with Subject Matter — 213
  - Organization of Classroom Teaching — 214
  - The Development of Children's Conceptions in Relation to the Evolution of Animals — 221
- Related Experimental Teaching Projects — 222
- Culturally Sensitive Teaching — 224
- Addressing Assessment Challenges through a Double Move Approach — 230
- Final Reflections — 233

10 **Adolescence and Transitions into Early Adulthood** — 236
- Introduction — 236
- Understanding Adolescent Development — 237
- Identity Construction in Adolescence — 240
- Cultural Practices and Identity — 244
- Working Relationally for Adolescent Future-Making — 247
- Engaging Adolescents with Curricula — 250
- How Information Technology Can Support Learning in and out of School — 253
- Transitions toward Adulthood — 256
- Final Reflections — 260

11 **A Caring Relational Approach to Education: Implications for Practice and Policy** — 262
- Introduction — 262
- The Importance of Knowledgeable Practitioners — 264
- Creating Knowledgeable Practitioners — 266
- Moving Forward — 268

*References* — 271
*Index* — 295

# Figures

| | | |
|---|---|---|
| 1.1 | Different perspectives for analyzing children's development | *page* 8 |
| 2.1 | A model of children's learning and development through participating in institutionalized practices | 21 |
| 3.1 | An example of common knowledge mediating the unfolding of relational agency | 52 |
| 3.2 | A representation of a teacher–parent meeting | 62 |
| 3.3 | The Relational Agency Framework | 66 |
| 5.1 | Inunaq's UBUS 5 profile | 124 |
| 7.1 | The Quadrant Teaching and Learning Sequence: A tool for reflection (Edwards, 2014) | 154 |
| 8.1 | A model for how the psychologist consultant can be seen as a participant in developmental psychological practice development for children in a zone of concern (from Hedegaard & Chaiklin, 2011) | 181 |
| 9.1 | Models for subject-related content | 206 |
| 9.2 | Models for how the primary relation in evolution of species became extended | 207 |
| 9.3 | A child's drawing of what can be researched in biology, from the second teaching period | 216 |
| 9.4 | A child's drawing of how animals and nature belong together in Greenland, from the fourth teaching period | 219 |
| 9.5 | A child's model of how animals live together, from the 10th teaching period | 220 |
| 9.6 | The double society model | 225 |

9.7 The core model that guides the teacher's activities and the students had to understand (From Hedegaard & Chaiklin, 2005)   227
9.8 Researching the history of their community. A child's model of living conditions   228
9.9 Model for what a family needs living in a community   229

# *Tables*

| | | |
|---|---|---|
| 2.1 | Relations between demands and what moves at different analytical planes | *page* 22 |
| 2.2 | The relation between institutional practice, developmental age periods and motive orientation | 36 |
| 2.3 | Questions to evaluate a child's social situation from the interaction and demands he meets in different activity settings and his motive orientations in different social situations | 46 |
| 5.1 | Showing the difference between three- and five-year-olds in area (2) *social competence and interaction* in how the child relates to other people and creates contacts | 122 |
| 5.2 | Showing the difference between three- and five-year-olds in area (4) participation in sensation and movement activities in how they relate to other people in moving around and paying attention | 123 |
| 9.1 | Principles for Developmental Teaching | 210 |
| 9.2 | The Goal-Result-Research Procedure | 212 |
| 9.3 | Example from the questionnaire of Mathematics in Grade 3 related to the Ministry of Education's Common Goals | 232 |

CHAPTER I

# *Taking Children and Young People Seriously*
## *A Caring Relational Approach to Education*

### Introduction

This book is about children, their learning and development as active agents with motives and intentions. It is also about what practitioners can do to support children's learning, development and well-being. It is therefore relevant to adults who work with children in different age periods from birth to late adolescence, both within and beyond formal institutions. We also intend it to be useful to researchers and other professionals concerned with children and young people.

Our aim is to look forward toward children's futures and how they can be supported to benefit from and contribute to what society has to offer. We argue that, by taking children's intentions and emotions seriously, we can create an education that benefits children across the age range. Practitioners, families and other carers are therefore key. We shall offer them tools for analyzing children's development in ways that also capture practices, activities and children's experiences. We also recognize that as children move through the institutional practices that society creates for them, they will learn, acquire new motives and develop. Therefore, the tools that we offer will allow carers and practitioners to tailor their support to children in different age periods. These ideas underpin a relational form of pedagogy, which is particularly, but not only, important when children are dealing with changes in society's expectations for them. These changes occur as they move, for example, between family, day care or school or when new challenges arise in familiar situations.

One of our starting points is our concern that so many of society's expectations for children are backward-looking, trying to fit children into institutions that have changed little. Sadly, these expectations do not recognize what children bring to situations from their life experiences or their motives for engaging with what education offers. We of course value powerful knowledge and, for example, want school-age children to be able to work knowledgeably on problems. But approaches to education that don't pay attention to emotion, motive and agency, and which do not allow rounded pictures of children, are short-changing them. The result is that many children fail to engage with formal learning and other opportunities offered by society, so that their alienation and dropout are major problems for societies globally. Society is therefore also being short-changed, as it loses the contributions that these children and young people might make.

We therefore take two themes through the book. One is about being sensitive to *children as agentic*, with feelings and motive orientations, potentially able to propel themselves forward as learners. Their agency is central to how they negotiate their way in settings inhabited by the family carers and practitioners, who guide them toward adulthood. In these negotiations, children are seeking meaning, building their meaningful understandings of the practices they inhabit. Creating this understanding intertwines cognition with affect, embracing the child's emotional engagement. We shall trace the mutual development of cognition and affect from infancy to late adolescence and show how emotional engagement may be expressed in different ways in different age periods. The second theme is *what practitioners can do* to work with the explanations we offer, especially in critical situations such as when children meet new expectations. We want to support professionals both in recognizing the emotional aspects of learning and development and in working relationally with children, by taking children's emotions and motives seriously.

In order to look forward we look back to the cultural-historical psychology of Vygotsky (1896–1934) and those who have since worked with his legacy to relate it more closely than he did to education. We particularly draw on his ideas about children, learning and development and connect them, through our own work and that of others, to how children can be supported as curious and intentional beings.[1] Vygotsky was a developmental psychologist whose central arguments were that the unity of the child and her environment characterized children's development across in different age periods. Importantly, this means that we should not locate a child's difficulties within the child, but instead examine the

---

[1] Even though Vygotsky's theory was formulated nearly a century ago in Russia, it is relevant for today's research and education (Dafermos, 2018; Stetsenko, 2017). Vygotsky's texts were banned in Russia until 1956 (i.e., until Stalin's death). It wasn't until 1962 that they started to be translated into English and several other languages. His work is still being translated, re-translated and published (Vygotsky, vols 1–6, 1994–2000, 2019, 2021).

*Introduction* 3

environments they are acting in and adjust them to better support the child.

Vygotsky (1989, 1998) described the dynamic unity we are advocating as a *child's social situation of development*. The extract below reveals the importance of agency in this dialectical relationship between child and environment and that the relationship changes as the child meets new social realities.

> One of the major impediments of the theoretical and practical study of child development is the incorrect solution of the problem of environment and its role in the dynamic of age when the environment is considered as something outside with respect to the child, as a circumstance of development, as an aggregate of objective conditions existing without reference to the child and affecting him by the very fact of their existence. The understanding of environment that developed in biology as applied to evolution of animal species must not be transferred to the teaching on child development.
>
> We must admit that at the beginning of each age period, there develops a completely original, exclusive, single and unique relation, specific to a given age, between the child and reality, mainly social reality, that surrounds him. We call this relation the *social situation of development* at the given age. (Vygotsky, 1998, p. 198)

Vygotsky's colleagues, D.B. El'konin (1972/1999) and A.N. Leont'ev (1978), and the next generation, including Bozhovich (2009), Davydov (1988–1989, 2008), Galperin (1969), Lisina (1985) and Zaporozhets (2002), have, in different ways, contributed to and extended this theoretical approach by studying different aspects of children's social situations of development in different age periods.[2]

One of the developments of this cultural-historical view has been Hedegaard's emphasis on institutional practices and how they mediate the demands of wider society. Leont'ev described the dialectics that underpin a cultural-historical approach to human development with the statement: "[S]ociety produces the activity of the individuals forming it" (Leont'ev, 1978, p. 7). Hedegaard refined this definition by inserting the idea of institutional practices into this notion of society. She asks us to pay attention to what she describes as "the conceptualization of the historical institutionalized demands that mediate this [transformational] progress" (Hedegaard & Fleer, 2013, p. 200). Edwards captures this meaning by describing practices in institutions as "knowledge-laden, imbued with

---

[2] We shall draw on English translations of their work throughout this book.

cultural values and emotionally freighted by the motives of those who already act in them" (Edwards, 2010, p. 5).

This development of Leont'ev's work to focus on institutional practices is central to our intention to help practitioners help children. Hedegaard's refinement means that practitioners and other carers have two tasks: making adjustments to practices to enable the unfolding of children's agency and guiding children's motive orientations so that they engage with activities in ways that reflect what matters in the practice. The focus on institutional practice also means that we can examine how practices give shape to the activities that comprise them and what is involved when children move between practices as they go from home to school to sports clubs and so on. Throughout this book, we therefore show the value of studying children's learning and development through a lens that recognizes the dynamic and evolving unity of child and practice.

## The Cultural-Historical Theoretical Underpinnings of Understanding Children's Development

Vygotsky differentiated between children in different age periods. By age he did not mean chronological age, but the expectations in a society for how children in different life periods (early childhood, school-age and adolescence) should act. Importantly, he argued that the meanings connected with a child's emotional experience may be different for children in different age periods, because they may have developed different needs and attributes and therefore are differently motivated toward the same situation. We can see this, for example, in how children of different age periods join in family interactions or games. Bozhovich later elaborated on Vygotsky's view of how children's emotional experiences are influenced by their age period. She argued that: "[I]t may be said that the function of [a child's] experience is to orient to the subject within his environment and consequently motivate him" (1969, p. 213).

When a child makes a major life transition, such as from home care to nursery, from kindergarten to school or from school to higher education, they enter a new institutional practice where a new age period is socially constructed and a new social situation of development arises. In these transitions the child or young person reaches out to what is meaningful for them in the practices and may engage with ideas that are valued by caregivers in the practice and develops commitments. A central purpose of education, we shall argue, is to care-fully ensure that these commitments reflect what is valued by caregivers, such as the societal values that embrace collaboration, sociality, mutual responsibilities and life-competences. A key concept here is a child's *leading activity*. Different institutions hold different expectations for children; while children's own development means that they experience demands in line with those expectations. For example, in most societies play is a leading activity in the preschool years, while learning in educational settings is the leading activity in middle childhood. The leading activity is therefore the interaction with the environment that produces the kind of development that is valued by society.

Throughout this book, we shall highlight the important role of adults in supporting children as they make these transitions. Key to that support is recognizing children's motive orientations, what they orient to in an activity. Hedegaard has described the development of motive orientations as follows: "Motive development can then be seen as a movement initiated by the child's emotional experience related to the activity setting" (Hedegaard, 2012a, p. 21). Motive orientations give direction to how people recognize, interpret and take actions to respond to the demands in a practice and are therefore crucial to learning and development.

Learning and development often arise from conflicts in motives. Conflicts can occur when children meet new demands in a new institution. They can also arise when children have acquired new competences that do not fit into the existing practice (e.g., when children start to walk) or when children get a new motive orientation because of being bored in the current practice (e.g., when children in kindergarten start to orient to school because older siblings go to school) Conflicts or crises in children's lives can therefore be seen as necessary, reflecting contradictions between a child's different motives or between a child's motives and the demands in the practices they are currently inhabiting. These crises may lead to a reorganization of a child's whole relation to the activities and people in his everyday life (Vygotsky, 1998). Development is therefore more than learning new competences or acquiring new motives. Development can be observed when children's social relations to other people are reorganized in each practice that the children inhabit (such as home and kindergarten) (Hedegaard, 2012b). Crises are nonetheless only potentially productive for a child. They can become detrimental if caregivers do not support the child to move forward and generate new motives and competences to meet new demands.

In general, parents want to do what is best for their children, and practitioners in kindergarten, school and other institutions want to engage children in the activities they offer. But they frequently find themselves concerned about children and their actions. Often these concerns can reflect crises for both adults and children, from which they need to find a way forward. Examples of crises include the challenge of caring for an infant who cries when being taken to nursery, while their parents have difficulty in leaving them there; or a toddler who, just learning to walk, moves into dangerous situations; or when an adolescent who is new to a school finds it difficult to settle. Concerns can also include children's lack of activity such as school refusal, or the anxiety of a shy child in a classroom setting, or a young person who is not able to communicate his intentions. We will not characterize such concerns as problems belonging to the individual child, and instead argue that they should be seen as relational problems belonging to new challenges or changes in children's social situations and which call for action by carers and practitioners.

In brief, these crises are potential growth points and when they are negotiated fruitfully a child learns and, for example, becomes a school child able to orient toward new demands in the new setting. All children need help with these transitions and the shifts in motive orientation that they entail, and, as we shall see, some children require quite intensive support. We shall argue throughout the book that practitioners need to work relationally and care-fully with children, to support their new orientations. Our overarching aim is to reinstate care into a pedagogy that enables children's agency in handling their social situations. Therefore, over the chapters we will describe a care-full process of reciprocity between a caring adult and a child as she or he negotiates their way forward and learns.

We turn to Lisina's (1985) research on infants and young children to explain how care can nurture agency. She writes about what has been translated as "love" in the following way.

> If we interpret love in the broader sense, as just not tenderness, but as demanding tenderness, as a constant readiness to persuade and explain, to share experience and knowledge. Then love can never be excessive. Love of this kind is an inseparable part of showing respect for young children and of the endeavor to achieve mutual understanding with them. (Lisina, 1985, p. 91)

Lisina sees the adult as the guide to development and writes: "[A] child can only acquire independence through his interaction with adults" (p. 91).

We are also in tune with Noddings' writing on ethics, care and education. Like her, we recognize that a climate of care underpins successful pedagogy (Noddings, 2013); but we add a more detailed focus on how that climate is achieved through relationships. We therefore also agree with her emphasis on confirmation in interactions with children.

Noddings explains the challenge: "To confirm another we must know and understand the other's reality. Given the structure of today's schooling, this may be asking the impossible" (Noddings, 2013, p. xix). We don't underestimate the challenge, but throughout this book we shall offer examples of attentive listening and care-full interactions to show that it is not necessarily impossible.

In the chapters that follow, we examine how children are helped to negotiate transitions between institutional practices and orient toward demands within these. The chapters are organized by age periods. This is not because our approach is based in an unfolding of innate qualities as a child matures. Instead, by analyzing conflicts between children's motive orientation and the different forms of possibilities and demands children meet in situations, we can reveal the crises that give rise to their development. We recognize that the demands connected to transitions both between and within practices will be different for children in different life periods. Our intention is to offer tools to carers and practitioners so that they can identify these crises and help guide children's engagement as they participate in new practices.

## A Wholeness Approach

So far we have focused on relationships between people and the demands of different practices. We are also aware of how practices, in families and schools, mediate the societal demands that arise through historically formed expectations and national policies. For example, in Denmark the objectives embedded in laws relating to schools focus on students' subject-matter competences, while the statutory requirements for preschool provision emphasize play and social competences over other learning goals. The examples and analyses in this book will recognize such societal imperatives but will focus mainly on the coevolution of the dynamic unities of children and the practices in which the activities they participate in are embedded. To do so we look below statutory demands to reflect how different institutions interpret and enact societal priorities and what that means for the children and young people in activities within the practices.

Hedegaard's work on what she has termed 'a Wholeness Approach' (Hedegaard, 2012b, 2014) has demonstrated how the practices of different institutions such as families, day care and schools mediate broader societal values and shape the activities that occur within the practices. Such mediation is fashioned by what matters for practitioners in each institution

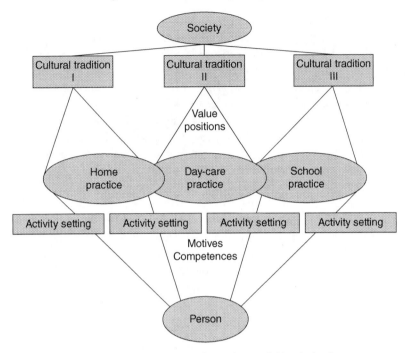

Figure 1.1 Different perspectives for analyzing children's development

and gives rise to the expectations held for children and young people as they engage in, and in turn shape, the activities.

Figure 1.1 (Hedegaard, 2012b) shows the interrelated analytic perspectives that comprise the Wholeness Approach. These are ways of entering an analysis of how societal priorities, such as those embedded in laws, national policies as well as values and norms in cultural traditions, are mediated into institutional practices such as those found in families and schools, and evidenced in activity settings within practices, such as mealtimes or classrooms. In brief, what matters in a practice gives shape to the activities within its activity settings and the demands the activities make on those who engage with them. For us the central analytic entry point in this book is how children enter activity settings, meet activities and bring to bear their own motives and competences when engaging.

As researchers who focus on how children learn and develop, our aim is to understand how children experience institutional practices and the activities in them, while recognizing that these practices are located in wider societal conditions.

In her work with families and practitioners over the years, Hedegaard has emphasized the need to relate to children, to try to see how they are experiencing and interpreting the demands to be found in activities that are situated in different practices. First and foremost, this relating involves understanding the child's actions from the child's perspective, how the child experiences the world. Here Hedegaard is following Vygotsky's observation (Vygotsky, 2019) that the world does not influence the child directly but is mediated through the child's emotional orientation founded in the child's social situation of development.

Vygotsky's developmental focus is important here. It reminds us that a child's perspective and emotional experiences in these practices are dependent on the child's age period (Bozhovich, 1969). Children's emotional development is connected with the development of the other psychic functions, such as imagination and memory, and cannot be understood independently of these. We elaborate the development of psychic functions in chapters that follow. Here we simply note that children's development of emotions involves making meaning through their growing understanding of cultural signs, such as the way language and facial expressions are used. At the same time, children learn to regulate their emotional responses in line with cultural expectations (Holodynski, 2013). Consequently, families and practitioners need to see children as active subjects with motives and intentions that influence how they act in different institutional activity settings.

A Wholeness Approach also recognizes that in a single day children can engage in several practices with other children and adults (Hedegaard, 2009). Consequently, a child experiences several social situations that together become part of their social situation of development. In this way a child's life is interconnected through their everyday participation across different institutional practices, giving rise to a multiplicity of social relations. A developmental perspective therefore sees a child's life as a pathway through central institutions such as family, nursery, kindergarten and school. Children's life courses, therefore, can be seen as pathways through the possible trajectories that a society affords its citizens (Hundeide, 2005).

This does not mean that their life courses are societally determined; our emphasis on agency and meaning-making ensures that we reflect the dynamic unity that is the social situation of development. One aspect of that dynamic unity is seen in the negotiations that children make when they move, for example, from the informal practices of family life with their own sets of expectations, to the formality of school and the need for motive orientations that allow them to interpret and engage with school activities. They also need to negotiate when engaging in afterschool sporting or other activities and interacting with peers, where expectations are again different.

The processes involved in connecting demands from school with motives and competences in the context of family life are revealed in Hedegaard and Fleer's (2008) family research. There, Hedegaard followed four children in a middle-class Danish family, the Frederiksberg family: Kaisa (4 years), Emil (6 years), Lulu (8 years) and Laura (10 years). Each child was seen as having a different social situation of development and different motive orientations, through being oriented to different practices outside the family. Kaisa and Emil were still in preschool practice, with Emil just starting in the transition class, class zero, which prepares him for formal schooling. Lulu and Laura were school-age children oriented to activities and friends in school.

Following the children during the week, the researchers found that the children participate in several practices. All of them participate in shared activity settings in the family; only Kaisa participates in kindergarten practices and only Emil in the transition class. Both Lulu and Laura participate in school, and Emil and Lulu are involved in afterschool practices. Only Laura attends club activities. Sometimes they visit friends and one evening each week Lulu and Laura go to gymnastics. We will return to this family in later chapters where we follow how the children's participation in different practices influences the shared family activities. One such example is how Lulu's school practice, through being given homework, influences home practice for the whole family. We will illustrate this here with an observation extract from a mid-week homework setting in the Frederiksberg family.[3] When analyzing the children in this activity setting, we can see that although in the same situation, each child's social situation of development is different and is reflected in their different motive orientations.

**Extract from observation 4. November**

Mother sits down at the dining table together with Laura who had started preparing a written text, a task for her mother tongue subject (Danish).

Laura says "I'm writing sloppily, because it is only a draft."

---

[3] In this research, four families were followed over a period of one year in three different periods of 30 days in each family, distributed into three periods by participant observations over 3–5 hours each time. In this chapter, we draw on the observations from the first period in the Frederiksberg family with four children to illustrate main points in Hedegaard's Wholeness Approach to development.

## A Wholeness Approach

Kaisa comes down from upstairs and says "I want to put on my pink short-sleeved shirt."

She asks Mother if she will help her to open her closet. Mother assists and asks if it is not too cold with short sleeves.

Lulu enters the setting to do her math homework.

Lulu says "Mom! I do not want to do homework."

Mother replies: "Sometimes you must do something you do not want to."

Mother asks what is 2x9? Lulu uses a multiplication table.

Mother asks if she is allowed [by the math teacher]to use that for her calculations.

First Lulu says "no," but then "yes" if you use it in a certain way. She shows how by explaining that if you have to calculate 9x4, then you start from 9x1 and count 4 down in the table, so you can see what 9x2 and 9x3 is before you find 9x4.

Mother says that she should try to remember the result, so it is on her back [a Danish saying].

Lulu takes the table and places it on her back and laughs.

Mother laughs and says "then, so that you can remember it by heart."

The observer asks Lulu whether she has much to do (for math homework).

Lulu answers not so much, but that she does not want to bother with it.

Emil comes and sits down with a toy cash register.

Mother shows how Lulu has to borrow in order to take 6 from 34, then Mother gives her a calculation task. Because they have talked about their grandmother, Mother asks her to figure out how old grandmother is and tells her the year when grandmother was born.

Lulu writes the year 1938 and then the current year 2006 in her booklet.

Emil has been playing with his toy cash register writing on small labels, which he pulls out from the drawer in the register.

Lulu says she cannot work out how to calculate grandmother's age.

Mother asks Lulu to continue and helps her.

Homework is a recurrent setting in the family with the mother as the center. In this actual setting, the mother tries to motivate Lulu to engage with her math homework. Laura and Emil also contribute to what is going on in the setting, through what they engage in and talk about. Mother influences Lulu's social situation but Mother's situation is also very much influenced by the children's activities, where she also has to take care of the youngest child, Kaisa, who is not oriented to school activities.

Importantly, children create their specific social situations of development; they are not passively determined by the conditions around them. In the homework setting, the four children each have their specific social situation of development, based in how they experience the situation with their different motive orientations. They each should be seen as active subjects who cocreate the conditions in which they live together with other participants such as parents, siblings, carers, professionals and other children. Children not only cocreate their own living conditions, as we can see from this extract; they also contribute to the creation and affirmation of the conditions of other co-participants.

## A Relational Approach to Education

We are advocating a highly skilled way of working with children. We see education as a relationship of reciprocity between a caring adult and a child or young person. But we do not see this in terms of the low-status, usually female, emotional labor of the kind Hochschild describes as relational service-based work (Hochschild, 1983). In contrast, we present this reciprocity, aimed at encouraging attention to motives and engagement, as part of the repertoire of skilled practitioners. In doing this we recognize that parents and other family carers will differ from practitioners in how they enact the reciprocity. But both will be oriented toward enabling the unfolding of children and young person's engaged agency as they address the demands and expectations embedded in activities.

This reciprocity involves taking seriously children's feelings, sense-making and agentic searches after meaning. We have also noted that their agency is nurtured as it unfolds in environments where what matters for the child or young person, how they are interpreting demands, is recognized. These are not simplistic arguments for child-centered education. Rather they challenge practitioners to enter into caring relationships where they work with the agentic energy of children, while helping them connect with societal values, including the opportunity to question those values. These relationships are professional and different from the close, caring connections that a child has with family members. They are at the heart of a sound pedagogy, and we shall discuss how it is accomplished by practitioners in chapters that follow.

## A Relational Approach to Education

The key concepts that describe what is involved in this kind of relational work with children are based in cultural-historical theory (Edwards, 2010, 2017), and are elaborated in later chapters. The concepts first emerged in analyses of how practitioners worked with women who were going through difficult times and attended an inner-city drop-in center (Edwards, 2005). The concepts were later used to explain how practitioners with different professional backgrounds collaborated across practice boundaries to support vulnerable children (Edwards, 2010, 2011) and recently they have framed analyses of pedagogies in schools (Nyborg et al., 2022). Interprofessional collaboration is detailed in Chapter 3 and a care-full relational pedagogy with children and young people is explained in Chapter 7. Here we introduce the relational ideas in the context of the drop-in center study, where we show a pedagogic relationship between a worker and a center user.

The central relational concepts are *relational expertise, common knowledge* and *relational agency*. Relational expertise is the capacity to elicit the motive orientations of others and to be explicit about one's own motive orientations in relation to a problem area. These orientations then comprise common knowledge, in the sense that each now knows what matters for the others, how they are interpreting the problem and how they might act on it. Common knowledge can then become a resource or, in Vygotskian terms, a tool that can mediate collaboration on the problem, which is now shared. This collaboration, while taking action on the problem, is the unfolding of relational agency. It is an unfolding that aims, when working pedagogically, to nurture and support the agency of persons as they meet new demands in new practices and learn something new.

One example from the drop-in center study is how a center worker supported a regular user of the center. The user had received a final demand for payment from her electricity provider and was in danger of being cut off from supplies. The worker exercised relational expertise by listening care-fully to the woman, eliciting what mattered for her, taking all her concerns seriously. She was also explicit about what mattered for her as a practitioner. She wanted the woman to find a way of paying and continue to use the center and contribute to its climate of support. The common knowledge built in the discussion led to jointly expanding their understanding of the problem so that it changed from being "I'm going to get cut off" to "how shall we sort payments?". This common knowledge was brought into play again as they jointly planned how to approach the electricity company. At this point the relational agency, joint agency of worker and user, began to unfold. This all took place before on-line contact with energy suppliers was the norm, so the worker and center user, together, visited the company office. While there the worker supported the user while she negotiated monthly payments of an amount she could afford.

Throughout the process, the agency of the center user was nurtured. First her concerns were taken seriously, and the worker reciprocated by being explicit about hers. The user's interpretations of the problem were respected as they jointly worked on interpreting and expanding the problem area. Finally, the user's agency was gradually enhanced, first through quite close joint work on the plan and then, when the user took the lead supported by the worker, at the electricity office. These relational processes are central to the relationships that we shall be advocating when practitioners work with each other and how they support children as agentic learners.

We shall propose that practitioners' support and guidance may benefit from building "relational expertise" (Edwards, 2010, 2017). Situations of concern may arise between practitioners and between practitioners and families. In brief, relational expertise involves respectfully recognizing and working with what matters (the motive orientations) for fellow participants and being open about what matters for oneself, while collaborating on issues of concern. Relational expertise, we shall suggest, can enable collaborations that focus on how to help changing children's social situations when caregivers are concerned about a child or young person.

As well as discussing relationships between practitioners and between practitioners and families, we will draw on these concepts to discuss nurturing the unfolding agency of the child or young person. Children are creators of their social situations of development in the different practices they participate in and are coauthoring their developmental pathways with families, practitioners and friends. We shall therefore take a dual focus to capture the perspectives and intentions of the child or young person and of their caregivers.

When working with children these interactions call for professional clarity and careful listening and observing. The practitioner therefore needs to ask questions that include the following:

*How may we learn about their current motive orientations?*
*What is the child or young person's motive orientation? Why are they orienting in this way?*

*What does the child or young person interpret as the demands in the activity in this practice?*
*What competences do they need in order to interpret the demands in other ways?*
*What are the implications for preparing for and supporting transitions that are developmental?*

The processes we are advocating involve care-full observing as well as sensitive conversations. We discuss the methodology and what needs to be captured in observations of a child and their social situation of development in Chapters 2 and 4. Here we simply note that Hedegaard's interactive observation method (1990/2013, 2008a, b, c) involves following the child, trying to capture how the child is interpreting the demands in practices and making meaning. This dual attention to actor and environment has led Hedegaard to suggest that a focus solely on the child is insufficient. Rather, we also need to examine practices and the demands in them that are being experienced by the child (Hedegaard, 2009, 2012b). In the next section we introduce our concern with social inclusion and the need to sustain this dual focus in order to create interventions that enable the participation of children in what society has to offer.

## Unfolding Agency for Social Inclusion

Our current sociopolitical environments are marked by huge discrepancies in wealth within nation-states and massive differences in access to health and education services across national boundaries. These differences are experienced by some children and their families as exclusion from the benefits that society offers those with greater social and material capital. In short, they are socially excluded. Poverty is the major cause, but racism can play a part as can social class. Part of the answer, we suggest, is to enable the unfolding of children and young people's agency so that they come to be active participants in society.

Shotter interpreted this aim as one feature of Vygotsky's attention to the dynamic unity of person and practice. He argued: "Vygotsky is concerned to study how people, through the use of their own social activities, by changing the conditions of their own existence can change themselves" (Shotter, 1993, p. 111). If this line is taken, our focus on the unity of child and environment and what practitioners can do to nurture agency, opens up possibilities for adjustments to practices that allow the unfolding of agency. These adjustments may enable children to change "the conditions of their own existence" (Shotter, 1993). We are not advocating social mobility for the few. Rather, we are arguing for a pedagogy that care-fully strengthens the agency of children and the communities they contribute to.

This agency is relational both in how it is nurtured and how it feeds a collective form of agency for the common good. Our use of the term agency owes much to the work of Charles Taylor. It unfolds in our actions on the world and in Taylor's view it rejects "the hegemony of disengaged reason and mechanism" (Taylor, 1989, p. 461). Values and emotion are central to how agency is enacted. Taylor was particularly concerned that the agency he advocated should not produce overweening selves who are disconnected from the common good (Taylor, 1991).

Vygotsky's concluding reflections in his early writings for teachers show how important skillful pedagogy was to supporting the creative agency of children so that they might build the new reality he was seeking for his fellow Russians.

> Life then discloses itself as a system of creation, of constant straining and transcendence, of constant invention and the creation of new forms of behavior. Thus, every one of our thoughts, every one of our movements, and all of our experience constitutes a striving towards the creation of a new reality, a breakthrough to something new. ... It is then that pedagogics, as the creation of life, will assume the foreground. (Vygotsky, 1926/1997, p. 350)

In this book we differentiate between social inclusion and school inclusion, while recognizing their connections. We give a cultural-historical account of resilience and interventions for social inclusion in Chapter 8, and throughout the book we discuss how a care-full relational pedagogy can aid students' school inclusion.

## How the Book Is Organized

Our focus is on relationships within different institutional practices and across the developmental pathways of children and young people. Our aim is to look forward, by (i) offering practitioners and researchers ways of understanding the changing dynamic unity of person and activity in different practices in a child's life course; and (ii) helping them recognize and support the emotional and motivational aspects of children and young people's engagement with demands that take their learning forward. In doing so we have emphasized the developmental potential to be found in the conflicts of motives that occur during transitions between the different leading practices of nursery, preschool and school, and the role of caregivers in helping shape children's motive orientations.

In this chapter, we have set out some of the key themes to be found across the next ten chapters. We recognize that some readers might like to focus on specific topics, such as the preschool years or adolescence. But these age-related chapters draw on chapters where core ideas are elaborated, in particular Chapters 2 and 3. In addition, because we shall be discussing how previous age periods contain signs of emerging motives and competences, we warn against taking too narrow a focus on age when selecting what to read.

In Chapters 2 and 3, we lay out the central ideas as they have been developed in our own work and those of others. Chapter 2 details our view of child development through childhood with a particular focus on Hedegaard's Wholeness Approach. In Chapter 3, we present four ways in which the three relational concepts can be used by practitioners in their collaborations with other practitioners and with parents or carers. The ideas in these two chapters permeate the whole book and give it coherence. Chapters 4 and 5 draw on research that takes the perspective of young children to explain their development as they negotiate the practices they inhabit. They deal respectively with the development of toddlers and preschool children.

Chapters 6 and 7 act as bridges to a focus on school-age children. In Chapter 6 we consider children's engagement with knowledge, seeing working with knowledge as an important element in our concerns with children's social inclusion. Chapter 7 is where we work with the three relational concepts described in Chapter 3 to explain a care-full relational pedagogy. We suggest that Chapters 6 and 7 are essential reading in preparation for the next three chapters. In Chapter 8, we discuss the agency and learning of children of primary school age and also address issues of resilience and social inclusion. In Chapter 9, we discuss forms of knowledge and what that means for children's learning and draw on teaching experiments that exemplify the power of Hedegaard's work on the double move in teaching. In Chapter 10, we move on to adolescents, their learning and transitions to adulthood. The final chapter is where we focus on what people can do to support children as agentic engaged learners. It therefore looks forward by discussing the implications of the preceding chapters for the professions that work with children.

Throughout this book, we give real-life examples from our own research as well as drawing on some of the foundational work of Vygotsky and the researchers who have followed and extended his theory over the last century. We also discuss the exciting cultural-historically informed work currently being carried out by our contemporaries. We are not alone in our conviction that a care-full relational pedagogy is good for children and young people and for society. We therefore hope that this book contributes usefully to a growing field.

CHAPTER 2

# *A Cultural-Historical Approach to Children's Development and Childhood*

## Introduction

In this chapter, we expand on the ideas on children's development introduced in Chapter 1 and explain the cultural-historical foundations for our approach. Our theoretical orientation means that we focus on the child's social situation by attending to the activities children engage in and what is meaningful for them, in different practices, in different age periods. In the chapters that follow, we then show how caregivers can work in and on institutional practices and the activities they offer to nurture the agency of children as they meet new challenges.

We start by discussing the importance of Hedegaard's introduction of the concepts of practice and activity settings to a Wholeness Approach to development (Hedegaard, 2009, 2012a, 2014). This move allows us to examine the relation between children's motive orientations and the demands that arise in the activities in which they participate. We also give examples of the demands children make on the other participants, thereby contributing to the conditions for their own development. This discussion is followed by explanations of how cultural-historical theory informs our understandings of how age periods and crises characterize children's development and the crucial importance of emotion to children's well-being and learning. The methodological implications of having a wholeness perspective when assessing children's development will then be outlined in the last sections of the chapter.

## A Wholeness Approach

A central concept in Vygotsky's (1998, 2019) theory of development is the unity of the child and environment. This unity can also be found in Kurt Lewin's approach to child development (1946). Both Lewin and Vygotsky opposed the view that environment alone could explain how a single person acts, learns and develops. Lewin (1946) suggested that, instead, a child's behavior should be seen within a social field, where both the child's needs and the demands from the field are recognized. Vygotsky (2019) took a more markedly developmental approach, arguing that a given environment can be emotionally interpreted by children in different developmental periods in different ways.

To grasp how a child is making sense of her world in order to guide and support her, the child has to be recognized as an actor within institutionalized practices, such as family life or school. Here Hedegaard employs a cultural-historical framing for conceptualizing development as a dialectical process, a recursive intertwining of person, institutional practices and society, which is more dynamic than merely taking into account the context. Hedegaard also goes further. She does not simply assume a child's relationship is with one practice in each age group, but shows how children participate in different practices – such as home, school and after school practices – each characterized by recurrent demands in familiar activity settings.

Hedegaard has therefore also taken our attention to the different activity settings within practices. Inspired by Barker and Wright, two followers of Lewin, Hedegaard elaborated their concept of behavioral settings (Barker & Wright, 1954, 1971). In doing so she distinguished between institutional practices and settings within different societal institutions (Hedegaard, 2012b). Barker and Wright, through their intensive observational studies of children's everyday life, described different community settings such as home, school, library, shops and medical clinics as important for understanding children's behavior. Their argument was that each setting affords different types of participant behavior. This prompted Hedegaard (2012b) to make a distinction between institutional practices and the settings within them, such as recess and classrooms in schools. She characterized the settings as activity settings. This added precision has allowed us to examine how children's agency may unfold in different settings within the same institution as well as how experiences in activity settings in different practices contribute to creating a child's developmental pathway as they move between practices.

Figure 2.1 is a representation of Hedegaard's Wholeness Approach. It shows how children's development at any point can occur in relation to three interrelated perspectives: societal, institutional and personal. Societal priorities and traditions are mediated by institutional practices and the activity settings within them. The activities within these settings are then experienced by children who develop the motive orientations and competences demanded by these settings and practices. A society's conditions for

# A Wholeness Approach

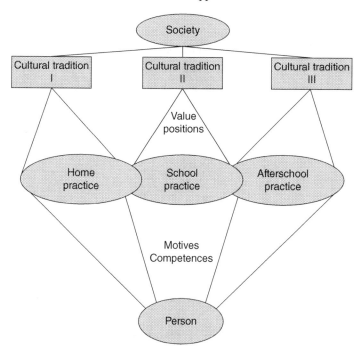

Figure 2.1 A model of children's learning and development through participating in institutionalized practices

an individual child's life course may thereby be seen as mediated through institutional practices and the activity settings in those practices, with their recurrent demands.

Within a Wholeness Approach, the focus is the child and her experiences in everyday life as she moves within and between different practices, but these practices are themselves societal products that are experienced personally by children. Children's life courses, as they move across practices in a society, are seen as their developmental pathways. The pathway created by an individual child can reveal how she interprets and responds to the demands and opportunities in different activity settings in different practices and how she negotiates transitions between practices. Children therefore create their own social situations of development as they carve their pathways across settings. Later, we shall be pointing out how adults can help with these transitions.

Participating in shared activity settings within family or school practices is a basic condition for children's development. Children appropriate

Table 2.1 *Relations between demands and what moves at different analytical planes*

| Structure | Process/demands | Dynamic |
|---|---|---|
| Society | Societal tradition- and value-demands | Societal conditions/needs |
| Institution | Practice demands for the type of participation | Value-laden goals/objectives/motives |
| Activity setting | Social situation's demands on both child and others | Situated motivation/engagement/interests |
| Person | Reciprocal demands for ways of participating in an activity | Motive orientation/intention |
| Higher psychic functions (perceptions, memory, thinking) | Physiological demands | Biological needs |

motives and competences through entering activity settings and sharing activities with other people within culturally formed practice traditions. In the different activity settings in which a child participates, she meets demands and challenges. But she also makes demands on the other participants and may challenge features of the activity settings and so contribute to how the activity settings are realized and how the practices evolve.

The different relations between concepts in Hedegaard's Wholeness Approach can be seen in Table 2.1. As we shall explain, the table can be read both horizontally and vertically. A horizontal reading usefully informs analyses at specific analytic entry points and reveals the key dynamic in play within that focus. A vertical reading shows the interconnectedness of these different analytic planes, such as how institutional practices mediate societal values and priorities and inform the demands that are embedded in activities in activity settings.

The Wholeness Approach raises crucial questions about the roles of educators, both formal and informal. This is because the activities they offer are created through the institutional practices that are found in families, nurseries, kindergartens and schools. These practices are shaped by adults' expectations of how children and young people should fit into these practices. However, we are also emphasizing the need for reciprocity between adults and children in a way that recognizes a child's contributions to activities in the different practices. In brief, we are arguing that children are shaped by the practice traditions they inhabit, but also contribute to shaping them. For us this dialectical intertwining is at the core of the relational pedagogy we shall be advocating in the chapters that follow. This relational perspective importantly alerts us to possible conflicts and differences in motive orientations between adults and children.

In later chapters, we shall emphasize the reciprocity between the personal perspectives of children, and the caregivers' pedagogic approaches. We will examine how children's motive orientations interact with the demands from the activity settings and how caregivers can relate to a child's motive orientation in a specific age period. The analyses in this chapter will focus on the differences between children's developmental situations in different types of practice in home, day care, primary and secondary school. We shall highlight how new demands, arising from children's moving into new institutional practices, may influence and change their motive orientations and participation in activity settings across practices. We shall also show that practices in a family's everyday life may also be influenced by children's activities within and outside the home, in day-care school and other institutions. Each child, by his or her activities outside home, contributes to practices in the home and also makes demands on their families in home activity settings.

## A Society Creates Conditions for Children's Development through Different Forms of Institutional Practices

Activity settings offer recurrent events in institutional practices of, for example, a family or school. They take place, for instance, in a family's morning activity settings such as breakfast and preparing to leave the house. As we saw in Table 2.1, an activity setting within a practice reflects the cultural traditions and values in a society.

Values between home and school may differ and there are clearly differences between similar types of activity setting in different institutional practices. For example, eating meals at home makes different demands on a child when compared with eating lunch at school. These differences relate to how societal cultural traditions and values are mediated by different institutional practices and how they produce activities and care for children. Importantly, what is expected in an activity setting does not only depend on how societal traditions are played out in different practices, but also on the people participating in and contributing to the setting. Activity settings afford activities that bring with them demands and possibilities. Participants respond to these demands and possibilities through their actions. Table 2.1 shows that an activity setting should be seen as a relationship between society with its cultural traditions, institutional practices and children's motive orientations and competences.

Through the prism of the Wholeness Approach, one can see how societal priorities both give conditions for and are mediated by institutional practices. A person participates over a life course in many practices. We shall concentrate only on the dominant practices connected to childhood. As we have explained, a child can participate in several practices within the same day. For instance a preschool child may participate in family and day care practice and later when a school child, in family, school and after school practice; while in adolescence they may participate in different community activities and employment practices. The different practices and how they interact over time give children different positions in different age periods. To analyze these different positions, our focus will be on the relationship between children and caregivers in different activity settings in different practices. These differences can be traced in how demands and expectations change for the unfolding of children's agency. These changes can be evidenced in their motive orientations as they engage in activities. Following these changes reveals the process underpinning Hedegaard's statement that "the relation between institutional practice and its objectives [and demands] and the person's motivated action within his/her social situation of development can be seen as the core in the conceptualisation of the developmental process as self-movement." (Hedegaard, 2012b, p. 12)

Practice in homes seldom has an explicit focus on the societal demands embedded in laws and regulations. The exceptions are of course the requirements that children receive an education and are not maltreated. In the home, family practices dominate, and it is the individual family traditions and values that set the demands in family practices. There are informal societal demands on families, but they are implicit through shared discourses in communities. Family members meet these demands from the extended family, in the community and the media in different ways. Grieshaber (2004, p. 64) described this as "regimes of truth," pointing to how, in the community and through different media, people discuss raising children and what parents should accomplish in relation to their children. Each family nonetheless develops more or less their own individual traditions of home practice. We will therefore argue that even though one can distinguish between national traditions, for the single family the participants are the central actors here.

## A Society Creates Conditions for Children's Development

Family practice is important for how children come to communicate, explore, play, learn and develop. To be able to evaluate these practices we have to be aware of how a family relates to the other institutions in society that care for children. We also need to examine how interactions take place in a family, how each child participates and what it means for the child. To do this we have to focus on the child's affective and motivational orientation to their position in the family, as well as the demands the child meets. We illustrate these points with an observation of the Frederiksberg family who we introduced in Chapter 1, taken from Hedegaard's studies of children' everyday life in Danish families. The extract shows that other institutional practices in the children's lives influence the activity setting of a family evening meal at home. What happens during dinner is created by the parents and by their children who are within different age periods (Hedegaard, 2018; Hedegaard & Fleer, 2013).

**Extract from the Frederiksberg family, November 6**
**Around the dinner table,**

Mother, Father, Laura (10 years), Lulu (8 years), Emil (6 years), Kaisa (4 years)

They are having spaghetti with meat sauce, a dish all the children like.

Father asks for Kaisa's plate and gives her a portion of pasta with meat sauce. Emil has been looking forward to the food and starts eating as soon as he has his portion. Father cuts Kaisa's portion into pieces. Lulu wants Father to cut for her. Father thinks it is not necessary [she can do it herself].

Emil says: "Does anyone need to go to the toilet? Why do I say that, because then they can pick up a spoon for me on the way back [which he can use for his spaghetti]?" Emil goes out and picks up a spoon himself.

Emil then asks Father: "Will you cut for me?" But Father does not hear him and goes out into the kitchen, so Emil says: "I can cut with a spoon." Father comes in with cheese. Emil repeats: "Will you cut for me?" Father cuts his spaghetti.

Kaisa asks: "Was it you, Dad, who did my lunch this morning?"

Father: "No, it was Mother."

Kaisa continues: "She did not have to do that, because I was at Villas' birthday. We got hot dogs, and candy bags, and the famous saltines."

Father repeats: "The famous saltines." He quotes a rhyme about the pigs who came to feast at the goose, which served pork, then the pig got goosebumps. They talk about goosebumps. Father says that goosebumps are called 'stand fur' in Norwegian.

Emil explains how he has goosebumps.

Emil wants another serving of spaghetti; it can hardly go fast enough. He says that if Father does not help him, he will call the children's adult center, to which Father does not respond. Mother laughs a little.

Kaisa is told to put away the balloon she is playing with at the table.

Mother brings up the birthday again, which Kaisa took part in at kindergarten. Kaisa says that Villas got a small skateboard that can be used with the fingers, and also tools.

Lulu asks if you can have time off on your birthday when you go to kindergarten. Mother says it is optional, but that in our family we let the children stay at home to celebrate.

Father asks Emil about school and who he is sitting next to now [he has moved desk position]. Emil says that he now sits next to Hector and Lise. Apparently, he does not like Lise and calls her "the little mitten." Mother tells him to speak nicely about others.

Lulu says she told her class the riddle Father told them yesterday. Father asks if they could solve it [it seemed so].

Lulu then tells them that she is going to the zoo tomorrow with her class. They are going to feed some animals and clean their places. Father laughs that they have to clean the shit out. He does not believe that they have to do this. Emil says it is disgusting: "Do you know what this is? It is to remove the animal shit and put it into a big pile."

Lulu agrees that they probably only have to give the animals food.

Lulu starts to tell riddles: "Why can a horse not be an electrician?"[1]

She continues: "Have you heard that the horse is a magician, an apple getting in one way and a pear[2] comes out the other way?"

Emil tries to make up a riddle, but does not get it out in a way that is understandable: "The ceiling looks at the floor; both say I am more than up."

Emil says then: "Now there is advertising."

---

[1] Horse dung in Danish, "hestepærer," means in this context, "horse bulbs." So when horses shit they lose bulbs.
[2] "Hestepærer" can also mean "horse pears."

Father: "You have certainly seen too much television."

Mother to the whole family: "Have you read the card from Grandma?"

Kaisa: "I have to go and make a shit, and you must not read while I'm shitting." She runs out and comes back and says: "I did not do any shitting."

Father: "Now we stop."

Emil wants a third portion of spaghetti.

Laura starts to rise from the table but Mother says: "We're not done, neither I nor Emil."

Being together at dinner is not something that is found across all societies (Hedegaard & Fleer, 2013; Nairn, 2011; Tudge, 2008). In this family, the dinner table is seen as an important setting where the whole family gather and it is a tradition that is shared in many Scandinavian families (Aronsson & Gottzén, 2011; Aronsson 2018; Demuth & Keller, 2011; Gotzen, 2018; Hedegaard, 2018; Holm, 2001).

The extract reveals the conditions that the parents offer their children and the demands they make on the children in the home practice. But it also illustrates both how a child transforms his activities when trying to live up to parental demands, and the demands that a child puts on the other participants in the family, especially the parents. In doing so, children contribute to creating conditions for their own further activities and learning.

In this dinner setting, the children engage in shared communication about their activities in other practices and are facilitated by the parents. The parents orient to what the children are engaged in, and both contribute to children's themes in the conversation and bring up their own themes related to the children's lives in institutions outside home. Kaisa is talking about a birthday of one of her peers in kindergarten where all the children visited the birthday child's home to celebrate. Lulu tells of a planned visit to the zoo with her classmates; and Father asks about how it went with a riddle she took to school. That leads to her offering a new riddle she has learned. Emil is also asked about a school event, and contributes to the word game. We see how the conversation supports children in recounting activities in the other central institutions in their lives.

What characterizes the communication at this family dinner is a play on words that is promoted by Father but followed by the children. The conversation demonstrates the difference between the children's relations to the world in their different understanding of what words mean and that words can have a double meaning. Lulu has just learned how to tell riddles and is eager to demonstrate her understanding of the double meaning of words. Emil does not understand the principle of the double meaning of words in riddles but anyhow wants to participate and plays with word meanings. The word "shit" is used by three of the children: by Emil, with disgust in relation to an imagined situation and by Kaisa, with delight in relation to her own activity of going to the toilet. She enjoys saying the word and does so twice (we guess, to test boundaries); this word for Lulu is included in a word game and seems not to be especially emotionally laden.

The parents make direct demands of the children. The demands on the two youngest are to use proper language, Emil when talking about a classmate and Kaisa when using a profane word (shit). She is also told not to play at the dinner table. The demands on the older children are for Lulu to master cutting the spaghetti herself, and on Laura that she is expected to demonstrate table manners, to not leave the table before everyone has finished.

Compared to a setting in school, at home the children have much greater opportunity to influence and guide the shared activities. This is so even though the setting in itself sets boundaries for what to do. In contrast to family practice, activities in kindergarten and school practices in most countries are guided by laws and regulations that are mediated by practitioners. Policies developed at a societal level may represent a mixture of priorities (Chaiklin & Hedegaard, 2009). In the English school system, for example, there is a focus on national priorities, such as teaching British values, and on the development of individual children with targets for expected performance at a given age. How institutions and the practitioners within them mediate these priorities will depend on how institutional practices have developed over time and how practitioners interpret the current needs of children and their families. But ultimately they are required to work within these heavily monitored and nationally set expectations and children bring these expectations into home settings when they discuss school events.

In Hedegaard and Fleer's (2013) study of children's transitions to school in Denmark and Australia, they focused on how children's days are shaped by the different institutional practices through the demands they meet and how these demands structure the different activity settings within these practices. Their analyses have also shown how day care and schools create conditions for the structure of the families' activities at home. This happens, for example, through the requirement that parents get children to kindergarten and school on time, that parents take extra clothes to kindergarten; and that children bring books and other materials to school. Parents are also expected to ensure that children get food before going to school, and that the child goes to bed in time to get enough sleep. In brief, this study revealed that school influences the everyday settings in families and not the other way around.

## Age Periods Framed by Leading Relations

As we saw in Chapter 1, Vygotsky (1994, 1998, 2019) described children's development in relation to age periods. Age periods denote periods in a child's life that have a biological foundation but are based on cultural norms and expectations for children's activity. Both Vygotsky (1998) and El'konin (1972/1999) observed that what counts as an age period has changed throughout the history of childhood and should not be understood as chronological age. This point has also been made by childhood historians, sociologists of childhood and cultural-historical researchers (Ariès, 1962; Poliavanova, 2015; Rogoff, 2003). Poliavanova (2015, p. 12) explains: "Age in cultural-historical theory represents a concrete historical category." She continues:

> This means that ages are considered as having emerged in the process of society's historical development. They are not given from the beginning or connected with any kind of inherent characteristics of the individual. Age is a period with its own special substance that can be expressed through some culturally or historically emergent goals that a person needs to meet. Developmental goals are different in every historical stage of a society's development. (Poliavanova, 2015, p. 12)

Different societies in different historical periods give different opportunities for developmental trajectories (Elder, 1997; Hundeide, 2005; Riegel, 1975). At the same time for the individual child, the age periods she lives through are defined both by the recurrent demands in the institutional practices in which she participates and the demands she makes on these practices in interaction with caregivers. Consequently, each age period in a child's life course is qualitatively different from the other age periods.

Vygotsky referred to Rousseau and argued:

> So just as a child is not a miniature adult, a preschooler is not simply a miniature schoolboy, an infant is not just a miniature preschooler, i.e., the difference, once again, between the individual ages is not simply that the ones at lower stages develop features that heavily favour the development of those at the senior level; the difference lies in the fact that preschool, school age, etc., are all unique stages in the development of the child, and at each

of these stages the child is a creature unique in quality that lives and develops according to the laws specific for the age and different for each of the different ages. (2019, p. 14)

This way of relating both to other people and to the material world in an age period, Vygotsky described as a child's *social situation of development*. It is created while a child participates in activities in institutional practices. A child's social situation of development is therefore characterized by a child's activity in shared everyday activities at home in cooperation with carers and siblings and in school and other settings with peers and adults. In summary, a child's social situation of development encompasses all relations between the child and social reality in a given age period. Vygotsky explained: "The social situation of development specific to each age determines strictly regularly the whole picture of the child's life or his social existence" (Vygotsky, 1998, p. 197).

Vygotsky described the transition from each age period to the next as a general reconstruction of the whole system of the child's consciousness. By this he meant that the relations between higher psychological functions such as memory, thinking and language are reconfigured. Children in the preschool age period think through remembering and may use images to help them remember. (That is why young children are very good at picture lotto.) When they reach school age, this changes and children start to remember through thinking, using language to reconstruct situations. Vygotsky argued that each age period contains two sub-periods: an unstable period where this restructuring takes place and a stable period.

Vygotsky described this restructuring as *crises*, which are indicators of changes in a child's consciousness and are signs of a new developmental age period in the child's life course. Crises indicate changes that result *in psychological neoformations in higher psychic functions*. These neoformations mark the shift where the relations between the psychic functions change in an age period. Other examples include when in early childhood the child starts to walk and acquire language, or in school when a child becomes able to read, in such situations the child's relations to the environment change drastically. Chaiklin interprets Vygotsky's conception of neoformation in relation to mastering different means in societal practices:

> Child development is conceived as a process whereby children grow into a societal practice through mastering external means, such as speech, writing, and mathematical operations, along with developing psychological capabilities such as will, intentional memory and conceptual thinking. (Chaiklin, 2019, p. 10)

## Age Periods Framed by Leading Relations

Vygotsky clearly defined a child's social situation of development in a given age period as a way of characterizing how children relate consciously to their environments:

> [A]t each given level, we always find a central neo-formation seemingly leading the whole process of development and characterizing the construction of the whole personality of the child on a new base. ... [T]he basic neo-formation we shall *call central lines of development*, at the given age and other partial processes and changes occurring at that age, we shall call *peripheral lines of development*. (Vygotsky, 1998, p. 197)

Crises are therefore indicators of the beginning of neoformation and changes in the child's higher psychic functions. These changes can be seen in how infants change from a neonate's passive orientation and on to voluntary activity, and later in how children in the preschool age become conscious of their own activity, and when at school age they start to be intellectually reflective. These changes in a child's conscious relation to the world, according to Vygotsky (1997b), are based in the leading psychic functions that structure relationships with the other functions. In early childhood, perception and voluntary activity dominate; in preschool, memory and becoming conscious of one's own activity becomes important; and in school, intellectual reflection on one's own activity becomes more central.

Bozhovich has built on these views in a way that informs our approach. She observed that there is one dimension in the child's relation to the world that has to be integrated into this analysis: children's needs and motive orientations (Bozhovich, 1969). She expanded on Vygotsky's view of how children's emotional experience is influenced by their age period by stressing the importance of children's experiences: "It may be said that the function of experience is to orient the subject within his environment and consequently motivate him" (Bozhovich, 1969, p. 213). Her point was that meanings connected with different emotional experiences may be different for children in different social situations of development, because they may have developed different needs and therefore also are differently motivated toward the same situations. This dimension also marks El'konin's extension of Vygotsky's developmental theory.

With D.B. El'konin's development of Vygotsky's analyses, the dynamic that propels development forward became theorized. His aim was to overcome a separation of cognition and emotion when explaining child development. He was critical of a focus solely on emotional development as can be exemplified by Erikson (1950) and of Piaget's (1955) relatively narrow focus on intellectual development. He argued that there were no objects that were not connected to social meanings and no personal relations that were not directed toward the material world. This led to his hypothesis that laid the foundation for his description of periods and stages in children's development toward adulthood:

> The child learns the objectives, motives and norms of the relations in adult activity by reproducing or imitating relations in his own activity, within the associations and collectives to which he himself belongs. It is remarkable that in this process of assimilation, the child confronts the need to acquire new object actions that are required for performing adult activity. Thus, the child sees the adult as the bearer of new and ever complex modes of action with object, of socially elaborated standards and norms that are necessary for orientation to the surrounding world. (El'konin, 1999, p. 21)

In his theoretical conceptions of age periods El'konin argued against casting *child adult* and *child thing* as dualities. He instead united them into what he saw as social communities of *child social adult* and *child social object*. These represented two interdependent stages in each developmental period of childhood. The key point was that a child's emotional and motivational orientation to adults came before the child's orientation to engaging with the object-world. Within that process, how the adult handles a child's needs as they orient toward acting in the world is crucial to the child's development. In this way, El'konin elaborated a dimension in Vygotsky's account of the social situation of development as changes in the child's consciousness of the world. This elaboration emphasized the contribution of social relations to development, arguing that changes in the child's leading relations implied both the social world of people and the world of objects.

El'konin, like Vygotsky, described age periods in children's development, but depicted them as three general periods, early childhood, childhood and adolescence with, as we have just explained, two stages in each. In brief, the first stage in each period is characterized by how emotional and motive relations unfold to dominate the child's cognition. The second stage is marked by the child learning how to approach the world, guided by the dominant emotional and motive relations toward people in this period. He argued that the dynamic between the child's emotions and motives and their intellect is the relationship that propels a child's development through the possible periods in the life trajectories that a society promotes (El'konin, 1999).

We now discuss these age periods in more detail. The first period, early childhood, starts by being dominated by the emotional communication between a child and their primary caregivers. It is these relationships, in the first stage of this period, that should provide a secure base for the child. The second stage in the early childhood period is marked by practical cooperation between adults and children. Here the child, through the cooperation, learns language because "he uses speech as a means for further cooperation with adults within the context of their joint objective activity" (El'konin, 1999, p. 23). In the second age period, childhood, the emotional aspects again enter into the child's relations, through play as a first stage, which then creates the motive for activities designed to promote learning, in early school age.

> It is only when an object action becomes incorporated into a system of human relations that we can discover its true social meaning, its purposefulness with regard to other people. This sort of "in cooperation" takes place in play. Role-playing is an activity within which the child becomes oriented toward the most universal, the most fundamental meanings of human activity. (El'konin, 1999, p. 24)

El'konin observed that the activity of play is not satisfying in the long run for preschool children. The motive for learning becomes prominent because the child wants to be able to act as they see adults acting. Adolescence, El'konin notes, is difficult to describe but here he also points to two periods. The first is an emotional motivational phase where intimate personal communication comes to characterize children's school life, followed by vocational or career-oriented activity. Since age periods depend on society and its conditions, the different age periods in childhood and especially adolescence may be quite different in different societies. Poliavanova (2015), for example, has observed that today adolescence, in some cultures, may last until the age of 30.

El'konin (1999) also brought the cultural aspect more directly into age periods through relating them to institutions in modern society.[3] He saw children's social relations to the world to be connected with the goals that adult–child relations introduce. Consequently, children meet and acquire new motives through participating in new relationships with adults.

But, although he introduced the importance of institutions to child development, El'konin only indirectly related institutions to practices and did not explain how objectives embedded in practices offer crucial goals or expectations for children's development. Hedegaard has remedied this omission with her focus on institutional practices, how children relate to

---

[3] Vygotsky also did this by promoting the difference between learning in school and in preschool (1984). Both Vygotsky and El'konin point to the societal conditions for age periods, but even though it seems obvious they do not introduce practice or practice traditions directly.

the demands in them and how that relationship promotes child development. As we shall note throughout this book, change in a child's social relations may come from a transition into a new practice or when new goals are inserted into an institutional practice that a child currently participates in. Hence, attention to the goals and purposes of practices is highly relevant to understanding and supporting children's development.

Hedegaard (2009), inspired by both Vygotsky and El'konin, described institutional practices and the goals and competences demanded in these practices as the ideals that children orient to in different developmental periods. These ideals may be seen as emotional ideals for acquiring positions in different practices, such as being regarded as a trustworthy person. They are also materialized ideals for acquiring competences, such as being able to do fractions in math. Importantly, both aspects are closely interwoven. The different activity settings within these practices are the social fields where children acquire new motives and learn new competences. Moving from one practice to another may lead to crises between motives and here again both Vygotsky and El'konin's theoretical insights are important for outlining these crises (see Table 2.2).

## Children's Emotional Crises Indicating Developmental Changes in Their Motive Orientation

The conflicts that can occur when entering a new practice or when changes occur within existing practices frequently relate to children's motives. When a child acquires new competences, such as when an infant starts to walk at around twelve months, or when a preschool child starts to orient to the demands of more formal schooling, their relations to their environments change and one can see the emergence of emotional crises.

Transitional crises, Vygotsky (2019) writes, may last several months. As we outlined earlier, Vygotsky described how age-related crises are connected with the development of higher psychic functions. The beginnings of the development of new lines in higher psychic functions are a precondition for neoformations in a new age period, where a restructuring of the child's way of functioning occurs. Writing about crises in the first years of life, Vygotsky describes three aspects connected to them. "Establishment of walking is the first point in the content of crises. The second point is speech. ... The third pertains to the aspect of affect and will" (1998, p. 243). Vygotsky elaborated: The crisis may manifest itself, when a child has been denied something, or is not understood. It can be observed as "a sharp increase in affect that frequently ends with the child lying at the floor screaming furiously, refusing to walk, and if he walks he stomps" (1998, p. 243). For Vygotsky, age-related crises are connected to emotional experiences of new social relations to the world.

The emotions connected to these crises are closely related to the development of motives that emerge with a child's new needs and interests (Bozhovich, 1969; Leont'ev, 1978). When preschool children begin to accomplish activities, meeting the demands in a new age period, they become oriented to how other people are evaluating their actions. Emotions become connected to a child's orientation to his accomplishments in these transition periods and play a significant role in the realization of new motives. Children gradually start to evaluate their own accomplishments in relation to the new demands and these self-evaluations may lead them to devalue previously valued activities.

The acquisition of values is, for us, a central concern when we discuss children's motive orientations and actions. Zaporozhets (2002) discusses a series of experiments with preschool children that revealed how children recognized what was regarded as morally right within the group through participating in group practices. As they moved through the preschool phase, they began to anticipate the implications of transgressing these expectations and their emotions acted as a check on their actions. He explained: "[T]he basis of emotional anticipation of the results of one's actions, plays an important role in the moral development of personality" (p. 63). This anticipation is crucial, as the child mentally acts out possible steps and their consequences for herself as a social being; while her emotions act as a reflective break on possible actions.

Zaporozhets argues that emotion is a "special form of reflection used for mental control of motivation" (2002, p. 53). The emotion associated with anticipation of the consequences of his action is what Zaporozhets described as "a new social motivation for activity" where "children gradually form more complex kinds of *anticipating* emotional regulation of behavior" (pp. 64–65). So the transition into the new age period is expressed through the child's self-evaluation through her emotional anticipation of her accomplishments. In this way, emotions can be seen to play an important part in processes of self-evaluation connected to children's way through developmental crises.

As we have already seen, El'konin's main focus was the leading activity in the three different age periods and children's relation to adults in these activities. These points are displayed in Table 2.2. Instead of change in psychic functions, El'konin focused on differences in children's relations to their communities and how they orientated to acquiring competence and

Table 2.2 *The relation between institutional practice, developmental age periods and motive orientation*

| Institutions with different practice traditions | Crises and developmental age Vygotsky (1998, p. 196) | Developmental age periods El'konin (1999, p. 27) | Motive orientations in different practice traditions |
|---|---|---|---|
| Maternity ward/Home | Crises of the newborn/Infancy | Early childhood: Direct and emotional communication | Orientation toward the caregiver (attachment) |
| Home/nursery | Crises at age one/Early childhood | Early childhood: Manipulation of objects | Orientation to explore objects and the spatial world (object play) |
| Kindergarten | Crisis at age three/Preschool age | Childhood: Role play | Orientation toward other children and to the adult world (role play) |
| Primary School | Crisis at age seven/School age | Childhood: Learning activity | Orientation toward mastering the adult world and to academic learning |
| Secondary School | Age of puberty/Crisis at age thirteen | Adolescence: Intimate personal communication | Orientation to friends and adolescent life |
| Work/Higher Education | Crises at around the age of seventeen/Adolescence | Adolescence: Vocational or career-oriented activity | Orientation to get a position in society |

reaching toward adult life. For El'konin, having the ideal for development in front of the child in form of adults' activities to guide the child's motive orientation, was crucial.

Hedegaard builds on both Vygotsky's and El'konin's theories but focuses more directly on the crises that arise from children's transition into new practices, where new motives and new psychic functions may become dominant. A new practice with new activities, motives and demands may create emotional conflicts in relation to earlier leading motives and result in crises. This is in line with both Vygotsky's and El'konin's theories, but Hedegaard sees the aims and purposes of practices as the core element in children's acquisition of new motives.

Table 2.2 summarizes key aspects of Vygotsky's and El'konin's accounts of development through crises and conflicts of motives. In particular, it

# Children's Emotional Crises Indicating Developmental Changes

depicts crises and shifts in motives in relation to developmental periods and different practices.

To illustrate some of these processes we return to the dinner setting in the Frederiksberg family with the four children, and reveal conflicts and crises in Emil's social situation of development. The extract shows six-year-old Emil in a state of transition between his previous motive orientations as a kindergarten child and his new orientations, as he begins to look toward formal school. He is in class zero, which prepares children for school. There is conflict between his earlier orientations and his emerging orientation to a position in a new and shifting social situation of development.

**Extract continued from observation on November 6**

**At the dinner table**

Emil talks about Hasse, who in school kicks people. "I'm scared of him."

"He told me I should open the door."

Mother: "Why are you scared?"

Emil: "Because he's better at hitting and kicking than Philip [his friend]."

Kaisa asks if she is allowed to go and watch children's TV. Father walks upstairs and turns it on for her, and comes back.

Emil has finished eating, and he crawls over on to Father's lap.

All the girls have now gone upstairs to watch children's hour.

Emil then talks about both Hasse and Sein. Sein is in his class; Hasse is in a parallel class.

Father: "Are you afraid of both? Is it Sein?"

Emil: "No it is Hasse."

Mother: "Why are you afraid of him?"

Emil: "He can fight, and he has thrown Philip from the green lane."

Mother asks: "Should I do something?"

Emil responds ambiguously.

Mother changes the subject and asks: "Emil, have you been to the [school] library?"

Emil says: "Yes." He retrieves his book and shows it to her.

38    A Cultural-Historical Approach to Children's Development

In the earlier situation, Emil used words to claim some competence by asking if someone is going to the toilet, if so could they bring a spoon for him, and he then answers himself; and he also wanted to make riddles. In this later situation, where he talks about two boys Hasse and Sein, he appears to want attention and care from his parents, moving to Father's lap like a small child. He does not want Mother to do anything about what he says he is afraid of; rather he wants to receive parental attention. When Mother asks about a school event, getting books from the library, he at once leaves Father's lap and finds the book,[4] and his competence as a knowledgeable school child dominates. Emil's relation to being a school child when he is home is still ambivalent and conflictual. We also can also see this in the following observation.

> **Extract from November 29**
>
> **At the breakfast table**
>
> Grandmother has been staying overnight and is sitting at the table eating breakfast together with the family. Emil is sad and crying, as he cannot stay home with Grandmother and Kaisa. He sits on Mother's lap. She tells him that he has to go to school. He then argues that his friends in school do not want to play with him and are bossy, and therefore not fun to play with. Mother tells him that he has to talk with them about this. Emil sobbingly says that it would not work. While Grandmother prepares Emil a slice of bread with butter and jam, she makes an agreement with Emil that she will pick him up after school, so he does not have to go to after-school care. Emil eases up a bit and accepts that he has to go to school.
>
> *Later this morning on the way out of the door to go to school 7.30 a.m.*
>
> Father tells Laura and Lulu that they have to be ready for school. Lulu tells Emil that they are about to go out of the door. Emil asks Father if they are about to go out of the door. Father says soon. Emil gets up from the sofa where he has been sitting next to the Observer looking at what he was writing. Emil finds his boots that are behind the sofa and puts them on. Then Emil tells the Observer they are about to leave. The Observer answers that he is ready.

At the table, Emil is again a small boy sitting on his mother's lap. But when he has to leave for school later in the departure situation, where the family is preparing to go out of the door, he becomes the responsible school boy who takes responsibility both for himself and the Observer who

---

[4] Emil is not able to read yet, which is not expected of any children starting in class zero in the Danish school system.

## Children's Emotional Crises Indicating Developmental Changes 39

is going to be with him in school. The activity also shows how the siblings' relations to each other are included in children's learning through recurrent everyday activities at home.

**Later in the classroom the same day**

> When Emil arrives at school, he no longer seems sad, and is not isolated. On the contrary, he has good contact with his friends and talks and giggles together with them. They get a drawing task that he and his friends Hector and Tom work on in their work group.
>
> The teacher comes to the boys' table and looks at their drawings. Emil continues drawing. The teacher leaves. Emil talks to Hector about the two of them being picked up today. Emil says that his grandmother is visiting and says to Tom's [his best friend] that he should meet her one day. Tom answers that he thinks that's a good idea. The teacher says the boys should be quiet now.

In this extract we see how Emil brings Grandmother into the school in his relations with his friends and he wants his best friend to meet Grandmother. It does not seem that he is sad and with no contact with his classmates. Also we see how the school situation is more structured than at home, that the boys are told to be silent and work quietly.

What is happening at home is that Emil's relations to his parents and siblings start to change, because he starts to see himself as a schoolboy, but he is also ambivalent about giving up being a small child, with the privileges that this brings (sitting cosily on his parents' laps, staying home from school when Grandma is visiting). However, it seems that Emil also wants to get a position as a schoolboy at home.

Looking at Emil's crises in these different settings we can see that they are created by his oscillation between trying to keep his relation to the parents as a small child and his orientation to a new demand of assuming a position as a school child. He explores his new situation through playing with words as we saw in the earlier observation extract. His parents support his new position by talking to him about school events. His mother, in the crises' situation, especially supports his new position, asking if she should intervene in relation to his school worries and by asking him about library books. She also tells him that he must go to school every day and that he should talk to his friends about their not being fun to play with. As we will see in a later observation, she also engages him in homework, though children in class zero do not have homework.

In the period of crisis during a major transition, the child opens up to entering into new relationships, both with new people and with those he is familiar with. For Emil, the framework for his social situation of development has changed from being a kindergarten child to now entering into relations as a school child. Consequently, his relation to both his mother and his sisters changes; he moves from the child who needs care to the child who is trying out his own agency and expressing his own will. Vygotsky (2019) explained that a child become a different child when changing the framework of his social situation of development, as is the case when he moves from kindergarten to school.

The theoretical perspective of crises and neoformation of a given age defines a new relationship for a child in three dimensions: to the world, to people and to oneself. For Emil this means he orients to new activities in a new way, not only in school but also at home, and he is supported by his parents while he creates his own position in the family as a school child.

Poliavanova (2015) writes that at the cusp of a new age period, a new ideal form opens up. Actions that are directed outward unexpectedly acquire a component aimed at the actor himself. For Emil this means that he not only acts differently toward his parents, but he also comes to feel he has a new position. As both Vygotsky and El'konin point out, in crises periods the child's attention is directed at the child's own actions and their experiments with new relations to caregivers.

## The Zone of Proximal Development Seen from the Perspective of Different Age Periods Characterized by Different Learning Forms

Learning, according to Vygotsky, is the foundation for development (1997b, 1998). Learning may be different in the different age periods, both in relation to form and to content. But what is consistent is that learning drives development by reaching forward, enabling the child to meet the demands of new situations and to develop new motives. The idea of the zone of proximal development (ZPD) reflects that developmental process. It is often explained in terms of how a more competent other can help a child do more intellectually than they might accomplish on their own. The developmental aspect of the ZPD has therefore often been underplayed. Chaiklin (2003) has argued that the zone of proximal development should be seen as a concept connected to change in children's social situation of development for children at the threshold to a new age period. He argues that Vygotsky's concept of the ZPD is not a learning concept as it has so often been interpreted, but a concept central to understanding the importance of social relations for children entering new age periods.

# Zone of Proximal Development Seen from Different Perspectives

Caregivers in different institutional practices have a responsibility for supporting children's orientation to the learning demands embedded in the activities in the practices. Developing motive orientations to meet new demands during periods of transition, we shall argue, requires care-full adult support. A child's way of learning is related to their age period, which is anchored in the practices they are participating in. These changes in the child's social situation of development are therefore qualitative. The adult helps by guiding children within new institutional practices so that they recognize the demands in new activities, where both content and form of learning differ from their previous experiences. This we again illustrate from Hedegaard's family research where Emil is included in a homework situation although he has no homework.

**Extract from November 16**

**Homework and afternoon snack**

Mother asks Emil if he has homework. Emil replies that she can look and see [in his schoolbag]. Lulu responds to her mother and says that Emil does not have homework. However, her mother just repeats the question: "Emil, do you have homework to do?"

Emil finds his schoolbag and retrieves his new cartoon-booklet. "Look Mom, it's my cartoon-booklet." Lulu asks what is a cartoon-booklet, and he shows it to her.

Emil gets his homework out. He says, "It's not something I need to do, but I may make mirror images [of figures]." He starts by drawing mirror images in his booklet.

His mother tells him that he is good at it, and this is exciting.

Emil quickly finishes his mirror task, and then he takes a tangerine and begins to peel it. Emil then asks his mother: "When will you help me to make a figure, I can make a mirror image of?" His mother says she needs a pencil and asks whether there are some in Emil's schoolbag. Emil answers that they are all in the bottom of the bag. His mother asks him to go and get one and to tidy up his bag [to put the pencils in his pencil case]. Emil says that his mother can do this. His mother answers that she is not going to do this, but ends up looking for a pencil in the bag anyway, without success. When his mother cannot find a pencil, Emil searches in his schoolbag. He finds one and gives it to his mother, who goes back to the table and draws a shape for Emil to mirror copy. She says that this one is difficult, and that he will never do it. Lulu says she can. Emil starts. "Is this how it should be?" he sounds a little uncertain. His mother supports him and says he is good at it. Emil had reflected the figure correctly. Now Lulu wants to do her homework.

> Emil says that he would like to do more homework. He says he will write all the letters he knows on a piece of paper. His mother then says she also wants to hear the names of the letters. Emil writes an *A* and names it. He further writes *Å, R, L, E, O, H, T*, and *B*. Emil does not know all the names of the letters he has written, and instead starts to talk about playing in their play hour at school.
>
> The observation continues, while Mother gets him back to work with letters and his older two sisters join supporting him.

The observation shows that Emil is eager to take the position as a schoolboy, and do homework, though in class zero they do not have homework. He creates a minor conflict with Mother about getting a pencil, but he solves it himself because he has become oriented to doing homework.

It is Mother who gets Emil oriented to homework, through the daily activity setting with snacks and homework and through asking him directly, but his activity is also supported by his older sisters who also engage in homework. In this activity setting, Mother clearly supports Emil in his ZPD, entering a new age period as a school child. By being together with his sisters in the homework situation, Emil has the ideal in front of him at home for being a school child, and Mother is meeting his demand of entering this position by giving him the same attention as she gives his two sisters. As we noted earlier, El'konin argued that caregivers may support a child to become oriented to new activities with new motives by showing them the ideal for the new activity and this may take different forms in different age periods.

Vygotsky alerted us to how differences between age periods mean that different types of learning dominate in different age periods (Vygotsky, 1984, 1987). For example, in early childhood, meaningful imitation is core to how children learn to use the tools and symbols that are directed toward becoming able to act in the material world and to communicate with caregivers. While in school, the teacher has to support the child's orientation to the systems of the different subject matter. El'konin (1999) again extended Vygotsky's points, arguing that children have the ideal for learning in front of them in the adults' activities. The adult as model is most evident when the child moves from one age period to the next and changes their emotional relations with adults.

As we saw in Table 2.2, these relations take different forms. In infancy and early childhood, children are oriented to communication with adults and to object play. In the kindergarten age they become oriented to playing at adults' activities. In school, learning activities in themselves become the focus. Children's learning in school is directed toward becoming competent adults able to work within the demands of different subject matters. Here the child may learn the standards within the different subject matters through following a teacher's actions as they model how to engage with activities, but also through their own experimentation. In adolescence, the young person again becomes oriented to emotional communication and to finding a position in society. In all of these age periods, the reciprocity in caregiver–child relations is crucial. Children, their meaning-making and their motives have to be taken seriously and the developmental shifts that occur should arise in the supportive relationships that caregivers can offer.

The modeling we have been discussing has affective elements. Bronfenbrenner (1970, 1979) pointed to how children from early childhood to adolescence learn through recognizing and attempting to replicate other people's activities. Bronfenbrenner argued that modeling is a more encompassing concept than imitation because, in modeling, the person the child imitates has to be conceptualized as a person. His argument is that modeling, as a part of learning support, has to be connected to the moral concerns of the adult and how they relate to the child. For both El'konin and Bronfenbrenner, the child doesn't just learn through meaningful imitation in Vygotsky's sense, but by including these wider characteristics of the model. In this way, a new dimension is related to children's learning. By being care-full and taking children seriously as motivated actors in their interactions, caregivers may influence children's motive orientations and their affective engagement. Bronfenbrenner (1970) particularly argued for the importance of adults taking an ethical responsibility in relation to children's opportunities to relate to their community and to wider society. From this perspective, adults' involvement as models for children in the school age and adolescence has the potential to lead to children's growing involvement and responsibility on behalf of their own family, community and society.

Children's ZPDs may therefore be seen as the space where caregivers work relationally with children in communication, play and learning, oriented to their next age period. How children's learning may unfold with support from caregivers and teachers in the different age periods will be central in all the following chapters.

## Methodology: Age Periods and the Child's Social Situation of Development

Our approach to child development, by recognizing the dynamic unity of child and practice, creates challenges for assessing development. We therefore suggest that when analyzing a child's development, one should start with examining a child's social situation of development. This can be undertaken by searching for the child's motive orientation within activities in practices. This search will include their primary relations to adults and how the child interacts with caregivers' demands and expectations. It will also reveal conflicts or oppositions, and the importance of attention to children's emotional connections.

Our approach involves analyzing children's development in their recurring everyday activity settings, where the focus is on children's motive orientation and engagement with activities. It also involves examining practices and capturing how the demands in activities in these practices create the conditions for the unfolding of children's agency in interaction with other people. These analyses should focus on how children relate to other people when engaging in explorative interactions, play and learning activities. Vygotsky's concept of the *social situation of development* is the core of this analysis. The analysis therefore aims at taking the child's perspective in activities, whether that involves meaningful imitation, explorative interaction, play, or a formal learning task.

Let us reiterate the key concepts underpinning this form of assessment. First, from a practice perspective, an *activity setting* is a social situation that a child takes part in. The child's *social situation* characterizes the child's experience in an activity setting from a child's perspective, revealing the child's motive orientation within the setting. The child's social situation of development captures how activity settings are engaged with by the child within a developmental age period. This focus will include the child's engagement across all the settings and the practices they participate in, and characterizes how a child positions themself and meets demands. As we saw with Emil, children's social situations of development also position them in practices and in society, such as being a nursery child, becoming a kindergarten child or a school child. Changes in a child's social situation of development reveal themselves as qualitative changes across different settings, in different practices, in their relation to other participants and in their activities. These different categories may be used to analyze the interplay between a child's intentions and agency in institutional settings and the demands a child meets in these settings. Table 2.1 depicts the relations between demands and motives at the different perspectives from which a child's social situation of development can be analyzed.

When taking children and young people seriously while examining their social situations of development, one has to be able to see the world from their perspectives, as well as from the objectives of the relevant institutional practices. This is the case for a researcher examining a child's life course, a caregiver or someone undertaking a formal assessment of a child's development. To take the child's perspective means to identify the child's intentions and motive orientation. To take the perspective of the purposes and priorities of institutional practices means to see how these are manifested in demands and possibilities in activity settings. It means identifying what demands a child meets in their different social situations in order to understand how the conflicts and crises that are part of children's life are created and take forward their social situations of development.

We very briefly outline how this kind of evaluation can occur in practice, by referring to the observations of the Frederiksberg family that we have discussed in this chapter. Our methodological approaches are discussed more fully in Chapters 4, 5 and 6. The data on the Frederiksberg family were gathered using participant observation, a version of the *interaction-based observation* (see Hedegaard, 2008a, b, c). This kind of observation is based on the idea that the researcher as an observer is always in the observation situations and has two roles, as an observer, and as another human being in the setting. The reason for this distinction is that the researcher as an observer can never be completely neutral, because they have to act both as a researcher and as a fellow human experiencing the social situation of the focus child and the other participants. The distinction therefore recognizes that the researcher's experiences are the foundation for the observation protocols that are written up. But the writing-up process is simply the first stage. To validate the observation protocols, they have to be interpreted using the theoretical framing that the researchers have selected. The process for this case is summarized in Table 2.3.

Observations can only speak to others through theoretical interpretations, as we have demonstrated with the extracts and their interpretations in this chapter. Preferably there have to be several observations of a child to indicate validity. In this chapter, by focusing on Emil's social situation of development as he starts school, we have been able to reveal the changes in a child's social situation of development while they move into a new practice. The concept used for this interpretation may be seen from Table 2.3.

Participant observation may not be the only relevant method. Video observations, interviewing and questionnaires may also be useful. What is important in relation to any methods used to examine children's social situations of development is that the data produced have to be interpreted. In this book, we argue for anchoring these interpretations in a cultural-historical-theoretical framework that builds on Vygotsky's work on the dynamic unity of child and environment, their social situation of development.

Table 2.3 *Questions to evaluate a child's social situation from the interaction and demands he meets in different activity settings and his motive orientations in different social situations*

| Activity setting | Focus on Emil's social situation |
| --- | --- |
| What demands characterize the dinner settings and the breakfast settings at home? What demands characterize the teaching settings at school? | What are Emil's relations to the other participants? How can Emil's intentions and motives be characterized? Is there conflict between Emil's motives and the demands he meets? |
| How do demands from other activity settings influence family settings? | Does Emil experience conflicts coming from other settings? |
| What are the pedagogical approaches to resolve conflicts? | How can Emil's learning be characterized? |

## Final Reflections

It might seem strange to devote one of the opening chapters in a book about an approach to education to the processes of child development. But if we are to take children seriously, we need to understand as best we can how they are experiencing their worlds. This is why we see education and child development as intrinsically intertwined. For us, development is not a predetermined unmediated unfolding of moves toward maturity. Rather, development needs to be seen in relation to cultural expectations. The idea of the social situation of development captures this, while recognizing the potential agency of the learner in relation to these expectations.

The reciprocity that marks the relational approach we are advocating therefore demands that those who aim to help children should access their experiencing, seek out the children's motives. In looking forward in this way we are reminded of Bruner's suggestion that we see education as a courteous conversation (Bruner, 1996). Bringing children from early on into such conversations will, we suggest, prevent their alienation from what adult help can offer.

Hedegaard's Wholeness Approach (Figure 2.1 and Table 2.1) with its three different perspectives – the societal, the institutional practice and the person's perspective – is central to how we try to understand children. The societal perspective, the conditions that a society with its cultural traditions and values create for children's participation in different institutional practices, is often underplayed in analyses of development. It remains important in our analyses, not least because our attention to how institutional practices mediate societal priorities and offer particular ways of being to participants.

From the practice perspective we have focused on children's participation in the different activity settings that characterize a given institutional practice like the breakfast and leaving for school setting, and the homework setting in the family. The demands children meet through participation in these settings are the focus for understanding children's interactions with caregivers and their social situations. From the person perspective we focus on the children's intentions, agency and motive orientations, recognizing that they may be different for children in different age periods. We have argued that age periods and the demands children meet as they move through different societal practices are crucial to understanding the core concept of social situation of development in our cultural-historical approach.

We also introduced Vygotsky's account of the neoformation of higher psychological functions and how their emergence in a child's consciousness changes a child's relation to their environment and in particular their emotional relation to their world. Emotional crises are indicators of development, but they may take several months before the age period they indicate becomes stabilized. The child's emotional relation to their world also should be seen in relation to the child's needs and motives and the position they have in their family and school. In discussing the process of motive development, El'konin, Bozhovich and Bronfenbrenner have argued that caregivers, such as parents and teachers, have important roles as models for the child to establish a new emotional relation to the world. We shall discuss the development of motives and change in children's motive orientation in the chapters that follow.

In brief, we work with Vygotsky's three methodological criteria for studying children's development. These are that the method should be holistic, able to encompass a social situation of development: "that should not be understood as a comprehensive study, nor a study which excludes analysis but as a particular type of analysis, one that does not use the method of division into elements but rather that of division into units" (Vygotsky, 2019, pp. 41–42). The second criterion is that the method should be clinical, by which he meant one should draw on detailed case studies of children in order to move between the concrete and the general in analyses. The third criterion is that a child should be followed over time in order to capture subtle changes in children's orientations, as Hedegaard did with Emil. These methodological aspects as developed by Hedegaard (1990/2013, 2008a, b, c) will be further discussed in Chapters 4, 5 and 6.

CHAPTER 3

# *Working Relationally with Other Professionals and Families*

**Introduction**

In this chapter, we turn to the adults, the professionals and family members who work care-fully with children. Our focus is how they work relationally together as adults. First, we explain the three relational concepts that are central to this book: relational expertise, common knowledge and relational agency and how they are used in the work of professionals with families. In doing so, we describe how they originated and how they have been developed by us and by others. Next, we show how these ideas can explain how professionals work relationally across the boundaries of professional practices and also with the families and other carers of children to support children as they create their social situations of development. We then point to the importance of institutional conditions for relational work and conclude by showing how the concepts can frame efforts at building collaborations aimed at supporting the learning and development of children.

Throughout the discussions, we highlight the importance of the motive orientations of the adults. We discuss how they connect with the demands and possibilities found in practices and how they give shape to people's interpretations and actions. We see practices as value-laden and inhabited by actors who learn to orient toward what is valued in them. We also recognize that practices such as family life or ways of being in a preschool or school are made up of activities such as breakfast at home or recess in school. The activities are located in and shaped by these institutional practices, which have histories and purposes. Of course, our dialectical analyses of learning and development also recognize that active participants impact on practices through their own intentional actions in and on activities. Practices are therefore not usually fossilized and unchanging. If they are not responsive to the intentions of those who inhabit them, we need to ask questions about whether they allow the agency of participants to unfold.

## The Three Relational Concepts in Work with Other Professionals and with Families

These concepts have been developed over almost 20 years of observing successful collaborations on complex problems, such as the life course of a troubled child. We offer them in this chapter as tools for understanding and promoting collaboration. In this chapter, we discuss how they can be used in three different ways. First, we examine how they can explain interprofessional collaborations, which also may include involving parents or carers in focusing on a difficult situation for a child. We then consider the concepts in terms of a professional's work with a parent or carer, which aims to help them see how they can support a child. Finally, we consider how they can explain how practitioners can work their way up a system to negotiate additional support for a child in a situation of concern.

We start by explaining the concepts in terms of interprofessional collaboration. A problem, like a troubled child's trajectory, is rarely simple and needs to be understood as fully as possible if responses are to be effective. For example, we might observe a child who is being very disruptive by frequently picking fights with others at school. But it would probably be wrong to deal with it simply as misbehavior and place them on a short-term exclusion. Instead, we should aim at a better understanding of what is going on in their life so that we can help them find a way of creating a more productive way forward for themself.

In cultural-historical terms, this move involves expanding our interpretations of the problem, the child's current developmental pathway, and we do this with others who also have a stake in supporting the child. These others may include family members, social workers, voluntary sector workers supporting the family and so on; and if the child is old enough, the child themself would be involved. Bolin has written about the importance of involving children in interprofessional collaborations (Bolin, 2015). Expanding interpretations of the problem involves each person using their expertise to add to the picture being built. A teacher, focused on creating a calm classroom, might observe that the behavior is worse toward the end of the school day; the social worker, focused on supporting the family, might know that a parent is facing court proceedings about drug use; the volunteer, focused on building the child's resilience, may add that the child is very protective of their younger brother.

Once there is a mutual feeling that the interpretation is as rich as possible, the next step is to work together to calibrate responses, who will do what and when? At this point, the knowledge of what is important to each person is crucial, this common understanding allows actions to be taken with everyone recognizing the reasons for them; and prevents actions that may cause difficulties for the others. It is at this point that the agentic responses of the participants can unfold relationally. So, the teacher may hold back while the social worker helps the child understand the court case and how they and their brother will be supported as a family.

The overarching concept in play in such a situation is relational expertise. It is an expertise, which is in addition to other specialist expertise such as teaching, or social work, or knowledge of a child as a parent. It can be found where practices intersect, where people who don't regularly work together are involved in jointly addressing a problem such as a child's current developmental trajectory, which appears to the practitioners to be directed toward the child's exclusion from the benefits of what society has to offer them. This responsive nonroutine work involves eliciting the motive orientations of the others, what matters for them, when they interpret the problem. It also involves being clear about what matters for oneself as a parent or practitioner. The skills that make up this expertise are therefore careful listening and questioning to elicit each other's' motives, together with a clear awareness of what matters professionally to oneself. It is an expertise that enables people to overcome mistrust and professional tribalism and often involves starting out by agreeing a broad goal, such as a child's development and well-being. The next step is for each participant to share ideas on what that goal looks like and to explain to the others about why that aspect of development and well-being is important. This is where the asking for and giving of reasons is crucial and where the different motive orientations are surfaced. We shall look in more detail at the asking for and giving of reasons later in this chapter.

The motive orientations that are surfaced need to be recognized and respected because together they comprise common knowledge. Common knowledge is not simply shared knowledge about a troubled child, it is knowledge of what matters to each person involved in the collaboration to support the child. It is built through the exercise of relational expertise and is made up of people's motive orientations as professionals or family members. For example, social workers are likely to be oriented toward supporting the family, while teachers want children to attend school and be calm while they are there. Common knowledge, containing those two motive orientations, enables the teacher to recognize why they need to stand back while the social worker helps the child understand what is happening in their family and how they will be supported. It also allows the social worker to recognize how the school is giving them space to do their work and will take the lead later in the process. In brief, common knowledge becomes a resource to enable sensitively aligned joint work on a problem. These carefully calibrated joint responses are the unfolding of relational agency in working on the problematic situation for the child. By working together on an expanded understanding of the problem, people can support each other rather than make interventions that may be contradictory. The concept of relational agency therefore captures how practitioners, who come together to work on a specific problem, can successfully collaborate while exercising their core professional skills. One outcome of this approach is that it values the core professional skills of each specialist practitioner. Here are two social workers explaining the impact on their own development as practitioners.

> So, you always have different perspectives, and that helps you grow, I think, professionally and you have more of this community feeling, to work together towards a child's or a family's wellbeing.
>
> It's helped me to think about what my core skills are as a social worker. (Edwards, 2009)

We now turn to how the relational concepts can explain care-full work with clients. While expanding interpretations of the problem and the resulting mutual support can enrich professional collaborations, it can also be extremely important when practitioners work with family members. As we outlined in Chapter 1, relational agency first emerged as a way of explaining the joint work that strengthened how women with mild mental health problems responded to difficulties, such as managing to pay bills. Here a practitioner would work alongside a woman, helping her to tackle a problem by reducing her anxiety, guiding her to identify what needed to be done and being there while she did it. In cases like this, relational agency is not simply an unfolding of professional agency mediated by common knowledge. Rather, it is a way of describing how the agentic responses of one participant can be strengthened by care-full attention to building confidence and a sense of efficacy (Edwards, 2005; Edwards & MacKenzie, 2005).

Hopwood and Edwards give an example of this mode of relational agency when they describe how Sophie, a nurse, worked care-fully with a new mother, Masha, to build her confidence so that she could interact relationally with her infant (Hopwood & Edwards, 2017). In the extract that follows, Masha is receiving a home visit to help her engage responsively with her son who is two and a half months old. Her interactions with him are inhibited by her high levels of anxiety about his safety and a

52    Working Relationally with Other Professionals and Families

sense of her own inadequacy, not helped by the intrusions of her dominating mother-in-law. In the extract, Sophie is demonstrating relational expertise while boosting the sense of agency of Masha, helping her to interpret the infant's responses to show that she is a competent mother.

> Masha: Now he likes the playmat a lot, he gets very excited.
>
> Sophie: What does he do to let you know he is excited?
>
> Masha: Oh, he smiles and laughs. When I'm holding him, we just look at each other for a moment and he smiles or giggles.
>
> Sophie: Those little stops, when you gaze together and wonder, they are like food for the brain. He's got this big, exciting world out there he's just getting to know and you're helping him connect all the stars.
>
> Masha: Oh. (Hopwood & Edwards, 2017, p. 113)

Here we can see Sophie eliciting examples of Masha's competence and augmenting Masha's description by adding ideas that reflect her professional motives in her work with Masha. In doing so, she is helping Masha to expand her understandings of her son's development as well as building her confidence in the face of criticisms from her mother-in-law. We presented the relationship between Sophie and Masha in Figure 3.1.

In Figure 3.1, we can see how the common knowledge that Sophie and Masha have generated about what matters for each of them in relation to the infant, allows the object of activity, or the problem space on which

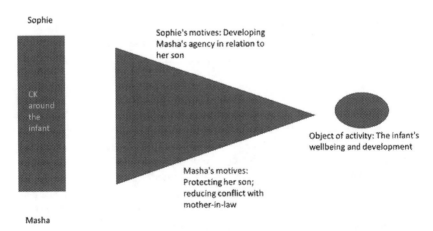

Figure 3.1   An example of common knowledge mediating the unfolding of relational agency

they are acting, to be expanded. This common knowledge mediates the expansion of the object and mediates how Sophie and Masha work together on the infant's development.

By working directly with Masha to help her become the solution to the problem, Sophie is not falling into the trap of objectifying Masha as a problem. There is, however, a danger that the relational concepts can lead to an objectifying of a child and her family or an anxious mother, as the problem to be worked on. We emphasize that professionals need to ensure that this does not happen. Wherever possible, family members, including children, need to be involved at every stage, from identifying the problem, clarifying what matters to them and working on the problem to take agentic control over it. Our theme in this book is that children need to be taken seriously, and nowhere more so than in this situation. As you can see from Sophie's interaction with Masha, this kind of relational engagement with families and children can have strong pedagogic overtones, which we return to in Chapter 7.

## Relational Support for Children in Transitions

Our examples so far have highlighted how to address relatively serious problems. But the relational concepts are also useful when considering how children are supported during their everyday lives as they make transitions between practices and need to adapt to the different demands they encounter. Here the collaborations are largely, but not exclusively, across the boundaries of home and school, involving practitioners in working with family members.

The Wholeness Approach, as we saw in Chapters 1 and 2, recognizes that as children move through a day or a week, they inhabit several different practices where various adults hold sway. These will usually include family life, preschool or school and maybe after-school activities such as sports teams or music-making. Hedegaard has long pointed to the challenges faced by children as they negotiate these transitions between such different practices, navigating their different expectations (Hedegaard & Fleer, 2012; Hedegaard, 2019).

Children will also make transitions that arise from how national policies structure expectations of development, such as the move from preschool to school, or elementary school to high school. These transitions are often at the root of the crises that Vygotsky saw as key to development. We have discussed developmental crises at length in Chapter 2; here we simply note that one feature of such a crisis is the need for children to move away from what mattered in the past in order to orient themselves to the new demands and opportunities available to them. Consequently, they are initially likely to feel disorientated. Vygotsky writes sympathetically of such disorientation. He explained that as a child experiences a developmental crisis, he (or she) "loses some of what he had acquired earlier. The onset of these age levels is not marked by the appearance of new interests of the child, of new aspirations, new types of activity, new forms of internal life. ... [H]e loses interests that only yesterday guided all his activity" (Vygotsky, 1998, p. 192). There is "a dying off of the old" (p. 194).

Children can also become disorientated through other changes that can form crises, including changes in family structures, illness, bereavement or moving neighborhoods. In all these examples of transitions, children can be helped by adults who have some understanding of what has been lost, what matters for the child now, how they are interpreting new demands and how they are orienting toward or away from them. In many cases, it is enough for an adult to work relationally with the child to facilitate their orientation to new demands and opportunities. When, however, transitions are troubling for the child, caring adults will often need to collaborate with others. Some of these changes will involve several specialist practitioners in offering support to the child, while other changes may call for particularly close collaboration between practitioners and families.

Hedegaard, taking a child-centered perspective, has labeled the sites for such collaborations as "the zone of concern" around a child (Hedegaard, 2019), while Edwards, working from a practice perspective, explains that these collaborations occur in "sites of intersecting practices" (Edwards, 2010). Both are places where people who inhabit different practices bring different knowledge and expertise to examining a problem or concern. Drawing on their own expertise, they mutually expand interpretations of the situation and negotiate joint responses to this enriched view of the concern.

Christine Woodrow and Kerry Staples have recently written about one such zone or space that was built as part of the *Futuro Infantil Hoy* (Young Children's Future Today) initiative (Woodrow & Staples, 2019). The project involved twenty early childhood settings over eight years in an isolated area of Chile, with families with limited experience of formal schooling. In many cases literacy cafés were established alongside the settings, as meeting places for families and teachers. These operated as locations for creating zones of concern or the intersecting of practices. They offered coffee, the chance to borrow children's books and games and the opportunity for families and teachers to talk at some length about the children, their families and what was important about the educational opportunities that were available. These conversations were zones or sites where what mattered in both family practices and educational practices were made explicit; common knowledge was built and became a resource that could be used to ease children's transitions into the settings and later as they moved on to more formal schooling. But the process did not simply impose school priorities on family practices. One marked finding of Woodrow and Staples' evaluation was how much the teachers learnt about the families, their strengths and priorities. They moved from a deficit view of the families and instead encouraged them to make their priorities, that is, motives, explicit so that the teachers could care-fully weave them into curricula that connected with children's everyday lives. Here common knowledge, built conversationally in zones of concern around children, acted as a bridge between home and school, reducing the disorientations of transitions, while also helping children orient to new demands in the practices of the settings. Woodrow and Staples explained the process they observed.

> By working with the idea of relational expertise, we could see that forming and sustaining relationships with families requires educators to recognize what matters in the expertise of families and make what matters for them as educators explicit. Over time, educators developed this relational expertise and, through this, gained new understandings of what was important to families. (2019, p. 139)

## Working Relationally across Roles and Positions

We now return to collaborations between professionals and the third way in which the concepts can be helpful when looking at collaboration: understanding how support is negotiated within an organization. Not all collaborations around a child involve practitioners from different institutions and distinctly different practices. In a recent study of how shy children are supported in Norwegian elementary schools, we used the relational concepts to explain how the class teachers of chronically shy children expanded their understandings of the shy child in and out of the classroom. These expanded understandings and knowledge of what mattered to themselves and colleagues, allowed the class teachers to negotiate support for a shy child from immediate colleagues or by taking the case of the child through a school's hierarchy to access additional resources. The expertise that these moves entailed was important because the class teachers held pivotal roles as 'first responders' to the needs of shy children

(Solberg, Edwards, & Nyborg, 2020a), but shyness did not automatically provoke additional resources to help the child. The class teachers therefore needed to create productive zones of concern by gathering advice and support (Solberg et al., 2020b).

Relational expertise was evident in all the class teachers' interactions with colleagues, listening to what mattered for others and being explicit about their own concerns about the child. With their peers in teacher team meetings relational expertise was deployed horizontally to build a richer picture of a shy child. Here is one of the teachers interviewed by Stine Solberg: "[W]e often discuss individual students when we have a need for information, or share our experiences, whether it concerns behavior or the home situation." The meetings would also be places where advice was given collegially or offers of help made, such as promising to watch out for a child at recess.

When peer support could not fully address the problem, class teachers needed to negotiate vertically up the school system to persuade the gatekeepers of resources to give help. To succeed in gaining an extra resource, such as a few hours of specialist support for the child, the teachers needed to know what mattered to the school leaders and middle managers who comprised the resource teams. Describing the child's difficulties in terms that would allow the release of support was key. These terms included falling behind in curriculum areas or concerns about elective mutism. In another study (Edwards et al., 2009), a practitioner described this ability as being able to press the right buttons. Armed with understandings of the motive orientations of the gatekeepers, the teachers could tailor their requests to match the concerns of the school leaders.

We found, however, that the vertical negotiations were in downward direction when we explored how school principals directed the teachers who brought their concerns about severe problems associated with shyness to them. In these interactions, the school leaders were skilled at eliciting what mattered for the teachers and then guiding them toward the appropriate external agency for help. Here a school principal describes one interaction:

> A teacher contacted me about a student who is very quiet. And then we talked about 'you need to find out what has happened to that student' (…) That was the activity; to converse with the teacher to really get at her experience of the situation and then converse with the student. Then the teacher and the student had a conversation, and then we took it to Child Psychiatric Services.

These vertical negotiations within schools were marked by imbalances in power, and pedagogy was employed to ameliorate the exercise of power. It was clear that when the school principal worked with the class teacher, she was being pedagogical. This was also the case when Sophie talked with Masha and when the worker in the drop-in center supported a center user. In each example, the more powerful person elicited the motive orientations of the other and was explicit about how they also interpreted the problem. The ensuing common knowledge became a resource that mediated action on the problem. But we also saw that this kind of relational work could lead to the more powerful actors learning from those with less status. The Chilean early years' teachers learnt a lot from the caregivers in the literacy cafés; while the Norwegian class teachers identified what mattered to their seniors as they pedagogically made the case for additional resources for shy students. The kind of relational pedagogy we are advocating is based in this kind of mutual respect, where the interpretations of all participants are taken seriously.

## Building Common Knowledge in the Space of Reasons

So far, we have explained that common knowledge, comprising the motive orientations of potential collaborators, is built through the exercise of relational expertise and can then mediate the unfolding of relational agency. But what is involved in the process of building common knowledge, how is relational expertise deployed in that task, how do motive orientations become explicit? The best answers that we have found lie in the philosopher Jan Derry's take on the "space of reasons" (Derry, 2013, p. 230).

In using the phrase "space of reasons," Derry is drawing on a long line of analyses that connect Sellars' coining of the term with Brandom's development of the idea. It denotes an environment where the asking for and giving of reasons is legitimate and expected: This asking 'why?' connects directly with our concern about eliciting motive orientations. In his work on the space of reasons, Brandom examined how we make our thoughts explicit and available to others so that they are open to scrutiny and reasons for them can be requested. Importantly, these spaces are places where everyone, regardless of status, has the right to ask for and give reasons.

Brandom also observed that being explicit in answering the question "why?" ensures that we articulate our commitments and in doing so can recognize any changes in them and the reasons for them. Highlighting one's commitments is clearly relevant to collaborations between professionals, whose work is underpinned by their distinct specialist expertise and professional values. The motive orientations that make up the common knowledge that they construct include these commitments. It is therefore worth examining the processes of making one's thoughts explicit and holding them to scrutiny that were proposed by Brandom and elaborated by Derry.

Derry comes at the space of reasons through her view that we should not think of learning simply in terms of moving to greater abstraction. Instead, we should recognize the value of building systems of inferences where connections are made between concepts. Here she is drawing on Vygotsky's argument that concepts are processes rather than entities, they are always in development through their interaction with the world. Derry explains, in cultural-historical terms, how creating a space of reasons allows concepts to be connected, so that systems of inference are constructed and referenced to experience:

> For Vygotsky concepts depend for their meaning on the system of judgments (inferences) within which they are disclosed. Brandom's careful study of concept use argues that concepts by their nature are not isolated from one another; 'to have conceptual content is just for it [a concept] to play a role in the inferential game of making claims and giving and asking for reasons. To grasp or understand such a concept is to have practical mastery over the inferences it is involved in.' (Brandom, 1994, p. 48; Derry, 2008, p. 17)

Derry's work on the space of reasons is explicitly focused on how we can enrich the system of inferences that connects the concepts that we use and is therefore relevant to building common knowledge. As we saw from the comments about their learning made by the two social workers earlier in the chapter, when building common knowledge practitioners are enriching their understandings and refining their systems of inferences. For example, when exercising relational expertise, a teacher might elicit a perspective on a troubled child from a social worker, which will lead to a fresh connection between their notions of troublesome and troubling behavior, helping them see that the child is in a situation of concern.

Derry's attention to the understandings that make up expertise and are so often held tacitly in practices is particularly useful when considering the construction of common knowledge. She draws on Joe Dunne's metaphor of "the rough ground" (Dunne, 1993), and suggests that the knowledge held implicitly in practices, the rough ground, has been overlooked

(Derry, 2008). Her solution is to create discursive spaces, where the asking for and giving of reasons is expected, and where what is important, but not articulated in the rough ground of practice, can be made visible and examined. To continue the previous example, a teacher may see disruptive children as troublesome and may react to them in a punitive way, without articulating or examining that belief. In a multi-professional space of reasons, which aims at making assumptions visible and questioning them, that belief can be examined. The outcome may be a more nuanced understanding of troublesome behavior on the part of the teacher, while a social worker may come to understand why calm and order is the *sine qua non* of school life for a teacher. The motive orientation of the teacher is clarified and becomes part of the common knowledge that will mediate later interactions.

We suggest, therefore, that it might be wise to create ground rules when setting up a zone of concern around a child or when participating in a site of intersecting practices. These ground rules should demand that people are explicit about what matters for them in relation to the problem they are addressing, what matters for them are the 'whys' of their practice. At the same time, they should elicit, with genuine curiosity and lack of judgment, the motive orientations of others. The asking for and giving of reasons should then reveal the motive orientations that can comprise common knowledge and at the same time participants' systems of inference are refined. Here is a practitioner talking to the National Evaluation of the Children's Fund in England (Edwards et al., 2006), explaining the importance of such a process.

> I think the very first step is understanding about what the sort of issues are. Professions have very, very different ideas about need, about discipline, about responsibility, about the impact of systems on families. . . . So I think the first step is actually to get some shared understanding about effective practices and about understanding the reasons behind some of them. Understanding some of the reasons why we are seeing these sorts of issues in families.

These processes are also important when building common knowledge between practitioners and families. In a study based in Rajasthan, Prabhat Rai has analyzed long sequences of conversational data between teachers and family members, which demonstrate the importance of being explicit about what matters for one as a professional while also eliciting and respecting what matters for a family. The data were gathered during his detailed study of the processes that made a small chain of elementary schools outstandingly successful with rural children (Rai, 2013, 2017, 2019).

The school where Rai based his study employed a community coordinator who visited families to discuss their children and ran village meetings for parents and teachers to discuss common concerns. In one meeting observed by Rai, the focus was the provision of a bus to make the journey to school safer for the older girls, enabling them to continue their education. Rai's analyses show that such a meeting was marked by how skilfully the community coordinator created a space of reasons, recognized the reasoning of the families and gave reasons for what mattered for the school. The school did not impose its views and acknowledged the validity of the parents' reasons. That particular meeting concluded with the school agreeing to take forward the solution offered by the families (Rai, 2013, 2017).

These meetings worked as spaces of reason because of the deep funds of trust that had been built between teachers and families. Just one example of that trust and how it was built is an exchange between a mother, the community coordinator and two teachers about whether the mother's daughter Rehana should leave school to get married now she was approaching 13 years of age. In brief, the family was under pressure from the local religious leader to take Rehana out of school, while Rehana wanted very much to continue her studies. One indication of trust was that the mother had invited the coordinator and the teachers to her home as she wanted help with this dilemma. The practitioners listened carefully while the mother presented the problem and respectfully probed the details of the dilemma from the mother's perspective and her need to please the cleric. Here is a very much abridged extract from the conversation between the community coordinator (CC) and the mother (M) about Rehana's future. After eliciting the mother's concerns and listening with care, the coordinator continues:

> CC: What is your plan? [CC is eliciting the agency of M]
>
> M: [. . .] Rehana is adamant to go [to school].
>
> CC: Rehana is very committed to her education; why don't you delay marriage for a year or two? [CC echoes M and presents Rehana's perspective]
>
> (M. reiterates the pressure on her from the cleric to prepare Rehana for marriage)
>
> CC: We are not against her going to Madrasa to learn sewing, if she wants to do so. You teach her cooking, it is fine. [CC is respectful of what matters in the parents' community]
>
> CC: If she is not willing to go somewhere, don't force her. If you let her come to school, which she wants to do, then you might be able to teach her

other things as well. [CC offering alternative reasoning to challenge and help M]

M: But what about her marriage? [M challenges CC]

CC: You remember our Rukhsar...She was good at her studies... [her parents] found a boy who owned a garage in the city. They got her married, but she insisted on completing graduation...Now she has passed her BEd exam...She earns more than her husband. You have examples in front of you. [CC offering an expanded version of a possible trajectory for Rehana]

Rehana returned to school in the following week.

In this extract, we see how CC made clear that he took seriously what mattered for the parents and their dilemma. He also made explicit his view on education and the reasons for them in ways that would appeal to Mother's concerns about her daughter's future. The conversation was managed so that the dilemma was clarified, allowing it to be seen as possible versions of Rehana's future. When addressing that problem, what mattered for the parents and the school had equal validity and could equally be held up to scrutiny. By eliciting and respecting Mother's reasoning (Rehana needs to marry early to have a good choice of husband), a conversational tone for the scrutiny of motives was set. Consequently, it was legitimate for Mother to reiterate her worries about marriage and for CC to re-voice what mattered for Rehana and to offer an example of an alternative future.

Rai (2013, p. 181) represented these teacher–parent meetings in a version of the way shown in Figure 3.2. In the case of Rehana, the problem was initially the dilemma presented by the mother; but it was soon expanded by the use of common knowledge: what mattered for the parents and for the school. The focus then became possible futures for Rehana, and Mother and CC jointly created this new version of the problem, which was her future life course. The building and use of common knowledge was achieved by CC through recognizing the reasons or motive orientations of the parents and offering his own reasons or motive orientations.

These processes were commonplace in the encounters Rai observed and had been so for decades. Consequently, parents were engaged as active and respected partners in what the school was trying to achieve, while the school was respectful of community traditions and strengths. We shall see how this common knowledge informed the pedagogical practices of the school in Chapter 7.

62    Working Relationally with Other Professionals and Families

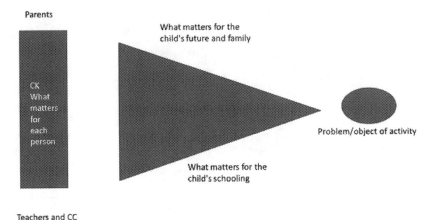

Figure 3.2   A representation of a teacher–parent meeting

## Working Relationally for Social Inclusion in and across Institutions

In the next two sections, we describe how the three relational concepts can be used to support strategies for developing collaboration. We start with efforts to overcome social exclusion. At the time of writing, reports from around the world are revealing massive discrepancies between the haves and have-nots and point to the dangers of social exclusion and its long-term impacts for children. The increasing differences in wealth and access to services to be found within and between nations are despite a raft of policy initiatives since the 1990s aiming at preventing social exclusion (Room, 1995a). During the 1990s, several definitions of social exclusion were offered to help plan these systems aimed at preventing it. Room's definition is one of the clearest and points to its detrimental long-term impact:

> Social exclusion is the process of becoming detached from the organisations and communities of which society is composed and from the rights and responsibilities that they embody. (Room, 1995b, p. 242)

The scope of this definition is much wider than school inclusion and the creation of inclusive classrooms through adaptive teaching, as important as these processes are. Consequently, schools have often found attention to social exclusion and its prevention somewhat challenging. Research in England in the first ten years of this century, for example, found that schools tended to establish quite strong barriers between themselves and the agencies that were aiming at preventing social exclusion. There were many reasons, not least the emphasis on academic outcomes driven by international comparisons of pupil performance. Schools' isolationist approaches were extremely worrying because, as universal services, schools were likely to be the places where the first signs of vulnerability to social exclusion could be seen and preventative strategies put in place. That schools were rarely involved with other agencies in interventions to prevent social exclusion was also paradoxical, as one of the most effective preventative strategies is education. This dilemma was recognized by policymakers in some countries and one of us was commissioned to report on efforts at overcoming the barriers to prevention-focused collaborations with schools across Europe (Edwards & Downes, 2013).

The review revealed an array of potentially fruitful relationships that eroded institutional boundaries. They ranged from placing social workers in Swedish schools (Bolin, 2011), through positioning multiagency teams on the boundaries of schools in The Netherlands, to place-based multifaceted collaborations in Germany. All of these interventions, from one-on-one collaborations in Sweden, to efforts to align the work of multiprofessional support teams with the aims of the school in the Dutch example and the more fluid ecological approach typified by the One Square Kilometer initiative in Germany, created sites of intersecting practices and the need for responsive nonroutine collaborations. One important reason for such fluidity in collaborations is that vulnerability is a dynamic state and children's need for support will change as they move from low to high need or back from high support to relatively low-level support.

In the report, we advised that practitioners should build common knowledge in interprofessional meetings while they discussed children's cases or planned changes in services. We suggested that meetings should be structured so that meanings were shared, for example, explaining what assessment means for different professions, so that professional dialects were translated, and taking the standpoint of the other was enabled. Our suggestions found support in Bolin's analysis of what led to successful collaborations between social workers and teachers. She described how they built 'common grounds' for the construction of 'collaborative relations' (Bolin, 2011, p. 126).

These efforts at eliciting what matters for others to build common grounds were also crucial at the level of systems leadership. In a parallel study, we explored the work of ten English Directors of Children's

Services, who were highly successful in reconfiguring services for interprofessional working to prevent children's social exclusion (Daniels & Edwards, 2012). One finding was that, alongside being clear about what their priorities were, attention to people's motives and taking the standpoint of the other were keys to their success. These two brief quotes were typical of the leaders we studied:

> I make a great play of listening skills and not being judgmental. I do deep listening and try to transpose myself into how others are listening. . . . I try to understand where people are coming from – their agenda and motives.

> You need to find out what is the grit in their shoes. Understanding that means you can get to aligning motives. You can talk in a way they will understand. (p. 37)

The institutional conditions for fluid preventative work are crucial. Over the years we have observed how practitioners, such as social workers, can feel that they have been parachuted into a set of alien practices when asked to work in schools. In one study, Edwards and Montecinos followed the work of social workers and psychologists who were allocated to four Chilean secondary schools as part of an initiative to promote interprofessional work to prevent social exclusion (Edwards & Montecinos, 2017). We examined what problems these practitioners were able to work on, who they could work with and how they worked with others. In the school marked by rigid rules and tight top-down direction there was no opportunity for the incoming practitioners to relate to and collaborate with other colleagues. Instead, children were referred to them and they did the paperwork to refer them on to other agencies. Success was mixed in two of the other schools, where there had been recent changes in leadership, but there were promising developments, as they could work in systems that were in some flux due to these changes. The most success was achieved in a school that had experienced a form of sustained leadership, which was values-led and gave leeway to all employees to work responsively with children. Their professional decisions were guided by a shared understanding of what was valued in the school.

In all but the first school we could observe the building of common knowledge. In the second and third school, there was an emergent form of relational agency. In the fourth school, there was strong relational agency between the social worker and the psychologist and with the teachers. Here is the psychologist describing a space of reasons, the building of common knowledge and how he benefitted from the reciprocity and challenge offered by the social worker:

I felt very fortunate when the social worker arrived, to know he is by my side, I can enter his terrain and he tells me "you are right, but I look at it from this other perspective". And he enters mine... there is trust within the team. That has been enriching because one learns from other points of view and that enriches your own. (Edwards & Montecinos, 2017, p. 243)

The psychologist and social worker went on to describe how they were able to set up structures for meeting regularly with teachers, how they worked alongside them to support children's engagement with school and how they could help children and families navigate other support services.

We discussed the interrelating planes of analysis that are derived from Hedegaard's Wholeness Approach in Chapter 2. If schools are to cooperate in tackling social exclusion alongside focusing on the inclusion of children in the flow of school life through adaptive teaching, attention needs to be paid to the institutional layer and the purposes of its practices. Otherwise, preventative initiatives may remain a series of parachute drops.

## Using the Relational Concepts to Assess and Develop Collaboration for the Support of Children

In focusing on leadership and the institutional conditions for encouraging relational work, we have moved some way from observing the efforts of individual workers to enhance the agency of children and young people. In this section we go further with our focus on collaboration between caregivers, to discuss how the relational concepts can be used to examine the extent to which practitioners are working relationally and responsively across professional boundaries to address situations of concern for children.

Marilyn Fleer and her colleagues were commissioned to evaluate an early years' professional learning program in Victoria, Australia (Fleer, Duhn, & Harrison, 2017). The program's aim was to enhance multi-professional working to support children and families among a range of different early years' practitioners. The program centered on practitioner enquiry, informed by new understandings of child development and shifts in Victorian policies for early childhood. The evaluation focused on 132 practitioners, who were collaborating in nine networks and who met in five workshops in each network over the eight-month program. Participant reflection sheets and facilitator progress reports from each workshop were augmented by nine focus group interviews and pre- and post-program questionnaires. To make sense of this vast array of largely qualitative data the research team drew on the three relational concepts to create the Relational Agency Framework, which we now describe.

The team found that the networks operated as sites of intersecting practices and were safe, but challenging places where ideas could be made explicit and tested and common knowledge built. The researchers did not use the term "space of reasons," but their descriptions of processes in the networks suggest that the scrutiny and challenge that mark such spaces was happening. They also observed how the discussion in the network meetings increased participants' curiosity about and respect for what other network members were "doing back in their specialist practices" (Fleer, Duhn, & Harrison, 2017, p. 217). Again, we can see how interprofessional collaboration can enhance respect for specialist expertise.

However, it was the team's use of the concepts we have been discussing in this chapter in order to evaluate the development of the networks that was a novel departure. The Relational Agency Framework (Figure 3.3 is an abridged version) captured whether and how participants exercised relational expertise, built common knowledge and experienced an unfolding relational agency over time. In Figure 3.3, Fleer and her colleagues offer eight stages of development from building a sense of belonging to a network through to engaging in collective activities. Building a shared

| Phase | Key Idea |
|---|---|
| Foundational | Building a sense of belonging to a network |
| Phase 1 | Finding out about each other's services |
| Phase 2 | Engaging in a common experience or process |
| Phase 3 | Building and expanding a common focus for the group |
| Phase 4 | Building a shared language |
| Phase 5 | Aligning one's own interpretations and purposes with that of others |
| Phase 6 | Thinking about one's own professional expertise and contribution in relation to what others with different knowledges and practices bring |
| Phase 7 | Enhanced professional practice where own contributions are viewed as part of the collectively identified professional inquiry or need. |

Figure 3.3   The Relational Agency Framework

language does, however, need to be explained. Participants did not lose their specialist language; but learnt to talk in ways that could be understood by people from other practices.

When discussing these phases, Fleer and her colleagues talked in terms of "network maturity" (p. 220), which was evidenced by activity at each of the phases shown in the Relational Agency Framework.

The Victorian government quickly recognized that the Framework could also be used as a tool for supporting the development and maintenance of these interprofessional networks and have started to use it not only in the early years' sector, but also in their work on encouraging interprofessional collaboration in and around secondary schools. The research team note that the Framework is particularly useful when examining and supporting new groupings. We would add that it also recognizes the fluidity in the formation of these groups, as personnel in the networks change and different configurations of expertise are needed to tackle different problems.

## Final Reflections

It will be clear by now that the three relational concepts, relational expertise, common knowledge and relational agency, have other applications within and beyond the areas we are focusing on in this book. There are many more examples of their use in different settings including citizen science (Bantawa, 2017); learning in higher education (Hopwood, 2010); and relationships in research (Hasse, 2017; Rickinson & Edwards, 2021).

They are powerful concepts that enable practitioners and researchers to elicit the often tacitly held beliefs and commitments of others. They could therefore be open to abuse by potentially more powerful participants. Consequently, it is not enough to say that people need to feel safe in the spaces of reasons where they reveal their motive orientations. Participants need to reflect on their own power as they enter these spaces and recognize that building common knowledge as a resource to mediate relational agency depends on ensuring that all motive orientations are valued equally. If they are not, then the common knowledge that is built will be lacking. We elaborate this argument in Chapter 7 where we discuss the role of common knowledge in a relational pedagogy.

In conclusion, we therefore suggest that spaces of reason need to be imbued with care-fully articulated and agreed sets of values. The sense of belonging as the first stage in the Relational Agency Framework and the importance of values in the most successful Chilean school both point to the importance of connecting relational agency to moral purpose.

CHAPTER 4

# *Very Young Children*
## *Taking a Double Perspective in Understanding Their Development*

**Introduction**

In this chapter, we address young children's development by taking a cultural-historical approach. Our aim is to give professionals a foundation for supporting parents and other caregivers so they may assess the development of neonates, infants and toddlers in their context and not as isolated beings. To accomplish this, we follow the spirit of Vygotsky (1994, 1998, 2019, 2021) by working with his approach to children's development, captured in the concept of *the child's social situation of development*, which we described in Chapter 2. In that chapter we also explained how Vygotsky's approach encompasses how the higher psychological functions in a child's personality, such as agency, imagination and memory, develop through a child's participation in societal practices.

This development can be seen as interconnected neoformations of these capabilities over a child's life course. This interconnection means that when focusing on one aspect in a child's development, other psychological functions must be interpreted in the new relations created by the neoformation in the child's personality. We are using personality, in line with Vygotsky's definition, to characterize the child's conscious relation to the environment, a consciousness that changes with the child's development of higher psychic functions.

The chapter will focus on how the first psychological neoformations arise in an infant's social situation of development through their changing emotional interactions with their caregivers. As care may lead to developmental changes, importantly, care also has to change in relation to a child's developmental changes. Also, a child may be moving between different forms of child-care, that is, home and nursery, and family and nursery caregivers may have different views on how to interact with babies. Institutional practices and care for children in the first years of life may differ in different societies and in different societal periods in the same society (Oswell, 2013; Rogoff, 2003).

One of the challenges for caregivers is how to interpret and evaluate neonates', infants' and toddlers' social situations of development. Our advice is to employ a relational approach to understanding young children's development (Edwards, 2010; Hedegaard, 2008a,b,c; Lisina, 1985; Stern, 1985/1998; Vygotsky, 1998). To clarify the distinctiveness of this approach, we will exemplify how young children's development has been assessed within psychology. We shall, for example, take issue with Piaget's stage description, arguing, that it is based in an essentialist ontology of childhood where the child is conceptualized as a genetically fixed entity (Wartofsky, 1983).

Our argument, as we have already indicated, is that children are situated in a dynamic relationship with their social conditions, where they find the motives and goals for their actions. This approach to assessing development means that both family caregivers and professionals need to be aware of the demands children meet, and how these interact with children's intentional actions and motive orientations. To illustrate what we mean by this relational way of working, we will draw primarily, but not exclusively, on Hedegaard's research program over the last few decades, where she has employed *the interactive observation method* (Hedegaard, 1984, 1990/2013, 2008a,b,c) for observing children in their everyday activities, instead of using test material. This method has allowed Hedegaard and colleagues to orient to a child's intentions and motive orientation, despite their lack of language.

When practitioners assess children's development in order to advise caregivers, it is important to see children's development as two dimensional. These dimensions are: (i) the dynamic unity between the child and their environment, which we explained in Chapter 2; and (ii) within that unity, how the higher psychological functions in a child's personality develop through a process of crises and neoformations over a child's life course to create the child's personality. In this chapter, we try to sustain this dual focus and capture the dynamic unity and its developmental implications across the different settings for very young children.

Our arguments will be grounded in examples from interactive observations of very young children with caregivers at home and in nurseries and with professionals working with parents on their concerns about young children's social situations of development. In the latter example, we will draw on Edwards' concepts of relational expertise, common knowledge and relational agency to understand how professionals work pedagogically with parents with their concerns about caring for very young children.

## Communication as the Key to Young Children's Development

The relational approach that we are advocating is based in our recognition that communication between caregiver and child is important. Our focus will be how caregivers create a communicative atmosphere for interactions with infants so that it becomes a foundation for an infant's intentional orientation and agentive relations with adult caregivers and the environment. All of which are central to the creation of the child's social situation of development. We will illustrate this with extracts of interactive observations of how communication between parents and children takes place in different age periods, from newborn to preschool child. In doing so, we will point to how crises in this communication may be indicating neoformations in the young child's personality.

Communication here is understood as wider than linguistic interactions. It includes meaningful synchronized interactions through the coordination of action between a caregiver and a child. Examples include when a child and caregiver smile together; or when a caregiver enters the room and talks to a baby and the movement of the infant's arms and legs intensifies; or when a baby is held and kissed and then snuggles into the caregiver's arms.

An infant's social situation of development is connected to the conditions for their communication with caregivers. These conditions can be dependent on: (a) the child's acquisition of capabilities such as orienting toward people and objects in their movements; (b) changes in daily home activities, for example, moving onto solid food; or from a crib to a cot; or (c) changes in the institutional practice, for example, moving from home care to attending nursery. Changes in practices may also come from changes in societal conditions such as changes in parents' work patterns.

A child's development is biologically driven, but as Vygotsky (1998, 2019) points out, a parallel cultural force is interwoven with the biological development that starts when a child is born. This force is, from the start of life, founded in care and love and is as important as biological needs. How this cultural force comes to work is through parents' affective reaching out toward the neonate. Vygotsky writes that it is affect that opens up development and is seen in the interactive responses to when a child expresses their needs, such as hunger. In response, caregivers create an emotionally caring relationship by holding and stroking the child, while also feeding them. As Vygotsky summarized: "It might be said that affect opens the process of the child's mental development and construction of his personality and itself completes the process, concluding and crowning the development of personality as a whole." (Vygotsky, 1998, p. 227)

Lisina's research has been important in extending Vygotsky's approach, since it explains how caregivers' caring communicative relations to children, from the moment the child is born, contribute to the child's development. She argues that children's motive orientation and cognitive development in infancy and toddlerhood, as well as later, are interwoven with their emotional relation to adults. Her communicative approach to young children's development is important for our care-full relational approach because she argues that professionals need to analyze children's development, from the first moment of life, from the perspective of the parents. This, therefore, implies taking a cultural perspective. This is not to ignore that children's development also has a biological aspect. But she emphasizes the importance of how caregivers relate to the child's biology as part of the child's social situation of development. This relating is through communication that takes different forms in different periods in a child's life course. In brief, Lisina sees the adult as the guide to the child's development and writes, "[A] child can only acquire independence through his interaction with adults" (1985, p. 91).

In the sections that follow, we shall demonstrate how a caring communicative atmosphere leads to different forms of neoformation in three periods of a child's development as a neonate, an infant and a toddler. For the neonate, it results in an *intentional orientation* to the caregivers that may be seen as a central neoformation in the first period of a child's life. This may be followed by the caregiver's communicative cooperation with the infant so the infant attains *an agentive relation* to adults and their environment as a central neoformation. In the following period, when the infant can walk, becomes a toddler and starts to communicate verbally, the young child will, through caregivers' support, enter into a *volitional relation* to other people as well as a *self-controlling relation* to her own activities.

We use chronological age to demarcate age periods. But they should be seen as cultural age periods. As Vygotsky (2019) points out, the periods of psychological age may be different from the 'passport age.' It is also obvious that there are variations between the different theories we draw on to delimit the periods in early childhood: Lisina (1985), for example, uses different demarcations from Stern (1985/1998). But Vygotsky, Lisina and Stern agree that one can never simply assess the child in isolation, one always has to examine the child's interaction with caregivers and how this reaches into the zone of the child's proximal development and the emergence of neoformations. Their research also shows that, for the human child, there are some milestones in development that can be aligned into a sequence, but how a child's development proceeds also depends on the traditions in the practices of child-care.

There was also a raft of research in the 1960s and 1970s within Western – largely cognitive – psychology, which foregrounded the intersubjective emotional relations between caregivers and infants. It revealed how the child's intentional and agentive orientation evolved in cooperation with caregivers (Bruner, 1968, 1972; Meltzoff & Moore, 2006; Trevarthen, 1993, 2011a,b). Much of this research pointed to the development of the competent infant. The idea of the competent infant can be seen as both inspired by Piaget's (1952, 1955) research and theory of infant development and as an objection to his interpretations of development.

Piaget, in his empirical work on infancy, observed his own children and through this built a theory about the importance of the child's sensorimotor activity for the child's cognitive development in infancy. The child's cognitive development, he argued, takes place as the formation of schemata of sensorimotor activities that, through their organization, gradually lead to the child's conception of the world. Piaget (1955) promoted the idea that the child's first actions are founded in the child's reflexes and are modified when the child encounters the world. Even though Piaget researched his own infants, he took a bird's eye or distanced perspective with his conception of schemata as inner representations of the child's exploration and adaption to the world. What is missing in Piaget's theory is a conception of how the emotional communication between a caregiver and a child influences the child's sensorimotor activity and how the child's actions also influence the caregiver's.

We take epistemological departure in Vygotsky's view that children's development should be seen as a dynamic unity of child and environment, where the world cannot be seen as static but also changes and develops together with children's development (Stetsenko, 2017; Vygotsky, 2019). We therefore see Piaget's idea of a one-dimensional unfolding of developmental stages as insufficient, not least because it does not indicate how *both* caregivers and child are conditions for each other's activities and development. We do, however, acknowledge that Piaget's research has been of great importance for promoting infant research about the agentive child.

In the next section we will focus on the neonatal period, the first months of life, where a relation to adults has to be established. This will be followed by the infant period where children cannot move around by themselves, but through the interaction with caregivers they start to relate agentively and begin to explore their environments. We then turn to the toddler period where the young child, supported by caregivers, has learned to walk and meets demands from caregivers that restrict their explorations. This is where the child starts to demonstrate a will, but also self-control. The emergence of language also happens. Before becoming a toddler, the infant expresses themselves with babbling sounds but with caregivers' support, they start to imitate the adult to express themself verbally and not only with gestures or screams.

## The Changing Dynamic between Caregivers and Infants in Different Phases in Children's Development

### *The Neonate's Social Situation of Development*

In the neonatal period, the child has become physiologically independent of the mother, but is not yet biologically independent because, for example, they cannot feed themself. Hence, all the child's needs are met via their caregivers. The activities that dominate neonates' lives are eating, sleeping, crying and silent attention. Both parents and children create conditions for each other. For parents the task is to find a way forward to coordinate an infant's needs with their own needs, especially for their own sleeping and eating, so they also can continue with other aspects of life. For the infant, crying, but also their silent attention, make demands on caregivers. Consequently, caregivers seek eye contact, cuddle, talk to and smile at the baby to get attention, and hopefully get smiles and other responses in return. In this period, it is important that caregivers create an affective relation to process the child's intentional orientation to them and other key people. Through her extensive analyses and formative experiments with infants, Lisina's (1985) research demonstrates that from the first days in their lives, the social relations with caregivers are the central force in infants' development.

Vygotsky (1998) has argued against the view that children's development starts as a modification of reflexes. Instead, he proposed that the origin of development is founded in the affective aspects of instinctive activities such as the baby's searching for the nipple of the breast. He observes how active and even upset the newborn child becomes when hungry and how the neonate calms down when sucking and getting milk. These affective tendencies, according to Vygotsky, become the foundation for the caregiver's emotional communication with the neonate, which helps to create the child's intentional orientation as the first neoformation.

The neonate's intentional orientation and emergent agency has been a central theme in cognitive psychology, researched among others by Bruner (1968, 1972), Connolly and Bruner (1974), Kagan (1973), Meltzoff and Moore (1983) and Stern (1998). These researchers also object to seeing reflexes as the origin of children's development. Bruner points to the first type of actions, such as the infants' head turning and sucking, as the origin of children's development. He observes that the newborn child masters turning the head to find the nipple and suck and in response to light and gaze. Kagan similarly points to how the child's attention, from the very start, is oriented toward objects through gaze and sounds. Meltzoff and Moore interestingly argue that children can imitate from the first days of life. They then propose broadening the idea of the neonate's attentive orientation to suggest that children, through imitating actions from the first days of life, come to communicate with caregivers and thereby differentiate them from themselves[1]. Bruner's (1968) cognitively oriented research has demonstrated that children have preferences and related capacities in the first month of life, such as preferences for their mother's milk and face, and act in relation to these preferences. It is this research that has led to the notion of *the competent infant*.

The idea of the competent infant is important and is also found in Vygotsky and Lisina's research, where they stress the value of caregivers' communicative interaction from the first moments of a child's life. In their research they focus on bodily communication, where it is the love from caregivers that propels children's competences forward. Lisina's analyses show that with constant communication from caregivers, in the form of supporting physical contact and warm verbal expressions, a communicative and affective atmosphere will be built around the child. In the beginning, caregivers take both roles in communication, their own and the newborn baby's role, when they treat the baby as a totally reasonable being, by talking to him and praising him for his reactions. In that way, they create a dynamic that brings the baby out of passive attention and to an active intentional orientation toward the caregivers. An important event happens when the infant smiles, in the third or fourth week of life, Lisina writes, because this indicates reciprocity toward the caregivers, even though the first smile may be a reflex smile, the smile supports the adult's emotional interaction with the child. She writes: "A smile is not linked to a primitive

---

[1] As can be seen in tongue protrusion (Ullstadius, 1998).

physical state, but to a completely new kind of pleasure of non-physical nature stemming from interpersonal contact with another being, who is capable of perceiving and assessing the child's happiness and who is ready to share that happiness and present to him in return his own happiness." (Lisina, 1985, p. 113) Trevarthen (1993) ascribes this smile to an inborn readiness for the child to discriminate and react emotionally to adults.

Both Trevarthen (1980) and Bruner (1968) have promoted an understanding of the newborn child as agentive in relation to the environment. They argue that the neonate's intentional orientation is a biological precondition for the newborn's development. Melttshoff and Moore (2006) see this orientation as crucial to children coming to differentiate other persons from themselves.

Vygotsky's and Lisina take a different line and argue that the neonate's intentional orientation is a cultural outcome, arising through the parents' careful bodily and verbal communication with the neonate. The consequent orientation of the infant to adults may lead to the neoformation of intentional orientation toward adults as humans. Neither Vygotsky nor Lisina sees the child's intentional orientation as inborn and naturally unfolding, which means that if it is not awakened it will not develop. But both Vygotsky and Lisina accept biological preconditions for the child to learn to orient intentionally. The adults build on these preconditions in their care for neonates, but caregivers need to create a communicative atmosphere for the neonate and become sensitive to the child's bodily communications in different activities such as eating, sleeping, crying and attentive orientation. Vygotsky writes that the infant's path to satisfaction of their needs always requires the involvement of an adult. "From the very beginning the infant is confronted only by situations in which the whole behavior is intertwined and interwoven into sociability. His path to things and to satisfaction of his own needs is always channeled through relations with another person." (Vygotsky, 1998, p. 230)

The neonate has not yet consciously separated themselves from its mother. Lisina argues that for this to happen, a child needs guidance and education from the moment the caregiver first holds the child. For the neonate, an adult's care – in the form of attending, holding, stroking and talking to the baby – is absolutely significant for bringing the neonate out of passive attention and creating the baby's interactions with caregivers. Lisina writes that if "the adult only confines himself or herself to feeding the child and changing his nappies then the child will come to a standstill at that initial stage of development and will be totally alienated from what is happening around him" (Lisina, 1985, p. 104). She observes that this is what happened to the children in orphanages that Spitz described (Spitz, 1945). Therefore, she stresses very firmly that "a child needs guidance and education from the moment his mother first picks him up" (Lisina, 1985, p. 113).

During the first, the neonatal, period of life, the child's emotions assume the basic form of their receptive interest in the outside world. This gives way in the next period to their active intentional interest in the environment. Through affective caring, the infant may be seen to be in a conscious shared unity with others, a state that precedes the development of a consciousness of their own personality. This Vygotsky characterizes as – "Ur we that is great-we" (1998, p. 233).

Stern (1998) similarly suggested that the neonate's consciousness is merged with the environment, and that the neonate experiences themself as an "emergent self," not separated from the environment. According to Stern, this experience changes through interactions with caregivers, so the child comes to experience a "core self" (Stern, 1998, p. 26). This shift means that the child enters a new period and starts to distinguish themself from objects and other people. In Vygotsky's terminology, the neoformation of intentional orientation will change the communicative interaction with caregivers and the neonate will enter infancy.

## *The Infant's Social Situation of Development*

Through the neoformation of intentional orientation, the path to the external world opens up for the child's activity but it is still through another person. Lisina noted that after a baby enters the second month they can reveal an astonishingly fine sensitivity to gradations of adults' attention. Thanks to the influence of adults, emotional experiences and reactions begin to appear in children's relations to adults. It is the adults' interpretations of the baby's movement in their interactions that propels infants' development forward. The infants' emotional expressions start to take form as active gestures addressed at other people. The child's attentive orientation toward the caregiver can be seen in the synchrony in their interactions. Trevathen's research (Kokkinaki et al., 2017) shows how infant and mother act to obtain complementary feeling and intersynchrony of actions. Bruner (1972) also points to the importance of the coordination of infant and mother through shared gaze. Lisina (1985, p. 114) names this first form of interaction a *situational-interpersonal form of communication*.

## Change of Dynamic between Caregivers & Infants

Of decisive importance for a child's development during this period is the fact that, thanks to the interactive communication between caregiver and child, the infant begins to reach for objects. Lisina noted that, at first an infant will shake their arms haphazardly simply as a result of excitement, and when a caregiver approaches, the movement of arms and legs will increase along with gurgling. The infant's arms may knock objects, and their attempts to reach out to grasp an object begins. At around four months children are able to confidently take hold of a toy, with the help of adults. There now appears in the child an interest in objects in their immediate environment. In this period the caregiver may construct the environment so that the child has opportunities to come into contact with play-objects, by placing the infant in a position where they can reach for them. The infant's emotional expressions start to take form as active gestures addressed at other people. A new type of dominant activity emerges – *object-directed manipulative activity*, which leads to a new period with neoformation where the dominant line in infants' development is agency in relation to object manipulation.

This new orientation and the role of the caregiver can be seen in the following example in a Danish home setting. We can observe six-month-old Morten's orientation to new objects and his agentive interaction with his father. At the same time, we can see how a caregiver may orchestrate the child's new orientation, so that it becomes an enjoyable situation for both of them.

> It is early morning January 2019. Morten has got his bottle of milk and Father has sat him down on a blanket on the floor. Morten moves away from the blanket toward a bag with different toys. He pulls several times at the bag and each time a sound from one of the toys occurs. Father moves Morten back at in a sitting position at the blanket, sits down next to Morten and gives Morten the toy – a plastic book that makes sounds and lights up when touched and when the pages are turned. Morten explores the book by pressing and tasting it. He falls over still holding the book and makes some fuss. Father says wait. He raises Morten to a sitting position again and gives him the book again. Father finds another book with animal pets and points to the pets while naming them. Morten claps on the book's pages. There are some other books in reach and Morten reaches for them. The observer moves the books away and Morten falls over and hits the edge of the coffee-table. He cries. Father comforts him and he stops crying and gets a pacifier. Father tells him what there is on the front page of a book he now holds. It is a Winnie the Pooh picture book and Father starts reading the book. Morten claps on the page, Father reads. Father tries to turn the pages that Morten tries to grasp and succeeds and continues to read.

> Morten wants to turn the pages faster than Father reads. He has no pacifier any longer. He grabs the pages.
>
> Father: "Shall I turn the pages again?" He continues to read. Morten claps on the pages but also sits still and listen for a short while. Then he grabs the book, but Father raises the book out of reach and continues to read. Morten says some sounds (aaahh). Father says what there is on the page they look at. Morten succeeds in grabbing the page. Father holds him back. Morten alternates between looking and grabbing the book. Father continues to hold it so he can clap on the pages but not tear them apart. When Father has read all the pages Morten is allowed to hold the book and claps it. Then he tries to raise himself to standing by holding his father's legs and then turns forward and falls over his father legs.

In this observation we see how Father supports Morten in orienting to the objects, in this case picture books. Father uses language even though he knows Morten does not understand, he says what is on the pages and also reads to Morten. It is an activity that is ahead of what is meaningful for Morten, but the interaction of Father's reading, pointing and clapping and Morten's clapping and grasping the book make the interaction joyful for both child and adult. The caregiver, through his interaction with the infant before the child understands the language, brings the emotional expression of the child in line with a system of standards, accepted in their society. Delafield-Butt and Trevarthen (2015) describe this type of interaction as the start of the ontogenesis of narrative, moving from interaction to meaning. Adults shape the selection of gestures used by the child by encouraging acceptable ones such as glances and smiles, while trying to eliminate inacceptable ones such as excessively loud cries, squeals, angry waving of the arms. "Thanks to the effort of the adults, and children's willingness to comply with their desires, babies' expressions soon come to be signs comprehensible to the people in children's immediate environment" (Lisina, 1985, p. 128).

The adult's practical situated communication around the child will lead to cooperation around objects, and the following phase *practical communication as a central activity* will gradually take form. New modes of parent–child communication take place when the caregiver enters into practical play-interaction with a child. When this takes place, Lisina writes, the purely situational-interpersonal communication, which six months earlier had brought happiness to children, was now obviously burdensome to them.

If we return to Morten and Father half a year later in August, their way of interaction has changed. Morten can now hold and manipulate objects and starts to walk, supporting himself with the wall and furniture.

This morning Father brings Morten to the living room, and he is put down standing at the sofa. Morten turns toward the coffee table where there are three soft cloth blocks with bells inside. He grabs one of the blocks and shakes it saying jaa-jaa several times. Father imitates him and also says jaa-jaa several times and places two small figures in front of him, an owl and a bear, with knots on. (The figures belong to a puzzle where one can take hold of the figures using the knot.) Father says the name of the animals. Morten takes one and continues to say jaa-jaa. Father repeats and sits down on the floor while Morten remains standing at the table. He then puts one of the knots from the puzzle pieces in his mouth and looks at Father. Morten moves around the table and takes one of the other soft blocks saying jaa-jaa. Father takes the other soft block that Morten had thrown at the floor and responds with jaa-jaa. Morten moves over to Father, who now has some large LEGO blocks and put one on top of another. Father helps Morten to put a new one at the top. Morten takes the LEGO blocks apart, then plays briefly with them, trying to put some together. Morten moves to the toy-box, but then he turns around smiles and begins to wave his hand as if winking. Father does the same. They continue and both are turned toward the observer. The joint action is related to the soft music that is playing and Father begins to sing along. Morten waves again and smiles, then turns back to the toy-box.

Here we see again that Morten is intentionally oriented to Father but is also agentive in starting activities that, through Father joining in, become interactive. The neoformation in this period is the child's agentive orientation to explore objects in their environment and to move around. The child's agency starts to take form as self-initiated actions. These actions may be seen as signs of Morten's emergent motive orientation toward both objects and interaction with his parents. Object-directed enactive means of communication do not do away with the need for emotional support but are combined with it. They may acquire an agentive emotional flavor, as when Morten says jaa-jaa and Father repeats it, or when he turns around and smiles and winks supported by Father's winking.

In the practical communication between the child and caregiver, the infant may utter sounds such as when Morten expressed himself with jaa-jaa, Father imitates, but there is no talk. Father also imitates his waving. Trevarthen (2005) describes how adults' imitation of children may be joyful for the child as it was in the above example. Simple object-play in an infant's period of *situated practical cooperation* may result in the child's development of some kind of enactive imagination, seen in Morten's waving to the music, which can be interpreted as delayed imitation. This waving was an activity he and his father had done several times both to music and to saying goodbye. Father's emotional support to Morten's actions may be seen as the foundation for his first motive orientations, to repeat these actions, and to be brave in trying to walk.

In the following month Morten begins to walk. He becomes more competent, first by taking two steps toward Father's outstretched hands, then being by brave walking without support or outstretched hands even though he falls many times. After four weeks he walks confidently, though a little unstable, around in the living room and kitchen. Also, he has found out how to open the doors and drawers in the kitchen cabinets to take out the objects and to open the garbage can. These are activities the parents are not happy about and try to hinder him either by giving him other opportunities or by saying no-no. He reacts to the no-no for a short time, but then tries again.

Also, he changes from being easy to feed with porridge in the morning or mashed vegetables at lunch. Instead, he expresses his wish to feed himself and grabs the spoon with the mashed vegetables, so it ends up on the floor. The bowl goes the same way if his parents place it too close and do not watch him. The parents then start to give him whole pieces of food that he can eat himself. He expresses himself with angry cries when he is not allowed to feed himself. What we see in this period is a development of the child's will and motives for actions that are initiated by the aspects of the environment that he orients to, such as the doors and drawers that he can open. These aspects afford Morten opportunities for actions, but his parents' demands also start to make him control himself.

> We sit together, I (the observer), Father and Morten on the floor. Father has four new toy animals: a giraffe, a panda, a dolphin and a donkey that the observer had brought with her. Morten smiles at the panda that he has seen before and takes it to the coffee table. I (the observer) take the donkey, making donkey sounds, and let the toy donkey jump towards the panda. Morten laughs.
>
> Father leaves silently. Morten is preoccupied with the animals for a few minutes and then becomes aware that Father has gone. He starts to walk towards the stairs where Father had gone. I bring him back and distract him with the wooden figures for the puzzle that catches his attention. Then I sit down at the floor and start to put the large LEGO bricks on the table where Morten stands. He tries to put a LEGO brick on top of the other two I have put together on the table, but he does not succeed; instead he takes them apart. I take the animals, say their names and sounds, and he plays with these, and again orients to the LEGO bricks. I keep his attention for half an hour. He then gets up and walks along the couch and walks over to the stair safety gate. I carry him back to the coffee table and try to interest him in the

toys. He makes loud noises of dissatisfaction and immediately crawls towards the stairs where he expresses great dissatisfaction with loud howls.

I cannot keep him away from the stair gate, where he stands howling.

I lift him and go to the kitchen and put him in his highchair and peel an apple for him. It seems to work, but no, he takes it to his mouth once and then throws it on the floor. I cut a piece off and lay the piece and the apple in front of him, he throws both on the floor and makes himself completely stiff so he stands like an arch in his chair and expresses loud sounds of dissatisfaction. I have never seen him act like this before.

Father arrives and says he has been up since six am, so he is tired. When Father arrives, Morten stops the sounds of dissatisfaction.

Father carries him down the stairs and gives him a jacket and hat and puts him in the stroller. We walk toward the park. He is asleep in less than five minutes.

The end of infancy directly confronts us with the one-year crises, which are characterized by vigorous activity and the development of emotional life. In Morten's case, it is marked by the child's strong emotions as a manifestation of his personality – the first stage in the development of the child's will. The child's expression of his will can be related to the new form of self that Stern describes as the sense of subjective self that the child acquires through his interaction with caregivers.

> Self and other are no longer only core entities of physical presence, action, affect and continuity. They now include subjective mental states – feelings, motives, intentions – that lie behind the physical happenings in the domain of core-relatedness. The new organizing subjective perspective defines a qualitative different self and other who can "hold in mind" unseen but inferable mental states, such as intentions and affect that guide overt behavior. These mental states now become the subject matter of relations. This new *sense of subjective self* opens up the possibility for inter-subjectivity between infant and parents and operates in a new domain in of relatedness – *the domain of intersubjective relatedness* – which is a quantum leap beyond the domain of core-relatedness. Mental states between people can now be "read," matched, aligned with, or attuned to (or misread, mismatched, or mistuned). (Stern, 1998, p. 27)

The observation of Morten without his father shows that Morten does not want Father to leave. For some of the time his interests and motive orientation are directed at the toys, and the other caregiver delays his willful reactions to Father leaving. But it is obvious that he wants to be with Father. His protest may be interpreted as an experience that results in consciousness about being together with Father, and an orientation to wanting Father to return. As Stern writes, it opens up a state of intersubjective relatedness to specific people. Morten's willful reaction may be seen as based in his new capacities to experience shared objects of attention and to experience feelings for others.

When a child can experience that his own intention is different from a caregiver's, minor and major crises will arrive in their development. In Morten's case, his orientation to be together with his father does not align with what the other caregiver is oriented to, when she puts him in the highchair, and the crisis is solved only when Father arrives.

How caregivers handle these conflicts and minor crises will be important for the child's further development of agency, new motives, will and of self-control as well as for parents' peace of mind. Some crises are more central than others and indicate qualitative shifts in the child's relation to caregivers. In this period of development of motives and will, new caregivers may also enter the child's life through, for example, his move to nursery care. In this way the child meets distinctly new demands.

In this section, we have argued that the origin of children's development springs from the emotional relation between child and caregivers. It is from this relation that children's intention, agency, will and motives develop as neoformation in a child's consciousness. At the end of the first year, the adult can establish speech contact with a small child. But these verbal interactions are one-sided, as it is the adult who talks and the child who listens, though the child may babble. But, as the examples with Morten demonstrate, the young child has other ways of expressing his intentions and motives.

To develop the young child's verbal language, adults not only have to create a communicative atmosphere that takes seriously the child's communication needs, but they also need to provide models the child may copy. In this modeling, crises will emerge both as minor crises or as crises indicating neoformations, as sign of the end of the age period and the start of a new one. Trust in and love for adults bring forth, in a natural way, the child's urge to be like them and to merit their praise. "It therefore follows that, when working to develop their speech it is necessary to build up and extend co-operation with children on the basis of earlier emotional contacts with them and by providing them with experience in listening to oral speech." (Lisina, 1985, p. 171) Children start to learn language through imitating and modeling caregivers. The relation between adults and children changes when children starts to communicate verbally and they interact with more adults, such as when they enter day care.

## A Nursery Child's Social Situation of Development

It was commonplace during the 1950s and 1960s to emphasize the importance of the close bond between mother and child as key to child development. This view emanated from the research on attachment and maternal deprivation of Bowlby (1969) but was given traction because it fitted with contemporary national policy concerns, including discouraging women from working outside the home. As we have seen, Lisina's work shows that trusting reciprocal interactions with infants are not limited to those with the mother. Rogoff (1981, 2003), for example, criticizes the focus on mother and infant bonding as a middle-class Western concern, a view also taken by Schaffer (1990). Rogoff observed that family care and extended care may take many different forms in different societies. One of Rogoff's examples is sibling care, where she describes how the older children from quite a young age take care of the younger ones in Guatemala. In modern Western traditions, infants and young children may also show emotional relation to each other when in nursery care (Li et al., 2021; Quiñones, Li, & Ridgway, 2017). A condition would be that caregivers should cooperatively support young children as they reach out to other children and motivate them for using language and to play together.

We, too, have tried to transcend the focus on mother–infant bonding by examining the emotional connections between caregivers and child, in order to offer a broader perspective on how a child's life course moves forward as the child moves through different age periods. Our argument has been that once the child starts to become an active explorer of their environment, they do not do this alone through direct contact with the environment. Instead, their actions are given direction through their relationships with their caregivers. It is through these relationships that their orientation to key environmental features unfolds, enabling them to become intentional, agentive, motive-oriented and willful in their actions. In brief, it is through the adults' attention and demands in the interaction with the child that new capabilities develop. A reciprocal relationship therefore has to be at the core of pedagogic relations between children and adults. Lisina describes this as *coordinated cooperative communication and play*, in everyday activities.

Currently, in most Nordic countries, nursery care for children usually starts at one year of age and continues until moving to kindergarten at between two to three years. In many societies with no or very little maternity leave, child-care outside the home starts earlier (see, e.g., Meireles Santos da

Costa and de Souza Amorim (2021) on the situation in Brazil). When children enter nursery care, they meet an extended caregiver group, but importantly they will also meet other children. Over time, play with others becomes important, and demands to communicate verbally become more pressing.

But the relationships with adult caregivers remain important and those in nursery will differ from those at home. In nursery, the child may not confine themselves to waiting for help from adults; instead, they start following the adults' example, using them as models. While this is evidence of the child's learning, it may lead to several bumps and minor conflicts. To illustrate this, we will draw on the case from Hedegaard's *Play group project* that used *the interactive observation method* in nursery settings (Hedegaard, 1984, 1990 [second ed. 2013]).

## The Interactive Observation Method

There have been two broad approaches to researching and assessing neonates and infants. One is to take a third person, or a bird's eye, perspective; we have suggested that Piaget (1955) took this approach. The approach was also evident in accounts of the competent infant (Bruner, 1968), where the child is seen as an object of study. The other way of working is to take a first-person perspective inspired by psychoanalytical traditions, to focus on the child's experiences, as exemplified in Stern's (1998) interpretation of a pre-verbal self.

Hedegaard's approach is different again and takes a relational perspective where the focus is on the relation between participants, caregivers and children, in institutional activity settings in, for example, the home, nursery, kindergarten or school. Hedegaard's method of interactive observations aims at capturing the child's social situation of development and is based in the importance of seeing a child's emotional relations to other people. It is interactive in the sense that it incorporates the double perspective of child and observer. The background to this method is presented in the following vignette.

### A Vignette from Hedegaard's Early Research Career
As a young researcher in psychology, I wanted to follow the trail of researchers who had made recordings of their own children. Together with the professor in child psychology at my university we decided to make video-observations. She was trained in using *Cattell's Infant Intelligence Scale*, so I agreed to use this method. The tasks in this scale are oriented toward assessing the infant's sensorimotor reactions. In the 1970s, the scale

was used by clinicians in Denmark. Søren, my child, was 6 weeks old, the first time he was presented with tasks from this scale. Recordings also took place at 3 months, 6 months, 12 months, and 18 months. The sessions were video-recorded in our new video-laboratory between 1973 and 1975.

I felt very aggrieved by the testing after the first session, because the next day my colleague presented me with my child's IQ. I became upset about reducing his activity to a number. With the video recording of the testing, I had intended only to demonstrate how the child interacted with the world. I did not want to put labels on small children; instead I had expected that the different tasks would offer insights into important aspects of an infant's development. Analyzing the video of Søren at 6 weeks old, it was obvious that he oriented to aspects other than the presented tasks. In particular, his mother drew Søren's attention. The tester had to turn Søren several times because he looked at my face. When it was not possible to orient to my face, it was the people operating the video camera who attracted Søren's attention alongside the bright camera light. The focus of his attention was easy to identify because his waving of arm and legs ceased when focusing on something that was not the task the tester presented.

This testing event prompted me to look into how one could describe children in their everyday settings, seeing what they were oriented to and so get a valid impression of their development, where their emotional relation to caregivers was seen as important. In 1977, I started *The play group project*, which operated like a kindergarten with a professional pedagogue in its own room at the University with child-appropriate furniture and décor. It ran for 4 years with the same pedagogue (for further details, see Hedegaard, 2019b). Children participating in the practice were from 2½ to 5 years. This project ran for 4 years with 24 children. When children turned 6 and had to start school, they left the group, and a new child was accepted. No one left before they had to. The children were from university staff and the neighborhood. Ten children met once a week for 4 hours in the afternoon. Thirteen university students participated over the 4 years with a minimum participation of 6 months.[2] The project also involved two local nurseries and two kindergartens, where students had practice periods of up to three months, making description of children in their everyday activities. The aims were to find methods to analyze children's development by focusing on their activities in everyday life, and to develop ideas for an ideal play pedagogy. This project became the foundation for the interactive observation method.

---

[2] Only five students could participate at the same time. There were more students and more children who wanted to join the project than was possible. Several theses and publications came from the project.

The interactive observation method was inspired by phenomenological theory (Merleau-Ponty, 1962; Schütz, 1976) with a focus on people's intentional actions. Inspired by Schütz, the method demands that the researcher/observer has two roles, as a researcher distancing themself from the field and at the same time as a human being who relates to young children in a shared activity setting. The method is also influenced by the anthropological version of a participant observation, where the focus is on people's participation in activities in everyday life (Spradley, 1980). It is a special version of participant observation where the observer conceptualizes themself as part of the method. We therefore see it *as a second-person perspective method*, basing the assessment on both the observed person's experience as well as the observer's experience. Both phenomenological theory and the anthropological participant observation method emphasize seeing, evaluating and assessing children in their everyday activities; together with focusing on the intentional relations between people. The method is especially relevant when used in everyday situations to assess infants' and young children's social situations of development, because young children are not able to use verbal language to express their intentions or experiences.

Accessing their intentions and experiences can be accomplished through the observer's communication with the child in the assessment situation. The observer can check their specific understanding of a child's intentions through their communicative interaction with the child. They may also intervene if they find it is necessary, such as when a child is crying, or children are hurting each other. Verbal communication should not be the leading form of interaction. If the observer needs to communicate with the child it can happen through action, for example, in the form of support or care, or in a play situation where the observer does something to get the child's response. This way of doing observation presupposes the observer's knowledge about children in different cultural age periods.

The interactive observer is a participant contributing to the social settings they are observing, but by using systematic interpretation as a central form of analysis they transcend the situated setting to make a general assessment of a child's social situation of development. The process of interactive observations and their analysis moves through the following phases: (1) description entered in a protocol, (2) critical common-sense interpretation, (3) interpretations based on key questions and concepts related to child development and learning, and (4) assessment and suggestions for interventions.

# A Nursery Child's Social Situation of Development

The description is a written protocol that can be read, commented on and discussed with the caregivers. The interpretation is carried out in relation to the purpose of the observation first together with the involved adults as the critical common-sense interpretation, and then followed by the observer's theoretical interpretation led by questions such as: What are the child's intentions? What demands does the child meet? What is the communication between caregiver and child? What conflicts and crises can be found in the descriptive text? The significant difference between description and interpretation is that description is immediate, making connections with the activities as the child and observer interact (in a subject to subject contact), the interpretation is done separately and away from the observation setting. At this point, the description becomes an objectified text to be interpreted. The first phase of the interpretation process is to get a common-sense reading of the descriptions that may be used to check the observed activities in relation to other participants' impressions. Next, the observer/researcher works with the text to ask questions related to the purpose of the assessment based on research drawing on ideas derived from foci in the theory.

Following these interpretations, one may come to a judgment about a child's social situation of development that includes the child's motive orientation and the development of new capabilities – neoformations. The next step is to identify where the child needs support in the development of his motives and capabilities. The final step is advice on changes in the daily activities of both caregivers and children, as will be illustrated in the following example of a nursery child, Simon, taken from Hedegaard's early work with the method.

## Assessment of a Nursery Child's Social Situation of Development Using the Interactive Observation Method

Simon is almost two years of age and is followed while he is in the nursery, from arriving at 8 am in the morning to being picked up at 4 pm in the afternoon on two different days. We will use extracts from the observations to illustrate the interactive observation method as a tool that allows analyses of children's activities and social situations of development in everyday settings. We will also show conflicts that may indicate age-related crises in a nursery child's social situation of development. The extracts illustrate key activities in daily life settings in a Scandinavian nursery: (a) parents' delivery of their child to nursery, (b) play activities, (c) lunch time.

**Extracts from the Observations of Simon, Morning Tuesday in May, 8 am**

*Participants: Focus child: Simon; other children: Mikkel, Sune, Torben, Rene, Anne, Minna, Tavs, Erik. Pedagogues: Asta (PA), Lone (PL) Mariane (PM), Rikke (PR), Mother*

**Arrival in nursery**

The mother arrives holding Simon's hand. She goes to a table where PR is and starts to chat with her. Simon stands close to Mother. After a while Mother asks him: "Should we find a chair where you can stand and wave goodbye when Mother leaves?" Simon: "No!"

Mother: "You can stand on this chair. I have to drive Grandma, she is in the car, so she will not be late for work." PR: "Do you want to hold on to me?"

Mother: "You should not use the pacifier, your chin will get red."

Simon walks with his napkin (comforter) over to Mikkel and Sune, who are playing with a train and snatches something. Then he walks back to Mother

Mother: "You have to give back what you took."

Simon goes back and returns what he took. Then he takes a toy baby bottle. Mother tells him how to use this.

Anne takes it. Simon tears it out of her hand. Anne screams.

Simon plays with the toy bottle, and PR picks him up and they wave goodbye to Mother.

Simon says something and PR says: "I cannot hear what you are saying when you have the pacifier in your mouth". Simon repeats and PR puts him down at the table, where he starts to look at a picture book.

**Play Activity**

Mikkel arrives at the table and plays with the toy bottle. Simon tears it from him and Mikkel looks frightened.

The observer says no Simon, Mikkel had it now. PL: "Can you hear what the observer is saying Simon?"

Simon does not react.

PL asks Mikkel to come over to her, so they can play with a spinning top. Mikkel walks over to PL, Simon also walks over to her and wants to take the

## A Nursery Child's Social Situation of Development 89

top. PL: "No Simon it is Mikkel's to play with." Simon just looks at Mikkel's play.

PL: Come Simon we have to put the pacifier away. We have to put it into your bag.

Simon does not react.

PL: "Now I will come and catch you." Simon laughs and runs away from PL into the playhouse. PL runs after him and asks: "Do you want to come with me?" They leave the room together.

Simon comes back, steps on Mikel's foot and says "Gok." He moves and finds a doll's pacifier and put it into the doll's mouth. Then puts it into his own mouth, and then he tries to put it in PL's mouth. PL: "No this we cannot use this, it is for the doll."

Simon moves over to Mikkel who is playing with some chairs making a train. Torben has arrived and sits down on one of the chairs. Simon pushes him away. Torben's father says: "You should not take the chair Torben." Torben finds another chair which he adds to the train.

Simon leaves the train and takes a dolls' pram and drives it into the train. Then he enters the train again and makes humming sound, higher and higher.

PA asks him to be a bit quieter, and then "Where are you driving to?" Simon: "To the other city train." Simon takes Torben's chair and pushes it across the floor.

PA: "No Simon you are not allowed to take the chair Torben uses. Simon: "But I have to go to the fish store." PA: "You may ask Torben if he also wants to go to the fish store." Simon: "No!" PA: "Then you cannot take his chair."

Simon throws himself on the floor and cries. PA take him onto her lap and explains that he cannot take other children's things. Simon is still crying. PA: "Do you want to go and play with the train again?" Simon: "No I don't."

Minna comes over and shows something to PA, who still has Simon on her lap. Simon stops crying and PA asks "Shall we find you a book?" Simon: "Yes" PA finds a picture book and again takes him on her lap. Anne comes over and takes the book. PA: "Take a chair Anne so we all can see." Anne turns the pages and talks about the pictures. Simon sits still and smiles.

A little later Simon leaves PA and runs over to the train and bangs on the train and says: "Gong, gong."

Then he runs back to PA and cuddles into her. PA: "Do you want to play with the train?" Simon: "No". Simon runs back and forth between the train and hits the chair hard each time. PA: "You should ask if you may join the play."

Simon runs over and places himself on a chair and hits another chair. Then he runs into the playhouse.

Some children go over to the playhouse and shake it and scream. PA asks them to quieten down. Simon comes out of the playhouse and cries and cuddles into PA.

### *The Use of the Observation for a Critical Common-sense Interpretation*

An interactive observation has been written out and, the lines are numbered so it is easier to locate what the different participants focus on when discussing the observation. Observations are always given to the involved professionals. Preferably, the observation will be discussed with the leader of the institution and all the professionals who were included in the observation. The aim is that through the discussions of what the observation describes, a shared common-sense understanding of the relation between children's intentions and the adults' demand will be established. From here, discussions progress onto how to support a child in their social situation of development and what could be a goal of success that is possible to reach within a realistic time period.

Often through a reading of the description, the interaction pattern will be obvious and conflicts can be discussed as a mismatch between the child's intentions and adults' demands. Often there will be differences between the caregivers in their interpretations and that may lead to discussion among the pedagogues. A new observation may be followed by a second discussion before an interpretation of the observation protocol is established and a shared goal of success is formulated. We now present a third extract from the observations of Simon: A week later

**Lunch Tuesday in May, 11.30 am–1200 Midday**

Simon sits down on a free chair next to Tavs. He takes Tavs' plate. (He hasn't got one himself yet.)

PM: "Don't do that, Simon."

Mikkel is sitting opposite Simon and makes noises.

Simon: "Stop, stop, stop" knocks at the table.

Simon looks at PM who is cutting Tavs' food.

PR hands the potatoes to Simon, and says "Please."

Simon pushes the bowl away.

# A Nursery Child's Social Situation of Development

PM: "Then I give it to Erik."

Simon crying. "I want too, I want to have potatoes."

PR: "You now have to wait until the others have got some, because you did not want them, when I gave you the potatoes."

Simon sits crying and looks at the others getting potatoes, then gets up still crying.

PM: "If you want potatoes, then sit down on the chair."

Simon reaches for the sausages.

PM: "But now you have to cut your potatoes first."

Simon cries.

PM: "Why do we always have to have so much trouble with you?"

PR: "Where is your fork? Find it so you can quickly cut your potatoes, so you can get peas and sausage."

Simon crying: "Nooo!"

PR: "So you cannot get anything to eat."

Simon crying, reaches for the sausages.

PL: "You have to cut your potatoes."

PR: "Hurry to find your fork, so you can get something to eat."

PM: "Get your fork, so you can have something to eat."

Simon: "Nooo!" He leaves the table.

PM: "So you do not get anything to eat."

Simon walks into the playhouse, comes out and pushes a chair around. He walks in again and peeps out of the door opening.

Simon is still in the playhouse and crying.

PL: "Do you know what Simon, I think you should come out, so we together can cut your potatoes."

Simon comes out but walks to the other end of the room and runs over to the observer.

She lifts him up and suggests that they together find his fork and cut the potatoes.

Observer: "You should hurry and get your fork and then you can get something to eat. Soon it will be too late." She puts him down.

Simon pushes a chair. The fork is under the chair together with a small play object.

He puts the play object on top of the fork. After a short while he takes the fork and walks over to the table

PM: "Look, Simon, you can cut the potato with your fork."

PR: "You can get the knife and cut the potato with that."

Simon. takes the knife and cuts.

PR: "You can hold the potato with the fork."

PM helps him. He gets a piece of sausage and cuts it himself.

Simon wants some milk and PM goes to get him a cup.

Simon eats in silence.

The observations were presented to the involved professionals and a discussion took place with the staff, the student observer and Hedegaard at the time of the observation. The interpretation, conclusion and suggestions for intervention that are presented below were written later by Hedegaard and are her responsibility alone.

### Interpretation of Simon's Social Situation of Development

*What are Simon's intentions? What demands does he meet?* In the arrival situation Simon does not want Mother to leave, he tells her so directly, and also shows that this is what he wants by starting activities where he involves Mother. Mother is ambivalent in the situation because she involves herself in play with Simon, even though she explains she has to hurry. Mother also makes a demand on Simon, not to use his pacifier, which she does not follow up on. The pedagogue Rikke solves the problem about departure by taking Simon in her arms and waving goodbye. Simon understands the necessity and does not cry. Later he follows pedagogue Lone's demands to stop using his pacifier.

In the play activity Simon tries to enter into activities with other children, but in a very harsh manner, by tearing toys from Anne and later from Mikkel and by pushing Torben. Simon tries several times to join in the train play, without succeeding in interacting with the other children. Then he takes the initiative to enter the spinning top play, that pedagogue Asta started, again without success.

At the lunch table he takes the adult's role and wants another child to be quiet, as the adult does to him when he played at the train. He is oriented to eat, but he runs into several demands for how to act the right way.

The demands from the pedagogues both in the arrival situation and at lunchtime are mostly to stop Simon doing things, that is, to stop using his pacifier, to stop taking other children's playthings, to be quiet.

*Interactions and conflicts.* Mother's interaction and communication with Simon creates conflicts. Her explanation for why she has to leave seems directed more to the adult pedagogue Rikke than to Simon. The same may be the case with Simon's pacifier since she doesn't take any actions herself.

Simon interacts with the pedagogues by most of the time following their demands. He goes with pedagogue Lone when he has to give up his pacifier and return things to the other children.

Simon's interactions with the other children are filled with conflicts, and he does not succeed in playing with any of them. He is frequently scolded, so he ends up crying. Later he stops crying when pedagogue Asta takes him on to her lap and looks at a picture book with him and another child. He seems happy when Lone and Asta take care of him.

At the meal situation he tells another child to behave according to the rules of the lunch setting. When Mikkel is noisy, Simon wants him to be quiet in the way adults do with noisy children. The only time when the interaction is peaceful is when he sits on Asta's lap. He seeks comfort with her. Later in the meal situation he also seeks comfort from the observer, when he cannot handle the situation.

Simon's interactions with the pedagogues are very conflictual. At the meal three pedagogues interact with him, to make him do things in the right order at the table. He objects to the demands so much that he nearly does not get anything to eat. From the adults' perspective there is a trail of children crying around Simon, and he also cries himself when he cannot handle the situation.

### *Conclusion and Suggestions for Intervention in Simon's Everyday Nursery Activities*

We have only seen short extracts from three different settings in Simon's nursery day, but a picture emerges of an active boy who is oriented to other people, both when arriving, at play and at lunch time. However, there is the danger that he could be seen by the pedagogues as troublesome, a label that could stick with him for his whole time at nursery. Simon is oriented toward the adults' care and is able to seek comfort from the adults when his situation makes him cry. Therefore, Simon's way of acting could be seen as related to a developmental crisis, connected to his beginning to form motives for what he wants, and for creating new relations to children and adults, his conflicts may be seen as developmental and establishing new relations to adults and children. He may then be seen as developing his motive orientation to role play without yet having the capabilities to follow that through. Then the situation could be turned around, by creating new interaction patterns in the nursery that support Simon in his activities instead of hindering them.

Both Mother and Simon should also be helped by the pedagogues to ease their separation by engaging the child in a play activity on arrival. Simon is oriented to play but does not have the skills to interact with the other children; therefore, this is where he should be supported. At lunch it seems that too much energy is used by the pedagogues to make him do things in the right order. More flexibility should be shown so that he does not end up in situations where there is only one way forward, and the child has to be 'broken down' in order to do as the adults demand.

### Relational Expertise, Common Knowledge and Relational Agency: Supporting Families in Supporting Their Young Children

We are arguing that those supporting the development of children as agentic learners need to move beyond interactionism. Stetsenko (2017, 2018) offers a strong case in support of our view. The interactionist account of development has been a useful breakthrough in psychology but does not go far enough in explaining the relationship between a child's emotional experiences when interpreting and acting in the world and their development. Rather our dialectical view of development calls for a relational perspective that captures the connection between "intellect and affect" (Friedrich, 2021, p. 311). But before discussing how practitioners can help primary caregivers develop the capacity for these kinds of relationships, we offer a brief overview of those interactionist accounts that have usefully alerted psychology to differences in developmental affordances offered by families and communities.

Since the 1960s, developmental psychologists such as Rogoff and Chavajay (1995), Grigorenko and Sternberg (2001) and Stevenson-Hinde (2011) have been aware of what Super and Harkness termed "the developmental niche" (1986). Super and Harkness argued that the development of both cognition and affect was framed by three aspects: features of the social setting a child inhabited, the traditions of child care within the community and the psychology of the caregivers. Through experiencing interactions in this niche, children abstract the rules and expectations of their culture. Super and Harkness, taking an anthropological stance, observed interactions with the Kipisigis people of rural Kenya and compared these with what happened in middle-class urban homes in the United States (US). For example, the sharing of care was normal for Kipisigi infants, while in the US mothers were usually the primary caregiver, with the result that distress at the absence of the mother lasts much longer into late infancy in the US.

These anthropological accounts were useful in alerting researchers to cultural differences in the upbringing of children. For example, Caudill and Weinstein (1969) pointed to how Japanese mothers, who focused on calming their children, differed from US mothers, who tried to stimulate their infants. While Scheiffelin and Ochs (1991) observed how the Kaluli people of New Guinea aimed at connecting their infants with the wider community, by sitting with the child facing away from them and voicing the infant's intentions. This was very different from the face-to-face interactions of infants with their primary caregivers, so central to Western accounts of the development of intersubjectivity.

This attention to the impact of the niche on developmental possibilities marked an important break from universal notions of child development. But the niche was regarded as context. The perspective did not work with the idea of the dialectical unity of person and practice, so central to the idea of social situation of development. Sameroff's offering of a transactional model of development was one exception to seeing context simply as that which surrounds the child (Sameroff, 2009). Cole's (1996) book *Cultural Psychology* was, however, a key text in offering an explanation of the dialectics of a Vygotskian view of development to mainstream psychology. It is this dialectical notion of development that admits of the emergent agency of the child that underpins our arguments in this book. For us, the child is not only shaped by the environment, but also plays a part in shaping it.

We are suggesting that the three relational concepts, introduced in Chapter 3, relational expertise, common knowledge and relational agency, can help in understanding and developing the relationships that are at the core of our dialectical approach. The concepts involve taking seriously the motives of the other, being clear about what matters for oneself in the interaction and supporting the gradual unfolding of the agency of the child or client. We shall examine the approach in more detail in relation to pedagogies with children and young people in later chapters. Working with these concepts is a highly skilled form of practice. The examples that follow show how these concepts can explain practitioners' successful relational work both, with clients and when encouraging relational approaches between caregivers and young children. They are all located within English-speaking Western cultures.

In Chapter 3, we discussed how Sophie, a nurse, worked with Masha, a new mother, to encourage her intersubjective relationship with her son (Hopwood & Edwards, 2017). That study, led by Hopwood, examined how family workers in Day Stay and Home Visiting Services, in and around Sydney, helped parents to work in relational ways with their children to enable their unfolding agency. Here are two extracts from a conversation in a day-center also described in Hopwood and Edwards (2017). The participants are Sarah, a family worker, Bik, a mother, and Lee, her partner. Bik and Lee were worried about their nine-month-old daughter Rachel, who refused food that was fed to her and did not settle to sleep. They agreed that they were perhaps overattentive to her and that has made her more likely to refuse to eat or settle. Both extracts come at the end of a long set of exchanges during the day where the parents begin to see that Rachel likes being a little independent. In the interaction, Sarah points to the parents' role in enabling the unfolding of Rachel's agency, as she is now nine months, and the importance of a positive emotional response to the environment.

**Extract 1**

Sarah: Focus on each other and enjoy your food. She might be feeling under pressure if you're looking at her all the time . . . see she is exploring putting that cracker in her mouth. [Mealtime] . . . needs to be relaxed, no pressure, just the opportunity to explore.

Bik (to Lee): See that's what I say!

Lee: She keeps pushing it in [a large piece of cracker]

Bik: She'll work it out.

Sarah: Exactly! To work it out she needs practice. That gag reflex is a safety mechanism.

Bik: It is probably better for her to hold when it is bigger.

Sarah: Exactly! Around nine months that pincer grip will come into place. It's all about fun time exploring food. . .If she has a good time she'll come back for more.

Bik: Yes she is relaxed now (to Lee) because you are not shoving food in her mouth.

**Extract 2**
Sarah: As she is growing older now, she'll need your help to self-regulate, to control her emotions. And self-settling is an important part of that bigger learning process...

Bik: She is good at learning stuff. I rely on her working self-settling out.

Sarah: She'll work a lot of things out herself. But this is something you can help her with.

These extracts indicate how much crucial learning occurs at home and how important emotion is in the unfolding of agency and motive orientation. Rachel was beginning to create a motive orientation towards exploring food and eating; but needed a sense of her own agency and control in order to do so. Sarah's comments about 'fun time' reinforce her advice about giving Rachel space to act and develop her own motive orientations. One can also see how Sarah is using the common knowledge she has built with Bik and Lee about their concerns over Rachel and her own motives to enable the agency of Rachel to mediate her conversations with the adults. The two extracts reveal the unfolding of relational agency as Bik finds her voice and offers ways forward, encouraged by Sarah's use of "Exactly."

In a study Edwards undertook with Angela Anning (Anning & Edwards, 1999), they worked with staff in different nursery settings (from birth to almost five years of age) to support their development of cognitively demanding, yet play-based experiences, for the children. The study was intended as an alternative to then current expectations among policy-makers that nurseries and preschools should begin to operate like more formal schooling. In one nursery, in a highly disadvantaged area of a large city, the staff observed that the children aged between 18 and 36 months were not responding to potential joint involvement episodes (Schaffer, 1992). They concluded that the children had missed out on the meshing that occurs in sound intersubjective relationships and 'as if' conversations early in a child's life. These are conversations where an adult talks to the child as if they will understand. Earlier in the chapter we gave an example of this in how Morten's father spoke to him at six months of age.

Together with a speech therapist, the practitioners worked with a group of mothers to develop their abilities to engage intersubjectively with their children as a catch-up effort. First, the nursery workers modeled interacting with the children by getting on to the floor with a child, following the child's interests, giving running commentaries of the child's actions and helping the child to manage the objects they were playing with.

This modeling was augmented by a song book of paired action rhymes, such as "Pat a Cake," made by the nursery, which the parents could use at home. The practitioners also recognized that investment of time with a parent can influence the experiences of other children in the family. The success of this project stimulated similar efforts in other nurseries, where these joint involvement episodes came to be known as 'good one to ones' which were supported through song books, activity cards and so on.

The concepts of relational expertise, common knowledge and relational agency can be used to understand what was happening. While observing the workers with their children, the mothers were learning to take the motives of their children seriously so developing their own relational expertise. They could then use that expertise when they played the paired action songs and games at home. In time they learned to follow the child's interests and to capture their interests with joint involvement episodes and to build common knowledge. As they grew in confidence, they were able to support their children's explorations of their environments through an unfolding of relational agency.

The caregivers targeted by these nurseries needed help, but ideally the child enters a care-full intersubjective relationship at birth. Then, as they develop through infancy, their actions are supported through the unfolding of relational agency with their caregivers and gradually they emerge as an agentic actor in the family, being shaped by family practices, but also shaping them. Exercising relational expertise, building common knowledge and working relationally within the practices of the family are simply part of functioning family life throughout childhood and adolescence. We therefore argue that creating a curious, agentic learner who is oriented toward new experiences is how families can contribute to children's learning. Turning the home into school in order to enhance the development of children about whom there are concerns is not the best way forward. Instead, we need to consider how families are helped to work relationally to enable their children make strong emotional connections to opportunities for learning and to value their success at doing so.

Yates et al. have summarized the role of parents in relation to the unfolding of children's agency in a way that reflects the emotional underpinning of parental relational expertise. "We argue that the core of a developmental history of positive adaptation is a sensitive and emotionally responsive caregiving relationship. These exchanges foster the development of children's positive expectations of the social world, and of their self-concepts as agents of change within that world." (Yates, Egeland, & Sroufe, 2003, p. 254)

Describing such interactions simply as relational expertise perhaps downplays the emotional bonding at the root of these family relationships. When in Chapter 3 we discussed how the Sophie encouraged Masha, into emotionally responsive interactions with her son (Hopwood & Edwards, 2017), we noted that Sophie commented on Masha's attunement to her son and encouraged her to build on that strength. This attunement or intersubjectivity is based in a form of common knowledge that does not need to be overtly constructed. Rather, the mutuality of primary caregivers and children is marked by a shared understanding of what matters for the carer and the child, which can grow from birth in relationships of reciprocity, where relational agency is a consistent feature.

Attunement can be seen in the 'as if' actions of caregivers, through which an infant is brought into a family's conversational discourse. These exchanges also help children to orient toward their world to create what Schweinhart and Weikart (1993) described as dispositions, what we would term motive orientations. From these intersubjective exchanges where the focus is mutual engagement, the next step is Schaffer's (1992) joint involvement episodes. Here adult and child look outward and pay joint attention to something beyond their intersubjectivity. These might be "see the train!" or "here comes Granny." These exchanges help the child to look beyond their relationship with their caregiver and engage with features in their world in productive and emotionally supported ways, before tackling them alone.

However, not all parents have models of this kind of intersubjective relationship in their lives and may need help. Elsewhere we have argued that interventions that aim at preparing disadvantaged children for entry to school should focus less on preparing children for the academic demands of school and focus more on working with the strong emotional relations between family members and children to encourage the adults to enable the unfolding of children's agency (Edwards & Evangelou, 2017). We suggest therefore that practitioners who are working to support parents should reflect on the relational work that occurs at home and how that can nurture children's agency. We offer this suggestion as a counterweight to those interventions that aim at turning the home into an outpost of the school, a process that one of us has likened to the colonization of the home by the school (Edwards & Warin, 1999).

## Final Reflections

Vygotsky pointed to the origin of development in the emotions connected to instinctive activities, such as a baby searching for the nipple. With this he shows how active and even upset the newborn becomes when hungry and how they calms down when sucking and getting milk. These affective tendencies become the foundation for the caregiver's emotional communication with the neonate, from which is created the child's intentional orientation as the first neoformation.

We have also shown how the child's emotional orientation to the world in the first three years of life happens through communication and is characterized by developmental periods that encompass other psychic functions. Through communication with caregivers, infants and toddlers come to orient intentionally to the world and their agency begins to unfold, initially through sharing intentions with adults. Working in this way can be demanding for adults. Some may need help in learning to become a parent who interacts with their children to meet their changing developmental needs.

Although our aim has been to understand children's social situation from the child's perspective, we have emphasized the need to attend to the child's relations with others. We have therefore proposed taking a double perspective by focusing on both the child and the adults in their worlds. This is because the experiences of these very young children have to be seen in relation to how they are mediated by their caregivers. We have also advocated taking a double perspective when researching children's development, as the observations are mediated through the researcher's experience. When researchers orient to children's perspectives, they never access it as a first perspective but always as a second, relational, perspective. This also hold true for practitioners, parents or other caregivers who aim to understand a child's motive orientation. Edwards' work with the concepts of relational expertise, common knowledge and relational agency is an attempt to operationalize this double perspective in practice. These conceptual labels can help caregivers to see what needs to be done to take children and their motive orientations seriously, in order to support the unfolding of their agency as learners.

CHAPTER 5

# *Care and Education in Kindergarten with Play as the Core Activity*

## Introduction

At the end of their time at nursery, children have acquired many new capabilities. They can walk, use words to communicate and have become self-supporting in several ways. These new capabilities result in new relations to the environment that may lead to the kinds of crises we discussed in Chapter 4. These crises can arise from a child's new capabilities. For example, the child may act in ways that caregivers do not appreciate, or crises can occur because the child cannot act as they intend and needs caregivers' care-full intervention and support to help them handle new challenges. It is therefore important that caregivers take the child's perspective to recognize their intentions so that conflicts don't escalate. This kind of care is a very important part of early childhood education but is often forgotten in debates about education in early childhood (Winther-Lindqvist, 2021).

We also suggest that cooperation between parents and other caregivers is an important part of a caring approach to supporting children. In Chapter 3, we discussed how professionals can use *relational expertise* to orient parents toward supporting their children. Equally, parents can orient practitioners to what matters for them and their child. In kindergarten settings, this relationship can also involve keeping in contact with parents about how the child is progressing and any specific initiatives underway. The approach we are suggesting involves trust from both sides and is therefore more than information-sharing. Rather it involves building the *common knowledge* we discussed in Chapter 3, which consists of knowledge about each other's goals for the child and what education means for them. The common knowledge will then be the foundation for their cooperation over the development and well-being of the child as they take forward their social situation of development.

Both wider society and families have a stake in early childhood education and care (ECEC). From the societal perspective, it gives parents the opportunity to meet the needs of the job market or to upskill through education. From the parents' perspective, it gives them the opportunity to work and to continue a career. This can be particularly important for mothers, enabling them to be financially independent. Both society and families also take an interest in children's education to the extent that ECEC in kindergarten is a subject of debate in the Nordic countries and elsewhere (Hedegaard & Munk, 2019; Johansson, 2017). Discussions center on whether the main purpose of ECEC is to prepare children for school or whether it should focus on developing cultural competences, such as cultural ways of interacting and knowing how to act in different settings both in and outside kindergarten. The main concern with a focus on preparing for school is that the goals of formal education permeate kindergarten practice. See Anning and Edwards (1999) for an account of how this was counteracted in one initiative in England. We will argue that education in kindergarten is important, and that preparing for school and cultural competences should not be seen as in opposition, kindergarten should do both. Our aim is, however, to avoid the colonization of the kindergarten by the more formal approaches to literacy and numeracy to be found in schools and to explain what young children gain through play.

From a Vygotskian point of view, the central psychic neoformation in this age period in kindergarten is children's capacity to transcend their immediate situations through developing their imagination. This is a capability promoted by play activities. Kindergarten practitioners can contribute to these changes by creating possibilities for play, but also children will meet other children who are more play-competent and this impacts on their social situation of development. The adults' communication and cooperation with children is still central for supporting a child's development but being with other children becomes a central motive for the child's engagement in play and other activities.

Preschool institutions in Norway and Denmark are named *kindergartens* after the label given by the German philosopher Friedrich Frøbel (Eikset & Ødegaard, 2020; Kragh-Müller, 2017; Lindqvist, 1995)[1]. The term kindergarten indicates a place for children to grow. Frøbel argued that kindergarten should create a caring environment so children, through their agency, can achieve a free and self-managed life. He saw children's relation to nature and their playfulness as fundamental for human growth, seeing

---

[1] In Norway and in Sweden, the first kindergarten opened in 1840 based on Frøbel's ideas, and in Denmark in 1871.

play as a joyful activity (Eikset & Ødegaard, 2020). These ideas are still central to Nordic ECEC, even though several approaches introducing learning goals are also to be found in kindergarten. The challenge has been to maintain Frøbel's ideas about kindergarten, as open to children's initiatives, and at the same time to meet new demands for embedding learning goals in children's activities.

Children learn through all the activities in kindergarten: through play, communicating, meeting demands at mealtimes, in care activities in the bathroom, on walks outside the nursery and at naptime. What they learn will include: language while communicating, culturally expected ways of interacting and how to handle emotions. They will also acquire new everyday concepts such as color, number, the four seasons, different animals and so on.

Different societies present different cultural traditions for play and learning activities in their preschool programs (Faver, 1999; Fleer, Hedegaard, & Tudge, 2009; Rogoff, 2003). Play in the Nordic kindergarten is still seen as central for children's cultural development and the belief is embedded in the Nordic laws and regulations for kindergarten practice. The examples that we shall use to show what children's play activity means for their development, and in relation to wider society, come mainly from Hedegaard's and colleagues' research within the Nordic countries (1990/2013, 2016, 2018, 2012c; Hedegaard & Fleer, 2008; Hedegaard & Ødegaard, 2020; Lindqvist, 1995; Ringsmose & Krag-Müller, 2017; Schousboe & Winther-Lindqvist, 2010).

Several kinds of screening material have come on the market to evaluate both care and children's social and intellectual development in kindergarten. Toward the end of this chapter, we shall present an example of a relational approach to screening that focuses on the caregivers' evaluations of the actions and activities that constitute a child's social situation of development. We will argue that it is important to use the *interactive participant observation method* discussed in Chapter 4 in order to understand children's crises. We will also show how exercising *relational expertise*, establishing *common knowledge* between caregivers and using *relational agency* to create interventions can lead to changes in a child's problematic social situation of development.

## Ways of Learning in Kindergarten Practice

According to Vygotsky (1998), a young child learns through meaningful imitation both at home and in preschool. This meaningful imitation can be seen in children's modeling of the activities of key people in their lives, either directly or in play (El'konin, 1988). This is not mere imitation. When an emotional relation is established between an adult and a young child, the child may start to model the other person's activity and through this process come to orient to the motive of the activity. Bronfenbrenner (1979) observes that modeling is a form of learning that builds on the child's emotional relationship with a caregiver and it persists through to adolescence.

Children's learning through fantasy and role-play may begin when they start preschool. Meaningful imitation and modeling are still central activities, but role-play may become the leading activity in kindergarten, if supported. In fantasy play, children can rework their experiences in the different activities they encounter in everyday life and combine them in new and creative ways (Vygotsky, 2004). They can also orient to activities they are not yet part of and realize desires that are otherwise impossible for them to realize. Play is therefore a way that children acquire a conscious relation to the world, and this happens through shared imagination with other children and adults and in planning play actions.

Kudryavtsev (2017) argues, in line with Vygotsky, that consciousness emerges in play. Play-based activities never boil down to simply a subject's interaction with an object. There will always be two actors, two subjects that merge with each other, although one of them is virtual. These are the child and the role they take. The child thereby sees themself from the outside and may become conscious of their own acting. In this age period, children also may come to use egocentric speech as a support to planning their own actions when being alone. Vygotsky (1989) sees this as a step toward inner speech and thinking.

To support role-play and fantasy activities, practitioners should give children opportunities to explore both nature and different community settings outside kindergarten. These different experiences may stimulate their fantasy play, such as being a hunter following animal tracks, or a firefighter or nurse (Hedegaard & Lyberth, 2022). In play, children then may, with practitioner support, explore meaningful relations in nature and in activities that are detached from actual events. Kindergarten professionals may also create play worlds, as described in Lindqvist's research (1995, 2003). Here, through participating in children's play, they can support children's exploration of both the concrete and emotional aspects of life inherent in the different roles.

## Play as the Central Way to Learn in the Preschool Age

Although children play differently in different cultures, there is a biological basis for play. Play can also be seen among many animal offspring, where they tumble and chase each other (Bruner, Jolly, & Sylva, 1976). But human play is also more than rough and tumble. It is a learned activity that is closely connected with the culture in which the play occurs, and with other children who pass on play traditions.

Vygotsky (1967) has made crucial contributions to our understandings of the importance of play. He notes that play is the basis for children becoming symbol users. In play, children create an imaginary situation, they take on and act out roles and they follow a set of rules about how to act in these roles. In play, an object may become separated from its meaning and take on new meanings. This separation between object and meaning starts with the help of a pivot. When a child "flies" with a spoon, the spoon, as the pivot, becomes a symbol of another object, an airplane. Likewise, the child's running around with the "airplane" (spoon) becomes a symbol for the child acting as an airplane pilot. This separation between object and meaning and action and meaning creates a basis for children to be able to use symbols and, later, words in activities that are detached from the concrete situation. Play symbols and play rules provide the basis for children to be able to understand the meanings of the written word and cultural symbols such as traffic lights. Similarly, children, through play, get a basis for understanding stories that are not linked to their specific situation.

Just as children's learning through meaningful imitation and modeling continues when children enter school, play also continues when children start school. But it then takes new forms as rule-based games and experimentation with relations between events and ideas. These activities are important for creating motives for engaging with different forms of subject matter in school (Hedegaard & Fleer, 2013; Skovbjerg & Sand, 2021; Vygotsky, 1982).

## Adults' Role in Children's Play

Children in early childhood learn to play because the traditions of practice in homes and in day-care programs in modern Western societies support this activity. Most parents are oriented to offering their children opportunities for play and they may also join in the play. Playing with their children may start when they are infants, with different games, such as "give and take" or "peek-a-boo." Most children are also given toys from the moment they are born. In the observation extracts 1 and 2 in Chapter 4, we showed how Morten, as an infant, had toys that his father used for playful interactions. In these observations we saw how Father supported Morten's spontaneous actions with his toys through imitating his actions.

There is diversity in how children relate to the play initiated by the adults, and also, in how different families play with their children. In addition, children in different developmental age periods relate differently to parents' play strategies because their motives are different. The play that takes place in families with several children needs to overcome the age difference in their choice of play. In the Frederiksberg family introduced in Chapters 1 and 2, the mother played "hide the thimble" with her four children with an age range between four and ten years. Hide the thimble is a game in which children in different age periods can participate on equal terms together with adults. In this game, one person hides a thimble or other small object, and the others seek it. The one who has hidden the item, screams "it is burning," when one of the others moves close to it. In this family, the father also played with the children when they were gathered at the dinner table. He mostly created word games as we saw in Chapter 2. All four children in the family participated when he told riddles; the two older children were able to contribute to the father's language game by creating their own word games. The two youngest also participated. Emil (6 years) wanted to make a riddle, but he was not successful, so instead he imitated tunes and rimes from television programs. Kaisa (4 years) also wanted to be in on the language games but could not really understand what she was supposed to do; so, she tried to get her parents' attention by saying obscene words. The differences in how children relate to adults' play are connected to their age period and to the traditions for the adults playing with them.

The question is how the adults' role in play may continue when children have entered the lifeworld of shared imaginary play activity with other children. When adults enter preschool children's imaginary play, it is seldom as an equal partner, but as an adviser or pedagogue, something that may not be appreciated by children. Later in this chapter, we shall discuss play world projects (Fleer, 2017; Lindqvist, 1995) and show how adults can initiate and participate in play in ways that engage and motivate children to enter play world activities.

## Emotional Experiences and Feelings as Foundations for Children's Imagination in Play

Fleer (2014) and many other play researchers (Göncû & Vadebonceur, 2017; Grieshaber & McArdle, 2010; Lindqvist, 1995; van Oers, 2013; Winter-Lindqvist, 2017) agree with us that role-play is not a naturally unfolding activity but is instead learnt. But there is a logic in the development of children's play, as it relates to the development of children's capacity to use imagination to go beyond the concrete and use meanings connected to actions with objects. An example from Hedegaard (2008a) shows how three children wanted to play together but the two youngest, Jorn and Louis, were still toddlers and found it difficult to enter the fantasy play of the five-year-old Torben about Superman and his dog. The younger children had no experience of the comic book characters that Torben drew on in his ideas for playing. They were instead happy to sit in each other's company playing at drinking imaginary coffee together, inspired by what they had experienced adults doing, and by the dolls' cups that were in front of them. Torben became angry at their childish play and poured imaginary coffee on their heads while he scolded them. He then started to "shoot" at them, jealous of their playing together instead of entering his play.

Children's play changes when their social situation of development changes. In early forms of play, children repeat what they have experienced adults doing, such as drinking coffee. Children's play is initially more a recollection of images than imaginary play; it is more memory in action. This is followed later by imaginary play activities when children are more experienced in play and the rules become more explicit. In the following observation of a birthday play, play rules guide children's shared play activity.

In this imaginary birthday play, Kaisa is with two playmates Fanny and Lisa outside in the sandbox (Hedegaard, 2016). It was Kaisa's suggestion that they should play birthday. She had just celebrated her fourth birthday and she suggested that she should be the birthday child. To be like the real birthday, the play rules required Kaisa stay in "bed" (two small plastic chairs she put together), while Fanny and Lisa prepared the birthday celebration. But the birthday preparations took a long time (nearly half an hour); again and again Kaisa asked if they were ready so she could get up and participate. Fanny and Lisa argued, using the rules for how a birthday must prepared for, that Kaisa should wait. First, they had to make a layered cake with candles, then they had to make gifts, then they had to make dinner. While this was going on, Kaisa got up and played with another child for a short while and then moved back to her bed to wait until she could finally enter the party.

Kaisa's real birthday was a highly emotional event where she was at the center of her family's celebration, an event that Kaisa wanted to repeat in play. Therefore, she continued to participate in the play even when it was boring for a long period and involved emotional tensions. The rules from the familiar birthday activity were used to negotiate the different motive orientations of the three children. Kaisa's motive was the celebration of her as a birthday child. Fanny and Lisa used the power in the rules to take the lead, so much so that they created a rule about dinner preparation to prolong their dominance in the play. Dinner preparation is not part of the rules for a birthday celebration. Instead, the starting point is that one is woken up on the morning on one's birthday with song and gifts.

The birthday play shows how children create images to plan play, where their activities draw on real-life events. It also shows how these events lead to play rules that come to control children's activities. Schousboe (2013), drawing on Vygotsky, has pointed out that one can distinguish three spheres in play: the reality sphere, the imagination sphere and the planning sphere. These three spheres are woven together so that children in shared play move in and out of them to discuss, negotiate and plan their imaginary actions as well as to check them against what happens in the reality sphere.

The play rules in shared play may lead to both self-control and control of each other. We saw in the birthday play that Kaisa had to accept that she should wait before taking part in the play and should also overcome boredom and irritation, which would be difficult for her to handle in real life. In play, according to Vygotsky (1967), children are always ahead of their normal activity. In play they can imagine what they cannot perform, and they can adhere to regulations that they find difficult to implement in real life. The birthday example also demonstrates how power relations between children may change in play. Kaisa started by being the leader organizing the play, but Lisa and Fanny became the ones who enjoyed planning and imagining how things should proceed. The play also ended joyfully for Kaisa and fulfilled her wish for the play. She was at last celebrated at the play's dinner, got gifts, and was allowed to blow out the candle on the birthday cake.

Vygotsky's theory of play sees the child as agentic in the reconstruction of reality and in changing his relation to the world. El'konin (1988) developed this part of Vygotsky theory of play by using the concept of activity; in this way, he distinguished between the theme of the play and the content of play and pointed to the important role of practitioners in helping enrich children's play experiences. Themes can differ widely because they reflect children's actual life conditions and their needs and motives. Themes therefore change when a child's life condition changes, and the child becomes familiar with new experiences. The content of children's play, on the other hand, was described by El'konin as the child's motivational relation to people in their social worlds. Through several experiments, El'konin (1988) demonstrated that if kindergarten children were taken to visit special places, such as the zoo or the railway station, it would influence their play if the pedagogues helped the children to become attentive to the activities of the people in these settings. Examples may include the activity of the animal keeper in zoo or the conductor on the train. The children then incorporated the different roles into their play. The theme of itself, the zoo or train station, did not influence children's play. It was only when they were helped to be aware of the activities of key people in these settings that these visits influenced their play.

During the preschool years, children become increasingly capable of exceeding the concreteness of the immediate situation. This is because they experience a broader world through picture books, stories, TV, visiting places and participating in older children's play. Children with more experience use fantasy figures such as dragons in their shared play, and make up their own rules that are not as close to reality as that of younger children.

Grindheim (2020) described and analyzed a play-episode where four children made up stories of dragons fighting and being put in a cage, the dragons then manage to escape by blowing fire. She followed how children also changed roles while they were playing, from dangerous dragons to less dangerous firefighters and crocodiles. She interpreted the process of the play activity as indicating children's exploration of danger and borders. She analyzed the dangerous fantasies from three different perspectives: the perspective of being together in a play activity, that is, the personal perspective of being friends facing dangerous events; the institutional perspective of transcending the pedagogues' rules and following their own rules, demanded by the play fantasies; and the societal perspective of transcending educational values of how nice children behave.

In popular belief, fantasies are associated with young children as they are expected to be very imaginative. Vygotsky (2004) argues that the opposite is the case; that young children's imagination is not as complex as that of older children. This is because older children have had more time to experience different aspects of life both directly and through literature and other symbolic sources. When children's experiences become more complex, not only does role-play develop, but also new forms of pretend play may be found. Japiassu (2008) describes pretend play as a more complicated form of imaginative play, where children are projecting imagined people onto dolls, where the children may switch between the different perspectives that the dolls represent. An example of this is how two 10-year-old girls played soccer with Ken dolls (the male version of Barbie), where they each became a kind of puppet master, exploring in their play boys' activities such as playing football and fighting (Hedegaard, 2016).

Play is not only as joyful or pleasant as Frøbel's legacy may suggest. Vygotsky (1967) suggested that children's play is not motivated by seeking pleasure; several forms of play don't lead to pleasure. His argument was that play always is emotional as it is the fulfillment of children's needs, not of the immediate, but of more general wishes. Therefore, he found difficulties with those theories that did not recognize that children have motives when playing. He argued (Vygotsky, 1967) that analyses of play should start with the child's needs, inclinations, incentives, and motives to act.

From this perspective, it is the interconnection between emotions and intellect that gives rise to the development of imagination in play. Internal and external actions are inseparable in play. Imagination and will are internal processes underpinning external play actions (Vygotsky, 1967). In play, there is no opposition between imagination and reality; they are integrated in a dialectical relationship and imagination gradually becomes a form of consciousness that relates to reality in more than one way.

In the literature on play after Vygotsky's time, there is a split in conceptualizing preschool children's play. It is either seen as contributing to children's intellectual development or to their emotional development. This split is promoted through the differences in the focuses of the theoretical analyses of play. The emotional aspect is central in the psychoanalytic approaches of play therapy (Cuschieri, 2019; Lowenfeld, 1935/2008; Mook, 1994; Winnicott, 1977). These approaches focus on the emotional aspects of a child's play, seeing them as arising from an earlier event in a child's everyday social situation. Cognitive approaches are largely based on the work of either Piaget (1952) or Bruner (Bruner, Jolly, & Sylva, 1976; Garvey, 1977; Sylva, Roy, & Painter, 1980). But there are also researchers working with Vygotsky's legacy who primarily examine how play contributes to children's intellectual development (Bodrova & Leong, 2003). These more cognitive approaches tend to be taken up by those who are interested in how the competences children may acquire through play can prepare them for school.

Following Vygotsky, we have tried to overcome this split by integrating the emotional and intellectual aspects in our understanding of play, seeing play both as initiated by emotional experiences and as important for children's development of imagination and motives for learning. Through play, children develop imagination and can explore unknown situations. It also allows them to plan activities and, through detachment from the concrete situation, become able to work with meaning and to handle emotions. We will argue that play, as exemplified in the birthday example, is important both intellectually and emotionally for children's development, including how they approach activities in school.

## Emotional Tension in Children's Play

In play, children may also use objects to substitute for something they desire, for example when a toy animal becomes a substitute for a desired pet, such as a kitten. It is very common for parents to give an object, such as a blanket or soft toy, to small children to support the desire for closeness when they are put to bed. These comforters may, according to Winnicott (1977), become transitional objects that help children to become less dependent on their caregivers. The argument is that a transitional object helps children overcome anxiety about being alone and becomes part of a going to bed ritual where the comforter plays an important part. Importantly, the transitional object connects feelings and imagination as together they are projected into the object. The idea of a transitional object is helpful for understanding the role of pivots, such as a spoon for an airplane, for connecting imagination with feelings in play.

Children may be playing with their emotions through creating tensions in their play. Consequently, through analyzing a child's play, adults may discover what is important for the child and gain insight into the child's social situation of development. To illustrate this weaving together of experiences, emotions and motives in play, we now present an extract from a role-play about going to bed when the light is turned off.[2] In the extract, we follow a small group of children who have moved to "the

---

[2] The extract is from Hedegaard's project about *Play and life competence as a core in transition from kindergarten to school* (Hedegaard & Munk, 2019).

cushion room" a place that most kindergarten in Denmark have in one form or another, where children can play without direct supervision.

The play started with Elisa, Nobert and Nikki playing going to bed at night. Elisa and Nobert, the two younger children, were the children in the play; Nikki, an older child was the father; Jose, who is also older, joined in after the play had started. The light was turned off at some point. This could be scary for some children and in this case, it became so for the two younger children when Jose, invited by Nikki, joined the play as a tiger.

**Going to-Bed Play, Extract from 6th Observation (August) at the Oak Tree**

Children: Elisa, Nobert (4 years), Nikki, Jose (5 years)

I (the observer) walk around the hallway and the living room to see which children are where. In the hallway, I find Nikki, Nobert and Elisa. Nikki is standing behind a mattress that they have set up at the entrance to the small room off the hallway behind a doorway. In this small cushion room, Nikki has turned off the light. I look in and say: "Well, you're in here." Nikki smiles and turns on the light. Elisa and Nobert lie at the floor under a blanket. Nikki turns off the light again and I go to the Anemone Room.

Just after I have left the children, Nikki comes to the Anemone Room and talks with Jose.

Jose then goes with Nikki and I discover that he has joined the play in the cushion room.

Fifteen minutes later when I come back into the hallway the mattress is still standing, so that the opening into the room is blocked. The light is off, Nikki, Jose, Nobert and Elisa are in there.

I sit immediately outside the cushion room. Some of the children in there shout (not addressed to me): "There is peace! There is peace!" I sit so that I can only momentarily look into the room.

Jose moves from behind the mattress and out into the hallway. He crawls on all fours. He makes animal sounds.

Nikki says: "You cannot come in again."

Nikki comes out into the hallway. He goes down the hall and switches on the light, then goes back.

Nikki to the two children in the small room: "No honey don't be afraid." To Jose: "Can you see that these two got scared."

Jose makes growling noises.

Nikki says: "No tiger. Do not scratch any of the babies."

## Emotional Tension in Children's Play

Nikki: "Now it's night. We need to sleep." The light in the small room is turned off again.

Jose makes loud tiger sounds.

Nikki to the two small children: "Honeys, do you want chocolate? Chocolate in bed for you."

Nikki to Jose: "Shouldn't we say that you were our tiger and that you must not scratch any of the babies and you have to listen to the father."

Jose: "Then I walked away."

Nikki: "No!"

Nikki tells the two young children that Jose was their tiger and that he came back.

Jose: "No, because they do not close their eyes, and neither do you, father."

Nikki: "Just now, you went out on the road."

Nobert and Elisa have not said anything until now. Nobert says something about having fire behind him.

Jose emerges from the room. He lies down on the floor on his stomach with his eyes closed (as if he were sleeping).

Nikki also leaves the room. Nikki says something about – you did not realize I was carrying you. Nikki lifts Jose, who helps, still with closed eyes. They thus go behind the mattress and into the small room where the light is off.

Elisa: "Then I do not want to join [when the tiger is back]."

Jose: "Should I tell you. I do not eat babies. I do not eat girls."

Elisa (in a sad voice): "No!"

Nikki to Jose: "Then you cannot join us."

It becomes silent inside the room. Jose comes out of the room. He crawls on all fours. It is quiet inside the room.

Jose is lying on his stomach. He has closed eyes.

Jose sits up and put his knees on the mattress and pokes as he says ding dong.

At the other end of the corridor Pedagogue T calls: "Now we have to eat."

Jose turns over the mattress that covers the opening into the small room and says it's lunch time. The children spring up and run down the hall toward the lunch room.

In this play, we follow how children work through the anxiety of being in a dark room when they have to sleep. The tension in the play grew when Jose joined as a tiger, as we could see from their screams for peace, and Elisa will leave the play; for Jose, the tension is that he will not play, if he cannot be in the cushion room. It is difficult for Nikki to keep the playmates together because their motives are quite different. According to Vygotsky (1967), children's feelings indicate their motive orientation for their play. For Nobert and Elisa, their motive seems to be playing with the dangerous aspects of being in a dark room; for Jose, the motive seems to be being strong and dangerous. Nikki is the one who tries to keep the playmates together as the caring father who has a tiger; his motive seems to be like a parent who masters the situation.

The emotional tensions that children may feel in real-life events, such as when lights are turned off at bedtime, are what they try to overcome in play. Overcoming anxiety can also be seen when children play doctor or dying. Dying is formalized in many kinds of play. Some researchers have also pointed to a dark side of play, where play itself may lead to anxiety (Grieshaber & McArdle, 2016; Shousboe, 2013).

## Children's Lifeworlds and Adults' Creation of Play Worlds

If a caregiver sees that a child becomes scared in play, it will be difficult for her to interfere and keep the play going. She has to judge whether the child may be able to handle the feelings and overcome them or whether she needs to intervene. A reason why it is difficult to intervene in a shared play activity is that in play children create a shared lifeworld together (Johansson, 2017) that leads them to protect the play from intruders. In a shared lifeworld, children build a shared imagination of what the play is about (Fleer, 2017). Jose's attempts to join the *going to bed play* may illustrate this. Jose did not participate from the start in the play; therefore, he was an outsider who tried to be accepted in play that was already underway.

Johansson observes that from toddlerhood, children start to create shared lifeworlds where they play together and learn from each other. Inspired by Merleau-Ponty (1962), Johansson shows how even young children, through their actions and bodies, communicate and may create a shared lifeworld in play: "The other's actions embrace a particular meaning for us and allow us to understand something about his or her life. This meaning is not something hidden behind the actions; it is experienced in the other person's bodily movements, his/her posture, emotional expressions, gestures and words" (Johansson, 2017, p. 17).

Johansson argues that children, even as toddlers, start to protect their shared lifeworlds from intrusion from others when they have started to play. A nice example is given in Li, Ridgway, and Quiñones's (2021) description of three toddlers' parallel play as a team driving trucks on a bridge in a nursery. In the play they kept together, imitating each other even though twice other children interfered by taking one of the children's trucks. When the child got his truck back, they continued to cooperate through imitation without words.

If a pedagogue tries to intervene to help a new child enter an ongoing play in kindergarten, they have to be sensitive to the established shared play world. It is not enough to just tell the children to include a new child. When they do so, the newcomer is often given a nonsignificant role, such as the father who goes to work, or a cat who must leave the house (Hedegaard, 2020). Grieshaber and McArdle (2010) give an example, where an adult asked a child group to include a new child. The group agreed, but later the caregiver found out that the new child's role in the play was to be a carpet.

If practitioners find that a child is scared or hurt during play, they may have to stop the activity and talk with the children outside the play environment about what makes them scared. Another possibility is to create a *play world* together with children to explore the frightening area, as we will illustrate with Lindqvist's (1995) play world about fear. Lindqvist (2003) argues that in play central themes in the cultural life of adults may enter children's play worlds and can be found in dramatized aspects of children's play. So, for instance themes of travel and fighting and dying, may be shared themes of children's play and of adults' life. To approach these aspects of children's play, Lindqvist experimented with the creation of play worlds where adults start to dramatize thematic areas that for children are emotionally loaded. Here is an example in *Fear comes to Freja*.

### An Extract from Fear comes to Freja[3]

Adults: Monica who plays Fear and Karin who plays Rasmus. There is a bed in the room. The children are aged between three and six.

Fear is lying under the bed. Karin has put on her pajamas and a night-cap. She is now Rasmus, a boy about to go to bed. "What if there's someone

---
[3] Freja is the name of the children's group.

under my bed? I'm scared. Why is it so dark?" Rasmus asks. The dramatic overture to Beethoven's Fifth Symphony can be heard in the background. The children huddle closer together. They are sitting in a semi-circle around the bed. Rasmus whispers and lights a torch to be able to see. He starts back and hides under his blanket, but after a while he boldly makes another attempt. "Who are you? What are you doing under my bed?" "I am Fear and I am frightened," says a thin voice, barely audible. She spots the children. Some laugh uncertainly, others bite their fingers nervously. "I'm frightened of everything" "Who are you all?" Fear asks next. "I daren't come out, because children are quite dangerous." This breaks the ice, and some children laugh out loud. Fear has taken the torch and shines it in her own face from underneath. Her whole face is full of spots in different colors. She is wearing a small black hat, and all her other clothes are red. "When I get frightened, my whole face comes out in spots; red, yellow, and blue," she says. "But you are wearing red," says Stinna, one of the oldest girls. "Well, I have to get used to it," says Fear. "Do you want to meet my friends? They are just as frightened as me." (Lindqvist, 1995, p. 75)

When Monica has changed back in to her own clothes, she lets the children explore the clay figures in the box she brought. She says that they are her friends; she describes them as spotty ghosts and says they are called Frightings. Fear visited again a week later and again started a dialog with the children, where the adult and children meet in a shared play world. They had a party with adults, children and the Frightings, together with green snakes, dinosaurs and horrible monsters that the children had made from bread dough. This was followed by a period where they studied animals' lives, baptized the monsters and built a house where they and the animals could live. Through these activities, the children learned to handle feelings for strange creatures but also learned about how some of these lived. Later examples of Lindqvist's play world projects took different forms and were built around different characters or were about adventurous journeys. They were all structured as play dramas that contained tensions between reality, imagination and emotions.

Lindqvist (1995) argued that the emotional tensions in play may find their parallel in the psychological tensions in dramatic art. Lindqvist's play world projects were inspired by Vygotsky's ideas in *Psychology of Art* (1925/1971). Art, Vygotsky argued, proceeds from certain lived feelings, and in art, humans realize aspects of psychic tensions that find no expression in everyday life. Art is the social technique of emotion, a tool of society that brings the most intimate and personal aspects of our being into the circle of social life. The parallel between art and play is that in play children also bring their most intimate and personal aspects into the circle of social life.

Creating a play world starts with the professionals initiating a shared imagination by telling a story, or as in Lindqvist's (1995) first version of a play world "Fear comes to Freja," the practitioners directly play out a drama. Children are then encouraged, through the adults' acting, to enter the play world. In an overview of play worlds, Fleer (2018) explains that a play world starts with creating a shared story. The story may come from a novel such as in Hakkarainen's (2010) play world of Narnia or as in Fleer's play world research with the tale of Robin Hood (Fleer, 2018, 2021). The stories should initiate children's engagement with a play world.

To further support the imagined play world, practitioners may also use a ritual to mark the transition into a play world from the real world. Hakkarainen described how, in the play world of Narnia, they attached a cardboard box to the door frame, and when they went through the cardboard box, they entered the play world (Hakkarainen, 2010). In this way, they created a shared imagination of being together inside the Narnia play world.

Play worlds extend the idea of children's play from a self-initiated activity where they create a shared imagination in a small group of children, to practitioner-directed play where imagination is shared by the whole group of children. The pedagogue's intention in establishing a play world, which may run over several weeks or months, is to orient to both emotional care and children's learning about subject matter. In Lindqvist's projects, the emotional aspects dominate. Fleer has extended Lindqvist's approach by orienting the play world activity toward developing children's motives for engaging with science concepts; here the two aspects run in parallel (Fleer, 2018, 2020b).

When using the story of Robin Hood in Sherwood Forest, the adults and children in Fleer's study build a shared imaginary world of rescuing a baby dragon from the evil Sheriff of Nottingham. In one session, Friar Tuck brings a letter to the children about how a baby dragon was put in a dungeon. The children together with a pedagogue have to decipher the letter in order to rescue the baby dragon (Fleer, 2017). Later, they build a machine to rescue the peasants' treasures, which are stored in the Sheriff's castle (Fleer, 2018). Fleer argues (2021) that children's participation in this play world activity orients them both toward learning everyday science concepts and to working together as a collective.

Hakkarainen (2010) also pointed to the intellectual aspects of this kind of play, arguing that the story structure of a play world organizes children's thinking and reflection. This, he argues, is important for changing their memory processes from event-based perception to a narrative form of knowledge, where the events then can be remembered as a connected whole and not as separate perceptual events. In Fleer's and Hakkarainen's play world projects, the children were mainly in late preschool age, between five and six years old, so the play world activity can also be seen as an activity preparing children for school, where the teacher initiates and guides the activities.

## Assessing Children's Social Situation of Development Focusing on Activities

In this section, we turn to how a Wholeness Approach impacts on assessment. Assessment is a powerful tool that can lead to labeling and segregating children in ways that are detrimental to their futures and their long-term contribution to society. Our aim is to offer an approach to assessment that does not label a child, but which opens up discussions about how a child's development can be supported by others in their lifeworlds.

In doing so, we recognize the dilemmas faced by practitioners in places like Greenland, where society is undergoing rapid change and there is a need to sustain important cultural traditions, while also preparing for competent involvement in modern society. We gave similar examples in Chapter 3 when we discussed Woodrow and Staples' (2019) work with Chilean families and Rai's research in Rajasthan (2017, 2019). Our future-oriented argument is that the competencies children gain through play in ECEC and through their later learning in school offer wide choices later in life. These choices may mean that they can contribute to the communities in which they were raised and also meet new challenges that extend beyond the demands of these communities.

Children are expected to develop capabilities that are valued in the society in which they live. For example, day-care practitioners in Nordic societies expect a three-year-old to approach other children and adults with confidence, participate with other children in play and begin to communicate their wishes. They expect the child to want to run, crawl and jump, to play with water and snow, build with blocks, play with dolls and toy animals, explore nature, and have knowledge of how to celebrate simple cultural events, such as birthdays, and the big religious festivals. If they have had experience of playing with other children, around the age of five, children's play changes so that it becomes more planned. Here adult support can help, so that children learn that they can say no if others get too close, become more adept at dressing and undressing, can accept rules, can distinguish between fantasy and reality and have knowledge of key cultural events. These expectations of three- and five-year-old children are built into institutional practices. However, conflicts can arise between caregivers' demands' and what the children are oriented to. Such conflicts point to where children are developmentally and should not be avoided but handled so children stay engaged.

When one assesses children's social situations of development, one therefore has to examine the environments they engage with. This expectation can present practitioners with three challenges. When coming to judgment about a child's development, it is important to recognize that families have different ways of being, while also honoring the fact that children have to acquire the competencies demanded by modern societies. Second, when assessing a child's development, practitioners need to see a child as part of the whole group of children and not focus on them in isolation. Third, assessments need to be part of practice, where practitioners make demands on children and give them challenges. But these demands should not be boring for children; on the contrary, they should motivate them in their interactions with objects and with others. Assessments of a child's social situation need to capture how a child is allowed to participate in joint activities, how requirements are set, and how the requirements adapt to the child's development and experience.

When examining the support and expectations that children encounter while they are being raised, it is also important to consider how culture connects with their biological development, such as being able to walk and talk. This perspective is also key to how children with disabilities are helped to thrive. One of Vygotsky's (1991) important theoretical points is that children with disabilities have developmental processes, where participation in communities and communication are crucial for their development. The centrality of the social situation of development, the intertwining of person and practice, can alert caregivers to their roles in creating environments where children with disabilities can develop. Consequently, any assessment needs to include an assessment of how the environment supports a child.

In support of this view, Bøttcher (2012) has observed that caregivers who engage with children with disabilities need to recognize that the demands of kindergarten and school, which are aimed at developing important competencies, may not match the biological readiness of disabled children. This means that their development must be supported in other ways, with other means, to enable them achieve competencies that are valued by society and so give them a dignified life. Like all other children, they relate emotionally to the environment and need both support and challenge in order to develop the motives and capabilities to play and have fun.

In line with our aim to avoid labeling children and to build an understanding of the environments they experience, we will describe in some detail an approach to assessment that focuses on children's activities instead of their abilities. One consequence of this approach is that it can lead practitioners and parents to cooperate to create environments in which children's development and well-being are supported.

This assessment material was constructed at the request of the Greenland Government to secure optimum developmental conditions for young children. Hedegaard was invited to join a government task force to construct screening material to evaluate the health and social situations of development for all children aged three and five years of age in Greenland. Hedegaard was invited because she had authored *the interaction observation method* for evaluating young children's development in cultural settings (see Chapter 4). However, screening all Greenlandic children in the age range using interaction observation requires too many resources. Instead, the method was used to evaluate a sample of children in order to construct and test screening material that could be used by practitioners in kindergarten. The material was constructed to be used with children who were growing up in Greenland with its cultural traditions of being both an Arctic society and a former Danish colony. It was therefore presented in both the Danish and Greenlandic languages. In Danish it is named UBUS 3 and UBUS 5 (*Undersøgelse af 3 og 5 års børns udviklingssitation*); in English: Investigation of three- and five-year-olds' social situations of development.

The difference between *the interaction observation method* and the screening material is that the screening material cannot access children's intentions in activity settings by taking the child's perspective. Instead, UBUS 3 and UBUS 5 examine children's interaction with other children and with adults in daily activities. In that way, the focus is children's social situation of development from societal and practice perspectives (Hedegaard & Lyberth, 2019).

Before creating UBUS 3 and UBUS 5, the task force reviewed 13 recent assessment tools that might be used for evaluating preschool children's development. It was seeking a resource that could evaluate children's development from a cultural and educational perspective. They concluded that existing assessment tools focused too much on children's functioning, without attending to environmental and cultural conditions. It was therefore impossible to use them to assess children's social situation of development, and to use the assessment to identify how social situations might be changed to better support children.

The task group was clear that screening should reveal areas of concern and offer guidance for how to support and motivate children to participate in activities with other children, so that areas of concern could be overcome. The challenge was to construct a screening tool that was appropriate for all Greenlandic children in the age range, while also meeting the United Nation's criteria for children's development, which aimed at producing world citizens. UBUS3 and UBUS 5 were the outcomes.

The task force agreed that the screening should not be a neutral content-free evaluation of children but should become relevant for children in their actual worlds and be a tool that supports children in difficult situations. Therefore, the task force decided to use the cultural-historical approach as a foundation for constructing the screening material. Culturally appropriate assessment in Greenland did present a potential problem because there are big differences in living conditions between East and West Greenland. In Nuuk, the capital in the West, they have central heating, running water, sewerage and an expanded road network. In the settlements in the East, people have to fetch water, provide their own sewerage and heating, and contact with other communities is by boat or helicopter. Despite these differences, however, there is a common national language, news dissemination via radio and TV, and legislation on child care and education. The final material focused on activities that one expects three- and five-year-old children in Greenland to be able to enter into.

## The Design of UBUS 3 and UBUS 5

As we have been emphasizing, a child's social situation of development covers both the child's activities and the conditions that caregivers offer to enable the child to take themself forward as a learner. Based on this conception, the task force constructed screening material with six assessment areas. These represented the institutional expectations related to child-care in Greenland. They were built on Danish legislation for day care and were adapted to the special conditions for everyday life in Greenland.

The first assessment area is connected to the child's *health and well-being*. Its four subareas are: (1.1) vision, (1.2) hearing, (1.3) physical health and (1.4) well-being (the child feels happy and safe). The remaining five areas are connected to how the child relates to other people when participating in shared activities. These are as follows: (2) *Social interaction and competences*. Focus area: how the child relates to other people and creates contacts. (3) *Communication and language competences*. Focus area: how the child relates to other people through communication and language. (4) *Sensation and movement*. Focus area: how the child relates to other people by moving around and paying attention. (5) *Cooperation and initiation of activities*. Focus area: how the child contributes to shared frameworks and child-led activities. (6) *Knowledge of nature and culture*. Focus area: how the child relates to nature and cultural activities in Greenland.

It was decided that the assessment should be undertaken by a practitioner who has known the child for some time and can answer the questions in each of the six areas. In this way it should be possible to point to any *areas of concern* in a child's social situation of development. UBUS 3 and UBUS 5 also differed from other screening material in their weighting of *agency* and *communication* in children's participation in activities. To illustrate the difference over time, we will present how agency and communication may be assessed in two of the five screening areas within children's *social situation of development* in UBUS 3 and UBUS 5. The two areas are: (2) *social competence and interaction* and (4) *participation in sensation and movement activities* (Tables 5.1 and 5.2).

If the assessment shows areas of concern in children's developmental situation, the questions give clues to what practitioners should be aware of and where they should support new ways for a child to participate in

Table 5.1 *Showing the difference between three- and five-year-olds in area (2)* social competence and interaction *in how the child relates to other people and creates contacts*

|  | UBUS 3 area 2 | UBUS 5 area 2 |
| --- | --- | --- |
| Question 1 | The child may play with others | The child contacts other children with *ideas* for play activity |
| Question 2 | The child contacts other children to participate in play | The child accepts decisions and is led by shared rules (i.e., accepting guidelines and rules in play and games) |
| Question 3 | The child accepts being close to adults | The child master movement activities accepts bodily contact as well as contact at a distance, and can express wishes for nearness or create boundaries for this |

## The Design of UBUS 3 and UBUS 5

Table 5.2 *Showing the difference between three- and five-year-olds in area (4) participation in sensation and movement activities in how they relate to other people in moving around and paying attention*

|            | UBUS 3 area 4 | UBUS 5 area 4 |
|---|---|---|
| Question 1 | The child can differentiate between warm and cold, small and large | The child is aware of own body and act if they are too hot or cold or have pain |
| Question 2 | The child can climb stairs and mountains, dance and jump | The child experiments with balancing and climbing (i.e., in the mountains) |
| Question 3 | The child can perform movements (i.e., use building blocks, drawing materials) and dress and undress | The child can climb, jump, dance, draw, dress and undress (using buttons), |

developmental activities. Using the assessment, they can work out what they need to do so that the areas of concern gradually disappear.

At first glance, the health status of a three-year-old and a five-year-old may seem the same, but health problems may cause a big difference in psychological development. If a child has lived with poor eyesight or hearing or is failing to thrive until they are five years old, the problem may have greater significance for their social situation of development than for a three-year-old child. This is because the problem may have been there for longer. In the next example, we can see the impact of a health problem on a child's engagement in shared activities.

### Case: Analysis of Five-Year-Old Inunaq's Development Situation

The practitioner wrote that Inunaq has a hole in one eardrum and had a lot of fluid in his ears. He is very much in his own little world. Completing the assessment also created a profile, which enabled practitioners to see at a glance where there were areas of strength and weakness (see Figure 5.1).

Figure 5.1 shows that Inunaq's poor hearing has affected his interactions with other children, where he has difficulty accepting decisions and complying with rules (2.2). He also had difficulty in negotiating with others in play (5.2). Likewise, distinguishing between reality and fantasy was problematic (5.3), as was participating in common cultural activities (6.3).

When suggesting pedagogical initiatives based on this assessment, the most important step was to ensure, in collaboration with the parents, that

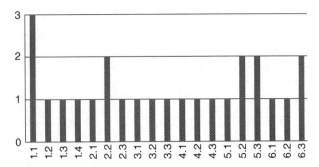

Figure 5.1  Inunaq's UBUS 5 profile The vertical axis illustrates the answer yes (can) (1), partial (2) and no (cannot) (3). The horizontal axis depicts the six areas. (1) health and well-being, (2) social interaction and competences, (3) communication and language competences, (4) sensation and movement, (5) cooperation and initiation of activities, (6) knowledge of nature and culture

Inunaq's ear problems were addressed by the health service. In addition, in their daily dialog and by providing information, adults had to ensure that Inunaq understood what was going to happen. The adults in kindergarten needed to support Inunaq to help him join in activities with other children. This involved caregivers in nurturing and encouraging his own agency through employing relational agency (see Chapters 3 and 7) to help him become involved in children's play. The adults also needed to talk to him about planning and rules in play as well as helping him to engage. Through conversations and experimentation, they needed to teach him to be more confident in his distinction between fantasy and reality. They should also help him to participate in cultural activities in the kindergarten by modeling how he should participate through drama and role-play related to Greenlandic myths, songs and music.

UBUS 3 and UBUS 5 are screening materials developed in Greenland and relate to Greenland's legislation and what is locally valued in day-care practices. It means that the material cannot be directly transferred to day care in other nations but should be interpreted in relation to other cultures' values for early childhood development and day-care traditions. Nonetheless, because of its basis in cultural-historical analyses, it is possible to learn from UBUS 3 and UBUS 5 when constructing screening material tailored to other societies.

Adaptations for other societies should also recognize the ways that adults can support children as they create their social situation of development, by working relationally with each other, with families and with children (Edwards, 2010, 2017). The assessment shown in a child's screening profile offers a foundation for this relational work. It can be a point of departure for cooperation between practitioners and between professionals and families. Discussions of the profile can produce common knowledge, and provide shared goals for success revealing what is important for both the practitioners and the family. This common knowledge can then mediate collaborations between home and day care. We cannot overestimate the importance of building common knowledge between home and practitioners as it allows ECEC to respect what matters in home cultures, something very important in Greenland. The same process can also be employed in collaboration with other agencies that support children in areas of concern and it can help with children's transitions from ECEC to more formal schooling (Hedegaard, 2017).

## Final Reflections

Children's development is not a natural process. It is a cultural process that is dependent on the institutional practices in which children live their everyday lives. The caregivers who responsively support children's participation in activities within these practices therefore have important roles to play. We have argued that because children's emotional engagement with people and with objects is crucial, care is important both in relation to the activities children may initiate and to activities that adults may initiate.

We argued in Chapter 4 that, in infancy and toddlerhood, agency is the central neoformation in children's development and it arises through communication between caregivers and children. The child's acquisition of language and ability to walk may be seen as part of their unfolding agency. In the preschool age period, the central activity is play, where the key neoformation in a child's higher psychic functions is imagination, which is crucial for their planning and experimentation. Other psychic functions also develop during the preschool period age and are interconnected with imagination. These include language, perception, and memory. In the preschool period, through play, meaning and symbol use become the core of the development of children's imagination, thinking and memory. As Wartofsky (1979) notes, human perception is always cultural as it is where meaning and symbol use connect.

Through play, young children become able to differentiate meaning from objects and actions, such as when the two small children Jorn and Louis drink imaginary coffee from dolls' cups. Here they extract meaning both from the objects and the acts. Play is therefore a way for children to acquire a conscious relation to the world, which is revealed in how they come to plan play actions and create shared imagination. Through role-play, children also become conscious of their own activity (Kudryavtsev, 2017) and may come to express feelings such as anxiety about the dark.

Children's shared play worlds are important for developing the complexity of their imaginations. For example, a specific object or action the child has experienced in their everyday life may be brought into imaginary scenarios. One outcome is that children may move in and out of reality while negotiating how the play may proceed, as happened in Kaisa's birthday play. It is the interplay between emotions and intellect in play that gives rise to the development of imagination. We have argued, following Vygotsky's ideas, that in play children bring the most intimate and personal aspects of their lives into the realm of social life, in the same way that adults may do through art.

We have also discussed how children rework their experiences in play and how this contributes to their acquisition of everyday concepts that are a foundation for their concept formation in school. Imagination also provides a way for children to work with symbols outside the sphere of reality, and to create narratives. Therefore, we see imaginative play as an important precursor to meeting the demands of subject matter learning in school.

We have also discussed the role of caregivers in relation to children's play. Caregivers may help children benefit from play activities by providing them with experiences that they may rework in play. Nonetheless, if they decide to enter young children's play, they should be aware of how children create lifeworlds in play that may be interrupted by newcomers. They can, however, create play worlds together with children, using narratives as in Fleer's play world research. Play worlds may therefore be seen to consist of activities that can support children's transition into school, as children learn both to follow the teacher's advice in explorations of emotions and, in Fleer's work, to orient to science concepts.

Children may use their imagination in the play world projects to relate experiences from everyday activities to the symbolic tools to be found in academic knowledge. But adults' support for learning in school is different from creating opportunities for imaginative play in preschool. In school, teaching orients children toward combining concepts they have acquired in everyday concrete situations, as imaginary symbols, with the scientific concepts of subject matter knowledge. Learning subject matter concepts should qualify children's everyday concepts, so that they become conscious tools used to understand and reflect about their lifeworlds. How this may happen will be the content of the chapters that follow.

CHAPTER 6

# *Engaging with Knowledge When Starting School*

## Introduction

In this chapter, we discuss how children engage with school knowledge and in doing so emphasize the emotional aspects of their motivated engagement. The chapter will focus on children's transition to school, and their first years in school. How they meet the demands of the new conditions that this transition presents, and how their engagement in subject matter learning can be supported. The school-age period is a time when conceptual learning and thinking is the leading activity. Taking a historical perspective, this developmental period is no older than school as an institution. The delineation of a special period for children as 'school age' originated in Western societies with the introduction of mandatory schooling in the nineteenth century (Ramirez & Boli, 1987). Until then, a developmental period between early childhood and adulthood was limited to the wealthier members of society and, for the majority of people, instruction for entry into adult life was done in the extended family or in workplaces (Ariès, 1962).

Schools have developed as institutions in response to the need to address societal problems. This has varied through time and in different societies (Afwedson & Afwedson, 1995; Ramirez & Boli, 1987, 1992). The purposes of school practices are anchored in societal and cultural traditions, which in turn shape the activity settings to be found in schools and the tasks that children encounter in them. This interaction is illustrated with the change in the practices of schooling in Denmark starting in 1814 with public schooling. At that point schooling was oriented to teaching children to read and write using the Catechism, with Bishops testing children once a year. As industrialization increased, its influence could be seen in the subjects taught in school. Math became a central subject, and reading and writing were divorced from religious teaching. Over time, changes in the Danish school law meant that until 1958 schooling largely differentiated between children from rural and urban areas. Another form of differentiation continued until 1975, this time by dividing children from grade 4 into either a practical route or an academic examination route. This changed in 1975 when comprehensive education was introduced. The curriculum also changed several times in response to public demand. For example, English is now taught from grade 1, whereas in the 1960s it was only available to older students on the academic route. Another important change globally is that, according to UNESCO, schooling is a right of children everywhere. The UNESCO statement is based on recognition that access to the best knowledge currently available is key to social inclusion and the ability to contribute to society. Schools are therefore for most children a central institution from around the age of six until adolescence.

In this chapter, we will focus on the characteristics of children as they enter this age period and how they engage with knowledge. We start by discussing children's transition to school, their motivation for school activities and what we mean by the subject matter knowledge they will encounter. Here we draw in part on El'konin's (1972/1999) theory of development and Leont'ev's (1978) theory of activity to analyze children's development of a learning motive, seeing it as central for children's learning in school. We shall also stress, in line with Vygotsky (1926/1997), Piaget (1955) and Bruner (1966a), the importance of understanding that children's way of thinking when starting school is quite different from how adults think, even though children may use the same words as adults do. We will show how Vygotsky (1987) illustrated very clearly that children's word meanings when they enter school are quite different from those of adults. That discussion is then followed by an account of the part played by emotions in children's development of these new psychic functions.

## Transition to School

Transition to school can be an emotionally turbulent time. Children meet new caregivers and new children and need to restructure their relations to old friends. Schools also create learning settings that are different from kindergarten because their objectives, practices and activity settings are different. These differences offer new opportunities for activities that make different demands on children. These new demands include being together with different children and the new learning demands in the new activities. To manage these demands, children need to develop new motives and competences that will reorient their relations to other people and their surroundings (Cavada-Hrepich, 2019; Hedegaard, 2012a, b; Hedegaard & Munk, 2019; Winther-Lindqvist, 2018, 2019).

Caregivers can help by orienting children to school while they still are in kindergarten, partly by telling them about what happens in school, but also by demanding independence in, for example, putting on and taking off their outdoor clothing and in toilet routines. But other forms of preparation are also underway in kindergarten. In Chapter 5, we pointed to the importance of developing children's imagination through role-play to prepare them for school in a variety of ways. The development of imagination can connect with emotion and create motives for the young child. They can imagine that they may acquire the competences in reading or numeracy that they see their parents, older siblings or friends having, and thereby become aware of a need to learn (El'konin, 1972/1999). Children themselves may express expectations of change in daily activities (White & Sharp, 2007; Hviid, 2018) and start to act to prepare themselves for school. They may become interested in letters, and supported by caregivers may write their name, recognize letters in their environment and ask others to read a word for them. They also may start to become interested in calculating through having money.

In the Frederiksberg family, Emil, who was in class zero, was invited to the homework table together with his older sisters, where he then often played with numbers or letters and so prepared himself to become a schoolboy participating in homework before he was actually given homework.

> *Continuation of Homework Observation November 4*, presented in Chapter 1. There the extract showed Lulu doing her homework in mathematics, while Mother tries to motivate her by calculating the age of Grandmother. In this extract we focus on Emil.
>
> Emil is sitting at the table together with his two older siblings. He is writing on small pieces of paper that he places in the money drawer of a toy cash register. He has written 100, but then writes 0001. Mother asks Emil what he is doing. He replies that he is making money. Lulu is also interested but comments that he writes receipts and not banknotes, to which Emil replies that he does make money. Mother explains to him that number one must be first before the zeroes. She shows Emil by writing a 100 on a note. Emil asks in relation to his note with 0001, turning the paper around: "What does it say now?" Mother says that there is no money that looks like that [She did not recognize that he had grasped the right idea, because in Denmark there is no 1000kr. note]

Emil leaves the topic and starts to talk about making a snowman and fantasizes about getting ginger nuts and a licorice pipe to make his face.

In these and the other examples from Emil's participation in the homework activities (Hedegaard & Fleer, 2013), it was obvious that Emil was playing with numbers and letters, and Mother's support was given in relation to his play. It was also clear that he was allowed to leave when he wanted, which was not the case for his sisters.

The new demands presented by school may therefore not be problematic; it may be exciting for children to meet the new world of activities and classmates. But it may be problematic if a child has *not* developed imagination of what going to school implies. Children should be supported to prepare for these changes by building images of what is going to happen so these images may function as motivational models for their future activities (Aidarova, 1982). If the child does not have an orientation model that guides their expectations, then the transition may become difficult. On the other hand, supporting children to acquire a motive orientation for going to school does not imply that one should start teaching children a watered-down version of the school curriculum.[1] Davydov and Kurdriavtsev (1998) argue that the transfer from kindergarten to school should not be seen as a continuity; neither should it involve shaping the social and pedagogical aspects of preschool education to accommodate the later demands of school instruction.

According to Davydov and Kurdriavtsev, education in kindergarten should be oriented toward supporting children's play and development of imagination, motivating them to build an imagination of competences they will need in school. Following Vygotsky we see children's development of conscious imagination as an agentic activity that is "not accumulated impressions but builds a new series of impressions of them and an image that does not previously exist emerges" (1987, p. 339). Davydov and Kurdriavtsev (1998) advise against bringing school learning into kindergarten. Instead, children should be supported to play and build images of everyday objects or actions and in that way become conscious of their everyday world.

When entering school, a qualitative change in children's learning occurs, from self-initiated activities to teacher-led activities. In school, teachers guide children into a world of concepts that are anchored within

---

[1] For further arguments, see Anning & Edwards, 1999; Hedegaard & Munk, 2019, Winther-Lindqvist, 2019.

a subject's conceptual system (Davydov & Kurdriavtsev, 1998; El'konin, 1972/1999; Hedegaard, 2020; Vygotsky, 1987). After starting school, children are gradually directed toward learning the powerful concepts that make up a subject matter area. This does not mean imposing formal teaching methods on young children. Instead, teaching in school should help children to relate their everyday concepts, acquired through imaginative play in kindergarten, to the knowledge systems of different subject areas, using and refining children's everyday knowledge through guided explorative teaching within different subject matter areas.

We shall be using the term *subject matter knowledge* in this chapter. By that we do not mean that six-year-olds will be making judgments about the right of William of Normandy to the throne of England. Rather, we recognize that school subjects are one way of organizing knowledge in a systematic way and that mastering the connections that comprise that knowledge is key to social inclusion and contribution to society.

## Children's Development of a Motive Orientation toward School Activities

Children's motives are connected to the type of activity setting that dominates in the practices of the institutions they take part in, such as play in kindergarten and building conceptual understandings of subject matter areas in school. The motives that shape the practices in these institutions, it is hoped, become children's *leading motive*. According to Leont'ev (1978), these may then become *meaningful* motives that give direction to children's actions in other practices.

To be able to explain the change and development of a child's motives, we distinguish between motives that characterize the child over a longer period and are connected to the dominant practice in a specific life period, and *motivation* that is connected with specific activities in the moment (Hedegaard, 2012a). An activity may invoke several motives, such as when Emil is with his friend in a homework setting and teases his sister Lulu by trying to erase her math exercise and thereby also tries to provoke his mother. This provocation may have several motives that guide his actions in the specific situation: to have fun together with his school mate who is visiting, to position himself in a powerful relation to his older sister, and to get attention from his mother (Hedegaard & Fleer, 2013, p. 76).

Most children participate in several common practices in early childhood such as living in families and going to some form of day care. As a result, they may share the motives that relate to their age period. It is therefore important for school-based practitioners to be aware of children's shared motives from earlier practices. These can be used as *stimulating motives* to motivate and engage children in the collective activities of school. It is, however, important that the teacher at the same time *orients* children to the leading motive in the new activity setting. The unwanted alternative is that children may create their own motives. In one example in Chapter 8, we discuss how two 1st grade children focused on becoming obedient pupils, taking the right actions, rather than risking failure by engaging with what the teacher hoped they would learn (Fisher, 2011).

It may also happen that a child does not orient to subject matter learning in school because the activities are emotionally challenging (Cavada-Hrepich, 2019), or because demands from home or other groups create emotional blocks or interfere with their engagement (Hedegaard, 1999b; Kohl, 1991; Varenne & McDermott, 1998). If this is the case, teachers need to find ways of building connections between children's knowledge and motives in everyday life and the subject matter knowledge in school. A classic way forward was shown in Moll's studies, where the funds of knowledge of Mexican families became resources for building engagement with the school curriculum in reading and math (Moll & Greenberg, 1990; Moll et al., 1992). We discuss a similar process in Chapter 7, drawing on observations in a school in Rajasthan (Rai, 2019). There we show how teachers built common knowledge that helped children connect the everyday farming knowledge of their families with the conceptual understandings they were building in school.

When starting school or being introduced to new subject matter, children may still use their everyday knowledge and imagination from play, but these processes should now connect with the conceptual systems that make up subject matter areas. The task for the teacher is to guide children into these systems through collective activities in the classroom and where positive emotion is key. When children start school, they may not have the motive orientation to, for example, learn to read, but emotionally positive experiences mediated by meaningful motives such as sitting together with friends or solving tasks together can lead to development of a motive that is oriented to the curricular purpose of an activity. Once developed, and if the positive feelings continue, this motive orientation can persist over time in relation to the activity. In, a reading activity, for example, the mediating or stimulating motive may be seen as a dynamic that guides a child's actions toward the motive-goal of the activity.

## Children's Learning of Word Meanings and Everyday Concepts

When starting school, children may use the same words as adults but will not have the same understanding of the words' meaning. Vygotsky (1987), Piaget (1955) and Bruner (1966a) all point to how children organize experiences in ways that are quite different from adults, when they interpret and use words. Therefore, when teachers simply present and explain concepts, it may be impossible for children to acquire conceptual knowledge except as the rote learning of labels. How to structure teaching to address this problem will be the focus in the next chapters. Here we will analyze phases in children's learning of word meanings and thinking and how these are different from adults' word meanings. To explain how children begin to grasp the powerful concepts that will allow them to engage fruitfully in societal practices, we turn to Vygotsky for the first analyses of children's thinking and concept learning.

To analyze the development of children's thinking, Vygotsky focused on their acquisition of word meanings as everyday concepts. Young children's learning of word meanings happens partly through conversation and partly through play. Vygotsky analyzed thinking as a dynamic system that constitutes a unity that integrates affective and intellectual processes: "Every idea contains some remnant of the individual's affective relationship to that aspect of reality which it represents. In this way, analysis into units makes it possible to see the relationship between the individual's need or inclinations and his thinking" (Vygotsky, 1987, p. 50).

For Vygotsky (1987), communication was the foundation for children's thoughts, first in the form of shared talk that may turn into egocentric speech that guides a child's external actions and then as thinking on an internal plane guiding his actions. But play is also important. In Chapter 5, we discussed how Vygotsky describes a process where word meanings become separated from objects and actions, through children's use of play pivots such as a spoon for an airplane. Consequently, children become able to use words on an imaginary plane.

Vygotsky (1987) repeatedly points out that adults and young children can use the same words and make references to the same objects, but the concepts connected with the words are qualitatively different. Because children and adults may use the same words, it may be difficult to follow how young children's word meanings (their everyday concepts) differ from adults' word meanings. Understanding of these differences is important for how teachers should introduce subjects to children.

Piaget (1955) also described preschool children's concepts as qualitatively different from school children's concepts. He described a child's first forms of cognition as sensorimotor intelligence, related to children learning to handle objects and move around. This period is followed by the preschool period where children use egocentric talk and their thinking is characterized as magical and preoperational, marked by the inability to follow concrete logic. For example, when water is poured from a squat jar into a tall jar, children at this point will say that the tall jar contains more water. Eventually, children acquire concrete operational thinking and the beginnings of rational thought. Piaget's view on children's cognitive development shaped early educational practice on children's transition to school for a long time in the Nordic countries and in Britain.

For many years, Piaget's influence meant that it was seen as necessary for children to have acquired concrete operational thinking before being introduced to subject matter teaching. This shift in thinking was expected to happen through children's self-initiated activities such as imitation, exploration and play (Piaget, 1952). This idea of readiness dominated early education. If a child was not an operational thinker, the advice in the Nordic countries was to not send a child to school until the child had acquired this competence, while in Britain teachers were expected to be alert to signs of readiness before moving children to engage with subject matter knowledge. This kind of advice may be seen in contrast to both Bruner's (1966a) and Vygotsky's (1998) view that children's development is founded in the interaction between adult and child.

Bruner (1966a) proposed three phases in children's acquisition of knowledge; these phases were seen as anchored in the child's acquisition of techniques for organizing experiences through interacting with other people. At first, the child's world is known to them principally by the habitual actions they use for coping with it. This form of representation Bruner named enactive. In time, children acquire a technique of representations through imagery that is relatively free of action, the iconic representation technique. Finally, through meeting the systematic aspects of language, math and logic in school education, children acquire a new and powerful method of translating actions and images into symbolic systems. Bruner (1966a) argues that enactive and iconic representations are the foundation for but are also changed by the child's acquisition of the symbolic representations they meet in school. This characteristic of the development of representations corresponds with Vygotsky's (1987) writings about the change from infants' perceptual orientation to kindergarten

*Learning of Word Meanings & Everyday Concepts* 135

children's imagination and, later, to school children's ability to act at a symbolic level.

The main difference between Piaget's theory of cognitive development and the approaches of Bruner and Vygotsky is in the weight Vygotsky and Bruner placed on speech as the most important communication form between children and other people and the role of speech in the development of children's thinking. Vygotsky saw speech as the central tool for mediating children's cognitive development. He explained: "Social interaction based on rational understanding, on the intentional transmission of experience and thought, requires *some means*. *Human speech*, a system that emerged with the need to interact socially in the labor process, has always and will always be the prototype of this kind of means" (Vygotsky, 1987, p. 48) [italics in the original].

The importance of concepts is that they support a child's organization of experiences into a knowledge system that the child may use to guide how they enter into activities and their actions in them. Throughout development, a child acquires different conceptual understandings that come to function as the child's everyday concepts. This starts as soon as a child uses words. Young children's everyday concept formation starts to become explicit when children use words for different objects or events and start to ask: 'What is that?' Vygotsky notes that children's first words already contain a generalization.

> The word does not relate to a single object, but to an *entire group or class of objects*. Therefore, every word is a concealed *generalisation*. From a psychological perspective word meanings are first and foremost generalisation. It is not difficult to see that generalisation is a *verbal act of thought;* its reflection of reality differs radically from that of immediate sensation or perception. (Vygotsky, 1987: 47) [italics in the original]

Children start their learning of everyday concepts through communication about everyday experiences. Morten (20 months), for instance, is happy when he sees a bird and he can spot them far away. He says "pip," when he sees a bird on the garden railing, and also when he sees a model of a flying dinosaur at the Zoo. The use of words becomes more refined as the child's experiences increase. Vygotsky argued that young children always move from the general to the specific; children have a general idea of the word's meaning and that becomes more specific with new concrete experiences.

Sara at four years corrects her grandmother when she calls Sara's bicycle helmet a bicycle hat or names her boots as shoes. She tells her grandmother that it is a helmet, not a hat, nor are they shoes, they are boots. Words have references, but words also have meanings, and for Sara this meaning starts to relate to certain aspects of specific objects and not to others. Sara has become conscious of relations between some objects that separates them from others and has acquired this capacity through communicating with others. "To communicate an experience or some other content of consciousness to another person, it must be related to the class or group phenomena. As we have pointed out, this requires *generalisation. Social interaction presupposes generalisation and the development of verbal meaning;* generalisation becomes possible only with the development of social interaction" (Vygotsky, 1987, p. 48) [italics in original].

Vygotsky explored how a child builds her first word meanings through the double stimulation experiment (Vygotsky, 1987, p. 127 ff). This experiment involved blocks varied in three dimensions, size, color and shape and each block had a meaningless three-letter word written on one side. He used the double stimulation method in the experiment. The blocks were the first stimulus, that the children would work on. The second stimulus was the signs the children employed while they sorted the blocks. What signs the children used to sort the blocks allowed Vygotsky to study the early processes of concept development across different ages of young children.

Children were asked to place together all the blocks that they thought would have the same word on the reverse side. After each attempt at solving the task, the experimenter corrected them and showed them the name on the reverse of another block, not in the set they compiled. The results showed that a meaningless word label helped the children in different age periods to organize the blocks differently. The youngest children simply produced random assemblies or what Vygotsky described as an "unordered collection or heap" (p. 135). Preschool children sorted the blocks by different features. Their sorting was driven by perception, but they were able to create categories. Vygotsky labeled this kind of sorting as complexes and identified five different kinds of complexes. These include associative complexes, where the child identifies a common feature, which may result in quite varied groupings and chain complexes where a child organizes objects into sets but moves on to create new sets by linking the start of a new set with a characteristic of the previous set, but with a marked difference. The older children, entering school, started to be able to use one feature of the blocks as a general principle when sorting them. This Vygotsky saw as a bridge from children's thinking in complexes toward the formation of concepts.

According to Vygotsky, pseudo-concepts involve children in using words that adults use while still thinking in concrete terms rather than abstract. He therefore used this experiment to support his argument that young children may use words without understanding their meaning in the way that adults do. His view was that it was not until adolescence that children began to work with what he termed true concepts. Reflecting on the experiment he wrote: "The experiment uncovers the real activity of the child in forming generalizations, activity that is generally masked from casual observation" (p. 143). He then summarized the role of adults in the formation of pseudo-concepts: "By addressing the child in speech, adults determine the path along which the development of generalizations will move" (p. 143).

What is missing in Vygotsky's analysis in this experiment is the dynamic and emotional aspect of children's concept formation: a problem that Vygotsky himself identified in his account of cognitive development. He argued: "The first issue that emerges when we consider the relationship of thinking and speech to the other aspects of the life of consciousness concerns the connections between *intellect* and *affect*. Among the most basic defects of traditional approaches to the study of psychology has been the isolation of the intellectual from the volitional and affective ascepts of consciousness" (Vygotsky, 1987, p. 50).

Although Vygotsky did not integrate the volitional and affective aspects in his experimental study, he was very aware of these aspects of children's learning. This is seen clearly in his accounts of the importance of play where he argued that children's needs and unmet wishes were what motivates children's play (Vygotsky, 1967). Through playing with other children, a child may learn ways to express their own needs.

### Emotional Imagination and Motive Orientation in Play: Children's Formation of Everyday Concepts

Children's actions, when involved in a collective role-play moving in and out of the play spheres of reality and imagination to negotiate the rules, contribute to how they become conscious of word meanings and create images. Their negotiations of rules may be emotionally loaded either with joy or anger (Schousboe, 2013). Nonetheless, the emotional images that children create when drawing on earlier experiences are important for their further concept learning, and for sustaining a creative aspect in concept formation. In Chapter 2, we introduced Zaporozhets' (2002) theory of emotion. There we explained that emotion may be seen as a "special form of reflection" (p. 53) that leads to an anticipation of one's own accomplishments and can help the child to regulate their own actions. Among preschool children this may be observed in how emotions unfold and direct negotiations in children's play.

In the same play, different children may organize their experience differently, reflecting both their conceptual level and their motive orientation. We illustrate this in the following analyses of three children's play in kindergarten. The focus is on Frida; she is about to leave the kindergarten and move to the school preparation class. The caregivers in kindergarten were concerned about Frida's way of interacting with the other children and were worried about how she would manage the transfer to school. Frida had little sustained contact with the other children around her. Through observations (Hedegaard & Munk, 2019) it seemed that she was strongly motivated to join in other children's play but had difficulty in finding how to be accepted. In the extract below, we follow how she both used her imagination capacity and emotions to join a shared play.

> **Observation Extract from Fifth Observation Mid-April**
>
> Frida walks to the carpet in the play corner, where Mikkel and Kaya (who are younger than Frida) are lying under a blanket with a pillow under their heads.
>
> Frida: "Can I be a baby?"
>
> Kaya: "No."
>
> Frida: "May I be a cat?"
>
> Kaya: "Cats only sleep in the morning. Cat, you may better go over to the table and draw. You may go to Tivoli (a fairground in central Copenhagen)."
>
> Frida crawls on all fours toward the table and away from where Mikkel and Kaya are located.
>
> Kaya says after a short while: "Now it's morning." (Frida is at the other end of the room.)
>
> Frida crawls, like a cat, toward them. She is now back with the others in the play corner on all fours.
>
> Kaya and Mikkel are still under the blankets with their eyes closed.
>
> Frida crawls toward the door of the play cupboard.
>
> Mikkel crawls over and retrieves a toy. He comes back and goes to Kaya who still is under the blanket. He then sings: "Today is Kaya's birthday."

Kaya and Mikkel are on the carpet in the play corner. They throw pillows at each other.

Frida is also sitting on the carpet. She throws a pillow once.

Kaya moves to the book corner. She says: "I am sitting over here and I am sad."

Frida moves over to the book corner and places herself next to Kaya. Frida says she could protect her with a shield.

Mikkel says immediately: "But I have a samurai sword."

Frida whispers to Kaya.

Mikkel, standing two meters from the girls with his back to them, he says: "There is a thief who has stolen a donut from me."

Mikkel goes over to Kaya and Frida. He pretends he unlocks handcuffs on Kaya.

Kaya rises.

Frida gets up, too, and shouts: "Now we have to catch them."

Mikkel goes away from the play corner.

Kaya and Frida say something to each other. Kaya asks if she can come home with Frida and eat.

Kaya says: "Frida, now you are in jail."

Frida sits down in the corner where Kaya was previously. Mikkel comes back.

Kaya: "Oh, you play Ramasjang-mystery (A children's TV series)?"

Frida hesitates and nods.

Mikkel: "So, I'm Christian. But who is going to be the spy (People from the mystery)?"

Frida says: "I am a Cat mystery (Another children's TV series)."

Mikkel says four times in a row: "Who must be Bruno (A person in the Cat Mystery)?"

Kaya rises: "Okay, I'm Bruno."

Mikkel: "Message from Christian to Cat."

Frida: "Try to see there is ketchup and jam on the plate – it must be him."

Mikkel: "Yes, it must be him. He jumps up and throws a pillow and runs to the other end of the room." (Hedegaard & Munk, 2019, pp. 36–37)

Frida's motive is clear; she wants to play with Kaya and Mikkel and is accepted in a minor role as the cat. The play gives an opportunity for Frida to enter the activity of the two children playing family. Through reaching out she gradually acquires a position in their play, entering into negotiating play rules, keeping her role as a cat. At the start her role is minor as the family's cat that is sent away (even as far away as Tivoli), but she is accepted in this role. She then masters making the cat role relevant by extending the play theme, so her contributions become accepted by the other two children. Mikkel and Kaya's elaboration of the content of the play take the form of chaining imagined events, where they change the play objective from family activities and a birthday to a children's TV series (Christian's mystery series) that is mingled with another TV series (A cat mystery series). Frida is the one who keeps the cat theme going across the different play topics. Her way of doing this may be seen to create a positive emotional situation, first together with Kaya and later with accepting that they play a Ramasjang mystery that combines with her role as a cat. In this way, she presents a way of organizing the activity that is close to Vygotsky's description of pseudo-concepts, keeping one general theme of the cat as the core for her in the play. In contrast, the two younger children jump from one event to the next in the mode of a chain complex.

The integration of the affect and intellect is also evident here, demonstrating how play is moved forward by the children's emotions. Mikkel makes a joyful birthday, but he also threatens Kaya, who immediately says that she is sad. Frida enters the scene to protect her. Mikkel then escalates the emotions by positioning himself as an attacker, but only briefly. He can see that Frida and Kaya are starting to join together and he does not want to be excluded, so he immediately moves to help Kaya and the three of them are united against an imaginary attacker. Both for Frida and Mikkel, the emotion can indicate that they anticipate events they do not want to happen. For Frida the emotional interaction makes it possible for her to become part of the play, for Mikkel it is not to be excluded by Frida through her relation to Kaya.

Both the Ramasjang Mystery and the Cat Mystery can be played as games, where someone in the game has to find the hidden person following some prescribed rules. This shift matched Frida's competences, so she could gradually take over the leading role. Children's ability to keep a theme going come to characterizes children's play when it turns into games guided by rules.

Some months later, Frida was observed when entering the school preparation class where she met a new group of children (Hedegaard &

Munk, 2019). For her the transfer was a leap forward. It seems that entering a new institutional practice with new activities and new ways of interacting was very positive emotionally for Frida and solved her problems of being excluded from the other children's activities. The new activities gave her opportunities to use her capacities for generalization and thereby to enter into new positions in school activities with new motives.

With Frida's case we have shown that children, through their emotional participation, can change the objectives of play and their motives for playing. In the longer perspective, children may create new motives and take forward their intellectual development (Kravtsova & Kravtsov, 2012). But for some children, the opposite may happen when moving to school. A child may end up in a new position and the emotional anticipation may become negative. This may be illustrated with a case from Winther-Lindqvist's (2012: 122–124) research.

She followed 12 kindergarten children's daily activities over a period before and after their transition into school activities. Each child had different ways of accommodating their transition. James particularly had difficulties entering school and finding his way forward in the new activity settings. He had had a high status among the other children in kindergarten because he was good at playing soccer. James is the 'king' at the playground, his best friend Ollie pronounced. In the kindergarten, the other children waited until he had finished his lunch to let him decide the teams. He made the rules and decided whether a goal counted.

In kindergarten, James also started to orient going to school. Winter-Lindqvist describes an event where James is sitting on a couch and his best friend Ollie asks him to come outside to play soccer. James answers: "Yes when I have finished reading this book." It was a spelling book. After the summer holiday Ollie and James started class zero in school, where playing soccer in the school yard was not possible. James still was slow finishing his lunch; when he entered the school yard the other children had already started to play Dungeons and Dragons, and only a minor role was left for him. His status as a leader disappeared. After six weeks his parents complained that he cried in the morning and did not want to go to school. After eight weeks when the teacher asked all children, "How do you like going to school," when it came to James he shrugged and would not say. When the teacher asked, "Is there something you miss from day care?" He answered, "I miss my friends."

The emotional feeling impacted on his more academic activities. Winter-Lindqvist reported that James says that lessons are boring and learning rhymes and singing are dull. Here we see what negative emotions may do to children. Even though James was fully capable of meeting the teacher's demand for participating in subject matter activities, the negative emotion connected with his school activities overshadowed his school life, his competences and his motive for learning.

What is crucial in both examples is how children's emotional experiences change qualitatively when moving from preschool to school. Following Frida over several months made it was easy to see that she changed from being a girl who contacted other children by pushing or other negative attempts at joining, she in school found a way forward out of her crises in relation to other children. James, however, still needed some support in order to create new relations to his environment.

Overcoming crises is central to development. Vygotsky makes the point in his lecture about *The crises at age three and the crises at age seven:* "That which was to the child essentially important, the guide rail, has suddenly become only comparatively so or unimportant at the very next step. For this reason, it seems to me that this restructuring of needs and impulses, the change in the value system, is the basic moment in the transition from one age to another" (2021: 215). This extract gives an insight into Vygotsky's understandings of how needs and motives are related to cultural values, values that may be seen as related to the practice demands and value-laden goals and objectives of the different institutions of families, kindergarten and school (see Figure 2.1).

## The Relation between Everyday and Scientific Concepts

Learning everyday concepts is not a natural process that unfolds between the child and the environment. As we have consistently argued, it takes place through interaction with other people (see Chapters 4 and 5). In the early years caregivers and teachers of young children follow the child's logic of action and support the child's spontaneous activities. One example was Emil with the toy cash register where his mother supported him and taught him about numbers. In school, in contrast, the child follows the logic of the teacher. By engaging with subject matter areas in school, children are introduced to conceptual systems. Vygotsky characterized the kind of conceptual knowledge we are calling subject matter knowledge as scientific concepts. The example of Frida and James showed that the competence children acquire in kindergarten may interact with how their emotional relations develop and may impact how their transitions to teacher-guided activities may take place.

Importantly, the subject matter concepts that children meet in school can only be understood and become functional for the child if they build on the child's everyday knowledge. Children, therefore, don't have 'real' concepts from the moment they meet subject matter concepts. Several phases may follow. A first phase of moving away from an organization of everyday experience into complexes is a form of generalization into the pseudo-concepts that Vygotsky described as a transitional phase. Increased precision in the use of concepts marks the move toward 'real' concepts, which allow children to use the signs and symbols that are central to the systematic knowledge that is the subject matter knowledge taught in schools and to abstract and synthesize within those systems. Vygotsky explained the importance of these processes: "The central feature of this operation is the functional use of the word as a means of voluntarily directing attention, as a means of abstracting and isolating features, and as a means of synthesising and symbolising the features through the sign" (1987, p. 164).

One of the important aspects of concept formation that Vygotsky (1987) advanced is that concepts symbolize both the concrete and abstract aspects of a subject area. The concrete aspect can be found in the images produced in children's imaginations. The abstract aspects are the generalizations that children produce when they acquire words and use them so that their meanings evolve. Vygotsky characterized children's conceptual development as an increase in the complexity of the relations between the concrete images and abstract generalizations of aspects of the conceptualized area. When teaching succeeds in creating these relations children will be able to use subject matter knowledge as a tool for analyzing and reflecting on their everyday activities. Subject matter knowledge becomes integrated with a child's everyday knowledge and develops into functional concepts for the child, where content and form define each other.

Vygotsky's analyses have been important for drawing attention to the fact that children, throughout their development, acquire different conceptual modes. For Vygotsky these were everyday concepts and scientific concepts, which relate differently to each other in different developmental periods. Everyday concepts may, in the preschool age, be connected to word meanings as a kind of action or visual image that takes the form of assemblies, complexes and pseudo-concepts. When children are introduced to subject matter concepts through teaching, their word meanings in the forms of images may become combined in different ways with subject matter concepts that are characterized by abstraction and generalization. These combinations are connected with a child's emotional experience.

Vygotsky's theory may be interpreted as offering a hierarchical organization of development with everyday concepts at the bottom and abstract concepts at the top. Vygotsky criticized this misunderstanding, arguing against idealizing abstract thought that was disconnected from context (Vygotsky, 1987). In his later work about adolescents' thinking and concept formation, he clearly stated that a concept is not a thing or a word, "but as a process, not as an empty abstraction, but as a thorough and penetrating reflection of an object of reality in all its complexity and diversity, in connections and relations to all the rest of reality" (Vygotsky, 1998, p. 55).

Children learn concepts while participating in different cultural practices, but the way of learning changes when they start school because of the systematicity in school education. When the child is starting school, caregivers no longer follow the child and their logic. Instead, teaching moves the child from acting to verbalizing to mental activity. But in the acquisition of concepts by children, adolescents and adults, these concepts become used as everyday concepts. Everyday concepts are the functional concepts throughout all phases of life, but these change qualitatively in different developmental periods depending on the practice where they are learned. In kindergarten, the change arises through pedagogues following the child's understanding and extending and verbalizing their activities. In school, the change happens through children working on tasks that are designed to connect their everyday concepts with subject matter concepts. For adults it happens mainly through participating in work practices. Everyday concepts guide learners' activities, both real and imagined, but their structure and content are personal and vary in relation to each person's life story.

When children acquire subject matter concepts, such as when they learn the logic of the syntax in language or principles in math, it is important to make them aware that both literacy and math relate to topics in the world. But at the same time, they consist of methods or procedures that are essential for working with these subjects. All too often in school, language and math are only seen as method subjects, in contrast to other subjects such as history or biology, which are usually taught as content subjects. After Schwab (Westbury & Wilkof, 1978), we see subjects to be made up of substantive and syntactic knowledge. The substantive knowledge is concepts that are central to a subject area such as weight in physics or character in literature. While syntactic knowledge is the ways of validating knowledge in a subject area, such as experimentation in the sciences and proof in math. The focus is the connection between the different conceptual content in subject matter areas and the procedures and methods for attaining and representing that knowledge.

Bruner (1966a) was in sympathy with this view, arguing that subject matter areas may be analyzed from the perspective of content and ways of knowing. In this way, one can see connections between the procedures for validating content knowledge and the nature of the content area. Bruner also helpfully reminds us of different forms of knowledge. Words have specific meanings within different subject discourses, just think about how the term 'times' is used in math, history and music. These different meanings are used to guide actions, but actions can also be visualized in iconic models such as figures and charts or may be symbolized in enactive representations such as break dance, ballet and sign language. These knowledge forms are not only making experiences visible, they relate directly to the objectives associated with grasping the substantive knowledge, the conceptual systems that comprise a subject area. In Chapter 7, we will expand on how children are brought into different subject matter discourses by teachers who are clear about ways of knowing and their relationship with the content of subject matter areas. In doing so, we draw on researchers such as Galperin and Davydov who took forward the pedagogic aspects of Vygotsky's legacy.

## Final Reflections

An important acquisition for children in kindergarten is their development of imagination. By the end of preschool age, both caregivers and children are looking forward toward learning in school. Children start to imagine activities they will experience when entering school and develop motives for these and may be supported both in home and kindergarten in this process.

In this chapter, we have focused on children's acquisition of knowledge, moving from imagination to concept formation. We have discussed how imagination supports children's generalizations of experience, so that it becomes possible for them to move between the general and the concrete in analyzing and using knowledge about the world.

In our analyses, we have drawn extensively on Vygotsky's theory. When discussing concept formation, he was at pains to avoid the idea that cognitive development was simply the outcome of the biological processes of organic maturation. Instead, he argued for a dialectical relationship between cognitive development, that is the formation of mind, and the culturally developed content the child encounters in her interactions in the world.

He observed that when children enter school, both the form and content of children's concept formation and thinking develop. He showed that children, throughout development, acquire different conceptual techniques (methods for acquiring and organizing knowledge). A child's acquisition of subject matter concepts in school can be characterized as concepts where the child can describe their core aspects when questioned, such as when they recognize how character is built in literature. Vygotsky based his explanation of children's development of school concepts on formal logic, but at the same time he acknowledged that these concepts also contain imagined aspects related to the child's emotional experience. In his last analyses, writing of adolescents, Vygotsky (1998) argued that through the acquisition of conceptual systems that relate to the social, societal and political aspects of life, young people for the first time can be conscious of the societal ideologies and of themselves as people in society and their self-consciousness develops.

But within the cultural-historical approach to learning and development Davydov (1977/1990, 2008) was the first to clarify how one should understand concepts as related within a subject matter system (see Chapter 7). The cultural aspects of children's concept formation were seen as characteristics of theoretical knowledge, while the development of their thinking was based on the ideas of dialectal logic put forward by Ilyenkov (1982). Dialectical logic is crucial for understanding the mechanisms of human mental activity where logic and cognition become integrated with the content and methods of subject matter areas. In contrast, formal logic only concentrates its attention on the form or method in knowledge. How this change in understanding of knowledge influences children's learning and development in school will be the content of Chapter 9. First, we will introduce our ideas of care-full pedagogy in school in Chapter 7 and in Chapter 8 we discuss what they mean in relation to elementary and middle schoolchildren. We turn to adolescents in Chapter 10.

CHAPTER 7

# *Caring Approaches to Pedagogy*

## Introduction

In this chapter, we discuss how the three relational concepts that were described in Chapter 3 – relational expertise, common knowledge and relational agency – can inform relationships aimed at enhancing pedagogy. Our examples will be largely school-based, but we recognize that much of the work of the caring professions is pedagogical, helping children to engage and move forward, and hope that this chapter will help understandings of school-age children. We shall largely take the perspective of the adult; but we shall not entirely ignore the child's perspective, because a relational version of pedagogy intertwines both. Our aim here is to set out the broad features of relational interactions that are common to learning-oriented exchanges. We shall start by briefly indicating how children can be supported relationally and care-fully in their development as agentic learners at home and then move on to discuss a relational pedagogy in educational settings.

As we saw in Chapter 6, the transition of starting formal schooling involves children in meeting the curricula that guide teaching. At the same time, in most jurisdictions, teachers have limited flexibility over curriculum content. This presents challenges for practitioners: they need to relationally support children as learners, while sustaining the required curriculum focus. We are advocating a care-full reciprocal pedagogy that takes seriously children's motives and connects learners with powerful knowledge in ways that allow them to grasp that knowledge, link it to wider societal issues and ask questions of it. We will introduce a teaching–learning sequence that can underpin the planning of teaching sessions and discuss its relationship with the work of Vygotsky, Galperin and Davydov. In doing so, we shall explain how these three relational concepts can help teachers develop their relational pedagogies.

In each of our examples, we shall highlight the emotional aspects of learning and the role of motive orientation. We shall argue that, while affect is usually central to family relationships, practitioners will find the relational concepts helpful when encouraging learners' positive affective relationships with the environments that they provide in their professional settings.

The importance of emotion to learning and development has been highlighted in earlier chapters, reflecting the importance Vygotsky placed on it. Two of Vygotsky's students, Bozhovich and Zaporozhets, have developed these ideas (see Chapters 2 and 6). Bozhovich pointed to the part that emotion plays in the dialectical relationship between people and the practices they inhabit as follows: "in order to understand exactly what effect the environment has on children ... how it affects the course of their development. The nature of children's experience must be understood, the nature of their affective relationship to the environment" (Bozhovich, 2009, p. 66). Zaporozhets' argument even more directly informs our efforts at bringing emotion to the fore when studying learning. As we saw in Chapters 2 and 6, he regarded emotion to be a "special form of reflection used for mental control of motivation" (2002, p. 53). He argued that the emotional anticipation of the results of their actions involves children in mentally outlining possible steps and their consequences for themselves as social beings. In that process, their emotions act as a reflective brake on possible actions.

This cultural-historical view of the importance of emotion was also partly echoed from a neurological standpoint by Damasio. In brief, his argument is: "Well-targeted and well-deployed emotion seems to be a support system without which the edifice of reason cannot operate properly" (Damasio, 1999, p. 42). While Damasio presents some interesting examples to support this statement, we take a rather different view. As we have explained in previous chapters, in line with Vygotsky, we see emotion as an integral part of higher psychic functioning and not merely a support to it.

All our examples will make clear that the goal of a relational approach to learning is that the learner, whether child or adult, becomes increasingly independent of the initial support given. But we are not advocating rampant individualism as the outcome; far from it. We recognize that agentic actions are rarely taken in isolation. Our actions are embedded in the practices of our communities, consequently, care for oneself and others is important. One way of developing that kind of responsibility is through taking children or adult learners and their emotions and motives seriously in an environment marked by care.

## Introduction

The pedagogy we are advocating builds on the view put forward by Vygotsky in his lectures to beginning teachers in Gomel in the early 1920s (Vygotsky, 1926/1997). There he explained that "[t]he student educates himself. ... For present day education it is not so important to teach a quantity of knowledge as it is to inculcate the ability to acquire such knowledge and make use of it" (p. 339). Here we can see connections with his dialectical view of the social situation of development where the child propels themself forward employing actions that are anchored in the practices which they take part in (see Chapter 2). It is also a very modern view of education, marking an important break with nineteenth-century opinion (recently revived in, for example, English education policy) that education involves filling the empty vessel with facts. At the same time, it calls for subtle expertise on the part of the teacher: It is not a call for a simplistic child-led education that purports to draw on Piaget's work. We have every sympathy with Piagetian scholars, as Piaget never intended his work on child development to be the basis of national education programs.

Vygotsky believed that teachers should guide students toward the central concepts in subject matter knowledge as part of his commitment to empowerment through education. It is this delicate set of moves, to take forward conceptual development while sustaining student engagement that we begin to outline in this chapter. These moves address the greatest challenge to teachers in formal education settings, bridging the gap between children's motive orientations and the knowledge that is valued in society. Engagement with knowledge is discussed from a cultural-historical perspective in Chapters 6 and 9. We will also be concerned with it in Chapters 8 and 10 because we need to address this engagement in relation to age periods and the educationally oriented institutional practices in which children are acting. In this chapter, our primary focus is the general importance of connecting emotion and cognition to release the agency of learners and how that can be done.

Agency is key to learning. Adult agency was discussed in Chapter 3 and children's agency was addressed in Chapter 4 in relation to motives and intention. We have also recently suggested that agency is an important element in the development and unfolding of motive orientation (Edwards et al., 2019) and is therefore key to learners' engagement. Children's agency is revealed when they are able to identify and evaluate what is important for themselves and others and to take action that supports those evaluations. Agency, however, is context-dependent: We see children's actions unfolding agentically in some situations and not in others. But even where there are restrictions placed on actions, their agency may be revealed in how they work around barriers or negotiate their intentions through them. Working with and channeling children's agency is the fundamental challenge for teachers, and across the caring professions.

Although Vygotsky did not use the term 'agency,' the concept is evident in his discussion of how learners are responsible for their own learning. Again, talking to beginning teachers in Gomel, he states: "The time has come to put the student on his own two feet" (Vygotsky, 1926/1997, p. 342). He, of course, recognized that releasing student agency called for skilled work by teachers and wrote at length about how demanding the job is, how not everyone is suited to it and how well-qualified teachers should be. In this chapter, we build on Vygotsky's foundational thoughts in two interconnected ways, one of which is to show how the three relational concepts – relational expertise – common knowledge and relational agency – can inform the kind of care-full relational approach that can release agency. The other strand in our argument emphasizes the importance of care in a relational pedagogy, which recognizes the emotional aspects of learning.

## Relational Work at Home

There are important differences between care-full relationships at home and those in more formal settings, although they may share the same long-term goals about children's well-being. More often than not, relationships at home are strongly underpinned by affect, by the emotional bonds that can tie families together, while in pedagogic relationships outside the home, care is part of a practitioner's repertoire of skillful interactions, marked by a necessary professional emotional distancing. Home and school consist of quite different practices and children are also positioned in them differently; we therefore caution against turning home into school and vice versa. Instead, as we argued in Chapter 3, we urge practitioners in the caring professions to see home practices as different but also valuable.

We suggest that practitioners should value the strength of the emotional bonds between children and their family carers, seeing them as assets for the child which cannot easily be offered in more formal settings. We saw, for example, in Edwards' evaluation with colleagues of the English Early Learning Parenting Project (ELPP), which aimed at ensuring school readiness among disadvantaged children, that the socially excluded parents we studied showed emotional warmth and support for their children's learning (Evangelou et al., 2008, p. 111). In another school readiness study in Chile, discussed in Chapter 3, Woodrow and Staples found that when teachers were able to talk in relaxed ways with parents, they formed fresh opinions of the strong emotional support the families offered their children (Woodrow & Staples, 2019). One important question arising from these observations is the extent to which parental interactions with children are oriented toward nurturing children's agency, enabling their curiosity, willingness to approach novelty and capacity to take action. As we saw in the Anning and Edwards (1999) study with practitioners working in English early years settings, which we discussed in Chapter 4, professionals can help families with recognizing the importance of nurturing children's agency as learners.

## Relational Work in Formal Educational Settings: Establishing Common Knowledge between Teachers and Learners

The transition from home and early education settings to formal schooling is a major move between practices. Formal schooling is quite different from nursery and kindergarten. In the latter, we can see that children may be captured to a curriculum and brought gently into enticing learning opportunities, while in formal schooling, they are unfortunately often simply recruited to the curriculum with little choice in what they must do. The transition requires children to create quite new motive orientations. We discussed this transition from the child's perspective in Chapter 6. Here we focus on the adult's perspective. We start with the obvious statement that all children are different and will enter school-based experiences with different prior understandings and different ways of orienting to the school environment. This premise points to the challenges of teaching and means that simple guides to best practice that list apparently failsafe teacher strategies tend to be doomed. Instead, we offer the idea of a relational pedagogy as a meta-level, or umbrella, framing of pedagogical relationships. In school settings, for example, a relational care-full pedagogy involves teachers in being alert to children's different motive orientations and guiding them toward those orientations that are most productive. It therefore involves practitioners in eliciting children's orientations and revealing their own.

In Chapter 3, we discussed how common knowledge is built between practitioners or between practitioners and clients. We outlined how it consists of respect for and knowledge of each other's motive orientations and is a resource that can be used to mediate joint action on a problem or task. There are, of course, power differences in collaborations, even between practitioners. A teaching assistant does not have the same professional status as a school psychologist, though she may know the child they are discussing much better that the psychologist does. The psychologist therefore needs to ensure that their interpretations don't dominate, and that teaching assistant's motive orientations are made visible and understood. Differential power relations are more clearly evident in professionals' work with clients.

In this chapter, we introduce another kind of negotiation of common knowledge, this time between teachers and learners. These negotiations are at the core of care-full responsive teaching. Building common knowledge for a relational care-full pedagogy requires teachers to: (i) be clear about what is important to how one orientates to subject matter knowledge, their motive orientations, and (ii) elicit the motive orientations of children. These processes are also relevant to relationships between all caring professionals and children.

In the previous chapters, we have emphasized that children do not learn simply through imitating actions; rather they also connect with the motives that shape the actions of adults who are significant to them. We have also stressed the need to try to access the motives of children as they negotiate their way through institutional practices in order to guide and support them. Vygotsky, writing on how children acquire word meanings, explained the importance of this mutual access to motives in the social interactions that support children's cognitive development.

> Understanding the words of others also requires understanding their thoughts. And even this is incomplete without understanding their motives or why they expressed their thoughts. In precisely this sense we complete the psychological analysis of any expression only when we reveal the most secret internal plane of verbal thinking – its motivation. (Vygotsky, 1987, p. 283)

Revealing the motive orientations of caring professionals and children is key. Most children will need to be helped to recognize the demands presented by classroom tasks in which subject matter knowledge is embedded and to be able to approach and tackle those demands. How a teacher orients to a task can help children see the demands in the task. Equally, eliciting children's orientations is crucial and the teacher's responses will guide and support the development of these motive orientations toward engagement with the demands.

It is important at this point to distinguish between common knowledge as used here and the common knowledge that is central to Derek Edwards and Neil Mercer's book of the same name. While Edwards and Mercer (2013) focus on how teachers bring learners to the same jumping-off point for introducing a new concept by careful reiterations of what was previously learnt, our version of common knowledge comprises the motive orientations of those involved in interactions. The former focuses on the importance of revision in building subject matter knowledge; while the way we use the term is concerned with motive orientations to and the consequent interpretations and deployment of new concepts. In short, our version of common knowledge adds attention to emotion in the learning process.

There is a wealth of literature on achievement motivation and avoidance and how avoidance impedes learning (Nicholls, 2017; Weiner, 1972) and on emotion and academic achievement (Pekrun, 2009). This broad body of research supports our attention to nurturing motive orientations toward grappling with the demands of subject matter knowledge as it is embedded in classroom tasks. Approaching demands in tasks is where emotion and cognition are very clearly intertwined and reminds us that teaching is not a matter of delivering a curriculum. Instead, it involves encouraging and enabling engagement with it.

The pedagogic exchanges that build and use common knowledge occur in different ways throughout a learning cycle as, over time, teachers pass responsibility for learning something new to learners. One would therefore expect teachers to be explicit about what matters for them about a new idea and how to work with the idea, while also eliciting how children are orienting to the idea. This kind of interaction occurs where a new concept within a thematic area is introduced. It involves working out how a child is orienting to the new idea and being explicit about what kind of orientation is best.

For example, a teacher starting a series of experiments in elementary school science leading to children understanding that to kill bacteria they need to use hot water when washing their hands might say: "Today we are going to observe what happens when we add hot or cold water to soap flakes. We will then draw pictures of what happens in each case. But first, what do you think might happen? Will there be a difference between the hot and the cold water?" The interaction that follows usually takes the form of questions and answers, where the children's responses are carefully considered and then built on by the teacher.

This exercise of relational expertise by the teacher produces a form of relational knowledge, the beginnings of common knowledge between teachers and learners, which teachers can use to mediate their interactions with children, either as individuals or as groups. In these interactions, the teacher guides children into competent actions within the target discourse. In doing so, they may work relationally with children to encourage the unfolding of relational agency and the growing independence of the learners. Or they may encourage learners' collaboration and the unfolding of their joint agency. These different exchanges are marked by an increase in children's responsibility for their own learning and their agentic control over their progress.

## A Sequence of Pedagogic Activities for Qualitative Changes in Children's Learning

We now turn to a sequence of pedagogical activities, developed by Edwards (2014, in press), which aim at supporting children's agentic engagement with subject matter knowledge. The activities form a sequence where children's learning is enabled by teachers who support changes in children's engagement with that knowledge. In doing so, we discuss how the three relational concepts, relational expertise, common knowledge and relational agency, come into play in the different phases of the teaching–learning sequence. Edwards has worked with teachers from primary and secondary schools using the quadrant sequence shown in Figure 7.1. The sequence moves from the introduction of key ideas in quadrant 1 (Q1) to demonstrations of children's conceptual understanding in quadrant 4 (Q4). It has been valued by practitioners because it gives an easy way to recognize theoretical underpinning to how they had frequently planned learning experiences. We are offering the sequence as a meta-level tool for professional reflection about the relational aspects of releasing student agency across age periods, not as a simple blueprint. As we indicated earlier, the detail of how the sequence can be used with different ages in different settings will be discussed in Chapters 8 and 10.

| *Intermental plane* | *Intermental plane* |
|---|---|
| Q4. Demonstration of grasp of key concepts and ways of enquiring. | Q1. Introduction of key concepts and modelling of ways of engaging with key concepts. |
| *Intramental plane* | *Intramental plane* |
| Q3. Open problem-solving tasks where learners use key concepts and ways of enquiring. | Q2. Tightly structured tasks demanding engagement with key concepts and ways of enquiring. |

Figure 7.1 The Quadrant Teaching and Learning Sequence: A tool for reflection (Edwards, 2014)

# A Sequence of Pedagogic Activities for Qualitative Changes 155

The sequence is based in the distinction that Vygotsky made between the intermental (public) and intramental (personal) planes in the processes of learning. He explained the distinction as follows:

> The higher psychological functions in the child, those properties that are specific to humans, initially appear as forms of collective behavior of the child, as forms of cooperation with other people, and only later do they become internal, individualized functions of the child himself. (Vygotsky, 2019 p. 83)

In Vygotskian terms, in Figure 7.1, Q1 (the teacher's introduction of key concepts) and Q4 (the children's demonstration of the grasp of these concepts) comprise the public or collective domain, the intermental plane, where the discourse reflects the knowledge and ways of representing it, which are consistent with current widely held meanings. In Q1, the teacher introduces a new concept, such as the measurement of area in math. She may challenge children's existing understandings to engage their curiosity, and then model the use of the new concept and the ways of knowing associated with the concept.

Quadrant 1 is where teachers' actions need to capture both key concepts and ways of working within a subject area. They therefore can involve a lot of planning. Q4 is where children demonstrate whether they can remember the key elements of what the teacher presented, perhaps through written work. The deliver and test models of teaching, found in many classrooms, involve moves between Q1 and Q4 without attention to the intramental plane and developing the in-depth understanding that comes with connecting new concepts with what the child already knows. The outcome is usually a superficial grasp of the topic.

The intramental plane is represented by Q2 (engagement with well-structured tasks where children can discuss and explore how concepts are used in concrete examples) and Q3 (the use of newly acquired conceptual understandings in open-ended problems). It is in the intramental plane that individual sense-making occurs. It is here that the work is done to connect the new to the old. Current concepts may be refined or replaced, as a child takes in new ideas and begins to reconfigure connections and current understandings.

In Q2, children are given tasks that have been tightly designed and resourced so that they need to employ the knowledge and knowing demonstrated by the teacher. This is often paired or small group work so that children use and explore the conceptual discourse when talking with each other. For example, in a session on area they may be asked to estimate the area of a book, a table, a mat or the classroom itself and then check their estimations using their measurements. Q3 is where students apply their new conceptual understandings to tackle an open-ended problem. In this quadrant, students combine a range of relevant concepts allowing them to explore their connections. A common sequence through the quadrants is to move between Qs 1, 2 and 4 in several cycles and to engage with problem-solving in Q3 when children are ready to bring to bear what they have learnt about the themes focused on in those cycles. But this is not a rigid sequence. Teachers of literature, for example, often want to start in Q3 with a reading of a text, which then becomes the stimulus for a move to Q1. Also, teachers often find they need to move from Q3 back to Q1 or Q2 to help students make connections between concepts or generally clarify the knowledge in play.

There is now a substantial program of research on children's talk, which is relevant to the sequence we have just outlined, and particularly to Q2, tightly structured tasks and Q4, demonstration. Initially based in Vygotskian understandings of the relationships between speaking and thinking, Mercer and his colleagues showed the impact of different types of talk on children's capacity for reasoning (e.g., Mercer, 1995; Wegerif et al., 1999). Three types of talk were distinguished: exploratory, cumulative and disputational. In brief, exploratory talk in which knowledge is made visible and publicly accountable led to stronger reasoning than either cumulative talk, which was additive, or disputational talk, which was argumentative. These analyses point to the importance of children's explorative activity but do not consider the emotional features we have been emphasizing.

The findings were replicated elsewhere, such as in the 'Thinking Together Programme' (Mercer & Littleton, 2007) with clear ground rules to be followed by children to lead them to exploratory talk. These approaches have also been refined by other research teams; for example, Rajala et al. (2012) distinguished between inclusive and exclusive exploratory talk among elementary school-age children, so bringing attention to motive. Inclusive talk is more productive and involves eliciting expanded responses from all participants. Strategies include asking each other questions such as 'What do you think?' and 'Why do you think that?' These questions fit well with our emphasis on motive orientation. In essence, by using inclusive exploratory talk children were expanding their understandings of what they were working on jointly by taking seriously the motive orientations of other group members and revealing their own.

# A Sequence of Pedagogic Activities for Qualitative Changes   157

Let's now reflect on the changing role of the teacher in the quadrant cycle and how the relational concepts help label what is happening. In Q1, the teacher is introducing new concepts and ways of using them and is initially the leader of the activity; but they will usually bring children into a relationally oriented whole class discussion through question and answer. These exchanges take seriously the children's current understandings and orientations and allow the teacher to emphasize what is important to themselves about the new concept. These processes are exemplified in Chapter 9, where children's talk about animals' adaptation to their environment and evolution is discussed. Here is where we can see the beginning of the construction of common knowledge, which will be made up of the children's motive orientations toward grasping the concept and what matters for the teacher in how that concept is used.

In Q2, the children are active within a carefully designed set of activities based on structured tasks, which require the child to orient to the task demands by employing the new concept. In Q2, therefore, the teacher needs to stand back and observe, intervene when children need help to keep them on track and use the conceptual language. She is therefore formatively assessing children's understandings and adjusting her feedback to help them engage. But she is primarily guiding students by how she has designed the tasks so that children orient toward the demands of the subject matter knowledge embedded in the task; and their agentic responses are limited by the constraints of the task. In brief, students take small steps toward agentic mastery in a safe environment. In Q2, one begins to see relational agency in action; the students' agency is beginning to be released, but with care-full support, they are not running before they can walk and risking failure. Vygotsky described education as: "a process of mutual and continuous adaptation of . . .[teacher and learner], where sometimes it is the guide or leader which represents the most active . . . side, and sometimes those who are being led" (Vygotsky, 1926/1997, p. 349).

In Q4, the demonstration of children's understandings happens. Here well-run plenaries can operate as a space of reasons (Derry, 2013) in the way we outlined in Chapter 3. In brief, they can be an opportunity for asking for and giving of reasons. In these sessions, children discuss their responses to tasks, what they have learnt and why it is useful. Through a focus on "why" questions, children can connect the target subject matter knowledge with their orientations to that knowledge. Plenary discussions can therefore help children to consolidate their conceptual understandings and give public voice to these understandings as well as affirm their motive orientations to the key aspects of the subject matter knowledge. The teacher's role changes yet again, as children's control over the discussion increases. She chairs the discussions, elicits children's perspectives and encourages children's relational expertise as they listen to and question fellow students. While they ask and respond to each other's questions they reveal their motive orientations and encourage each other's agentic engagement with the subject matter. During these sessions one can see children taking control of their own learning, the teacher is moving away from being the leader in the relational agency relationship. Consequently, it is legitimate for the children to question the teacher, to elicit what matters for her about orientations to the subject matter knowledge, why they are important. Plenaries can therefore become spaces for extensive discussions and for building common knowledge of each other's motive orientations, rather than a quick ten minutes at the end of a lesson to check what most of the children have grasped.

Quadrant 3 problem-solving activities take place when it is judged that the children are ready for independent action employing recently acquired understandings. Here children's personal agency unfolds as they interpret a problem and work separately or together in addressing it. At this point, the teacher is one resource among several, much of the work has been done in planning the possible challenges set for the children so that the children are oriented toward problems in ways that require them to employ new understandings. The children's questions should reflect their motive orientations and their engagement with how the teacher has demonstrated their orientation to the subject matter knowledge.

Teachers' responses in Q3 are mediated by the common knowledge built in previous plenaries; while the Q4 plenary session that follows the problem-solving allows children to give voice to what matters to them as they assess for themselves whether they have been successful. Self-assessment against criteria that are built and shared with learners is crucial to the unfolding of their agency. Being able to judge for oneself whether one has accomplished what was intended is key to agency. Taylor explained the importance as follows: "We think of the agent as not only partly responsible for what he does, for the degree to which he acts in line with those evaluations, but also as responsible in some sense for those evaluations" (Taylor, 1977, p. 118). Hedegaard (2002) made a similar point about self-assessment when she undertook a formative teaching experiment in Denmark (see Chapter 9). There are also strong links here with metacognition, which we will discuss later in this chapter, and with student self-assessment, which we also address in Chapters 8 and 9.

Edwards has noted that all the teachers who have worked with the framing in Figure 7.1 observe that it is during the more open tasks in Q3 that they do real teaching, responding to genuine questions from students who are ready to listen (Edwards, 2014). Teachers also report that although the interactions throughout the cycle involve a lot of preparation, they find teaching in this way far less physically tiring than the kind of teacher-led strategies that they had employed previously.

## From Orientation to Mental Actions

The Quadrant Teaching and Learning Sequence (Figure 7.1) was rooted in Vygotskian attention to how children take in new understandings when it was developed but was also influenced by early translations of Galperin's work. Those translations particularly pointed to how children's collaborative talk enhanced their engagement with knowledge (Stones, 1984). The pedagogical sequence was first put together because it reflected what Edwards had been trying to do as a teacher in both primary and secondary schools. But when she became a teacher educator, she found many examples of deliver and test approaches to teaching and needed some way of explaining quite simply to teachers how learning sequences could be planned. As we have seen, the sequence makes sense to practitioners and it was refined over decades as teacher action researchers worked with it and tested it.

In a special issue of *Learning, Culture and Social Interaction* focused on Galperin, Engeness and Lund (2020) translated and introduced four of Galperin's lectures. They summarized Galperin's work in relation to education as follows:

> [It] was based on three premises: (i) the leading role of teaching and learning in development; (ii) conceptual development involves material (physical objects) in materialised actions (using models, simulations, animations, schemes etc.); and (iii) a recognition of the centrality of cultural tools and social interaction in human development. (Engeness & Lund, 2020, p. 6; see also Arievitch & Haenen, 2005, p. 155)

Current Galperin scholarship is revealing the intricate detail of his approach (Arievitch, 2003; Arievitch & Haenen, 2005; Engeness, 2020; Engeness & Edwards, 2017; Engeness & Lund, 2020; Podolskij, 2020; Stetsenko & Arievitch, 2002). His pedagogy built on Vygotsky's concern with mediation and tool use and Leont'ev's work on action and activity, but he went further than Vygotsky, by examining the development of mental actions as learners acted with new understandings and so internalized these understandings. He did this through an extensive series of teaching experiments in classrooms, which tested and demonstrated the success of his approach. In doing so, he opened up a vibrant field of Russian pedagogical studies taken forward later by, in particular, Davydov and El'konin in the 1970s.

In brief, Galperin saw three levels of action as crucial to the processes of internalization, namely, acting at the material level, the verbal level, and the mental level. Arievitch and Haenen (2005) represented these types of action as steps in a spiral that starts with a child orienting to a task or idea at a very basic level; then, with guidance, orienting to key features of the task or problem using material artifacts including drawing models or orienting charts to represent the problem or task; next, discussing the task and relevant ideas with others; and finally, at the mental level, being able to manipulate new ideas to plan, evaluate and solve new problems. This spiral captures the six phases that Galperin saw as moving from a socially meaningful action to the capacity to take mental actions using what was learnt from engaging in the action. The phases or steps are: motivation, orientation, materialized action, communicated thinking, dialogical thinking, and acting mentally (Galperin, 2002). In this slow process of moving from the external to the internal, the internal remains connected with the external, as ideas are tested through externalization materially and verbally during the process.

We can see there how what he termed the orienting basis of the action as the starting point for learning (Engeness, 2020) is crucial. He subdivided the orienting basis of the action into three possibilities. These types of orientation were: incomplete, where learners lack guidance and operate through trial and error; complete, where learners are supplied with all they need to know in order undertake a task; and complete, and further constructed by the learners. The third type of orientation is the most productive, engaging as it does their agency as learners. It involves them in recognizing the essential features of what is to be done and the concepts underpinning their materialized action. As they move on to communicated and dialogical thinking, speech becomes increasingly important so that internal dialogues take the learner to thinking using the target concepts.

Galperin's premise was that these new understandings, mental actions, arise when learners are engaged in activities that are meaningful. To engender children's motivation to what is important and meaningful in an activity, teachers need to be adept at separating the essential and inessential aspects of the task, orienting learners to the essential aspects that they will need to engage with throughout a learning cycle. These aspects will include both key concepts in a subject area and methods of working in that area, or the substantive and syntactic knowledge of an area, which we introduced in Chapter 6. In doing this, the teacher also needs to help the learner recognize the value of the new knowledge. Hence the teacher should avoid breaking tasks down into elements that hold no intrinsic interest for children. If we relate this to Q1 in Figure 7.1, the introduction of new ideas, we can see how a teacher's modeling of what is to be known and their elicitation of children's questions are crucial to engaging children's motive orientation to the essential aspects of a task. Q2 paired or group work is where materialized action can occur and where communicated thinking starts and is followed up in consolidating plenary discussions in Q4. Q3 problem-solving is where dialogical thinking and mental actions come to the fore, while learners unpack the key features of problems and employ the target concepts to address them.

Arievitch observes that, by sustaining a strong connection between internalization and externalization, Galperin found a way of acknowledging the role of culture in learning and development without abandoning the individual (Arievitch, 2003). Arievitch and Haenen in 2005 argued that Galperin's approach indeed predated more recent attempts at recognizing the complementarity of the metaphors of participation and acquisition as ways of explaining learning that was put forward by Sfard (1998). His approach also underpins our intertwined focus on agency, motives, practice and culture.

## Developmental Teaching and Motives

Galperin's analyses were in turn built on by Davydov and El'konin in their explicitly pedagogic work on developmental teaching (see also Chapter 9). Together they emphasized motives and explained that motives are culturally constructed while a child engages in an activity within a cultural practice. Davydov's major contribution was to argue that existing modes of education that were based on acquiring knowledge were reproductive. Instead, what was needed was an education that could be productive. Instead of ascending from concrete phenomena to general representations, his approach was to lead children to ascend from the general to the concrete. This shift was because he wanted children to think theoretically, to be able to recognize the essential general features in phenomena. Also, like Galperin, Davydov used models to help learners in these processes and the processes were inherently social as children learnt how to learn together

(Davydov, 1990, 1999). Developmental teaching was implemented across the Soviet Union in the 1970s and 1980s and was successful. Children did become better learners. Importantly, Galperin, Davydov and El'konin saw motives and orientation toward subject matter knowledge as crucial (see also Chapter 6). We therefore see our concern with emotion in a care-full pedagogy as a development in the same tradition.

An interesting example of taking Davydov's ideas into Western schooling was the Radical Local initiative carried out in New York by Hedegaard and Chaiklin (Hedegaard & Chaiklin, 2005). This initiative connected what was meaningful for children in community life with essential aspects in theoretical knowledge in subject matters. At the core of the initiative was Hedegaard's "double move in teaching" (Hedegaard, 2002, p. 78). Inspired by Davydov, it was a move between a teacher's model of subject matter concepts and students' everyday understandings. Hedegaard describes the double move as "a spiral approach of problem solving," which starts with the teacher guiding "the pupils until they become acquainted with a subject domain. Gradually, through the process of learning, the pupils take over and guide their own learning processes and, in doing so, find their own problems" (p. 78).

We examine the double move and the principles in more detail in Chapters 8 and 9. Here we simply point to the radical way in which it gave children access to powerful knowledge and enabled them agentically to connect it to their local understandings, while echoing Vygotsky's view of the equalizing potential of education. It marks an important shift from the relativism of dumbed-down curricula that were supposedly relevant to the lives of disadvantaged students, and which were prevalent, for example, in the UK in the 1970s. At the same time, it recognizes the need to connect with children's lifeworlds.

Rai, in the study based in rural Rajasthan that we introduced in Chapter 3, drew on both the Radical Local initiative of combining core conceptual relations with everyday life activities in the students' community, and on common knowledge, that is, knowledge of each other's motive orientations. He explained how by harnessing children's motive orientations, the common knowledge that is built between the teacher and students can operate as a bridge between the conceptual subject matter knowledge work carried out in school and the lifeworlds of the children, without dumbing down the concepts (Rai, 2019).

His jumping-off point is his observation of a math lesson where the teacher is introducing the concept of area by first demonstrating, through care-full questions and answers, that the children's ability to measure a perimeter will not take them directly to calculating the area of a carpet in the classroom. This is a Q1 introducing the topic process. The class then moves on into Q2, working on a task, measuring the area of the carpet using their exercise books. This takes them to questions of unit and why we need uniform units to measure area and on to a Q4 plenary discussion. The lesson concludes with the teacher suggesting that the children ask their families about how they measure their fields. In the short extract that follows, we can see that the teacher values the families' knowledge and won't be persuaded to give them his answer. We can also see how his relational approach, taking children's responses seriously, has guided their motive orientation toward understanding the measurement of area and how he is encouraging their agency as problem-solvers. The translation is by Rai.

> Various children talking: You tell us how to decide (how to measure area); Yes how to decide; We want to know now.
>
> Teacher: I am saying, you think about it. Why don't you try to talk with your father or grandfather how they decide about the area of their fields? We used notebooks to find the area of the carpet, what do they use to find the area of their fields? Can we do this?
>
> Child 1: Yes.
>
> Child 2: My father doesn't know anything. You tell us.
>
> Teacher: Why don't you try to talk with your father and then I will certainly tell you tomorrow.
>
> Child 2: OK. You will have to tell, in case he does not tell me anything.
>
> Teacher: Yes, sure I will. (Rai, 2019, p. 159)

The next day, the children came back with measures of area. These were the basis of a discussion about which units to use for what size area and toward the end of the lesson the teacher brought the discussion back to the local units of area used on the farms. Rai notes that he later observed the children using different units for the measurement of area on their lunch boxes and during play sessions.

Rai, discussing how common knowledge mediated the teacher's interactions with the children (p. 163), suggests that:

> Teachers' awareness of where a child is coming from, i.e. their everyday understandings, gives them insight into how a child is making connections to the different practices they are inhabiting. These insights can support children as they create their own social situations of development as sense-makers, taking forward their own learning. . . . This awareness and support

needs that arise requires the teacher to align their pedagogic intentions with the demands in the tasks that they set and with the needs and capabilities of the children.

We shall discuss how the teacher in this study created a discursive space of reasons in Chapter 8. Here we simply highlight Rai's concluding statements. Having argued that common knowledge arises from how the teacher operated conversationally to allow the children to co-construct new understandings and to at times follow the lead of the children, Rai returns to the aims of the 2005 Radical Local approach of Hedegaard and Chaiklin. For him Hedegaard and Chaiklin's initiative was a valuable move from attempts at the kinds of cultural sensitivity found in multicultural education, to "a more nuanced approach to where subject-matter knowledge could be related to children's everyday life" (p. 166). He then suggests that common knowledge is key to those pedagogies that allow children to propel themselves forward, connecting everyday and more powerful concepts in productive ways.

Practitioners do need to keep a professional distance, while also nurturing children's agency as learners. A focus on motive orientation rather than emotional ties allows for such distance, while also sustaining an environment of care and contingent support. We therefore offer the concepts, embedded within the Quadrant Teaching and Learning Sequence, as a framework for realizing a care-full relational approach.

## Working Relationally for School Inclusion

Taking children seriously therefore means helping them to recognize that they have rights, including the right to a good education, alongside the responsibilities to others that go with those rights. The main outcome of engaging with education is that children learn to agentically propel themselves forward as learners, while connecting to and supporting the well-being of their communities. A key step in this process is engaging them with the benefits that education can offer. For some children, this can be a large step and most education systems have responded by emphasizing school inclusion with the intention of giving all children in mainstream schooling equal opportunities to develop as learners.

But equal opportunities need to be augmented by the help needed to allow children to access opportunities. Education is an intervention that is tailored to a child's strengths and needs, which means that for those children who have difficulty in engaging with education, pedagogical support needs to be tightly targeted. Difficulty in engaging can include statutory recognized special needs such as autism, but also an unsupportive home background, a difficulty – such as chronic shyness – that does not reach the threshold for statutory intervention, or a current, but short-term, disruption to home life such as parental illness. Consequently, teachers can be dealing with a class that comprises a diverse range of difficulties and where attention to the affective aspects of engagement is often paramount.

Tailoring pedagogy to these difficulties does not mean using a different pedagogy with each child. A seminal review of research on special education in the UK (Lewis & Norwich, 2005) has dismissed that suggestion. Instead, the emphasis is on teachers' flexible adaptations of their pedagogies and peer-to-peer support (Nind & Wearmouth, 2006). Our argument is that a relational pedagogy is well-suited to the emotional support and flexibility required.

We illustrate our argument with analyses from a Norwegian study of how shy children are helped to participate in classroom activities (Mjelve et al., 2019; Nyborg et al., 2020). Shy children are particularly interesting because their internalizing behavior means that, unlike disruptive children, their difficulties can go unnoticed; yet they may suffer high anxiety, which can lead to their academic underperformance.

We present some data from post-observation interviews with a class teacher and with a shy child in her class. The teacher was among 19 who were selected to participate in the research because their success with shy children had been recognized by, for example, educational psychologists. The research team's initial readings of all the interviews revealed how well the teachers knew the shy children and enabled them to increasingly engage with the oral demands of primary schooling. Edwards then employed some of the concepts discussed in this book, motive orientation, relational expertise, common knowledge and relational agency, to analyze the relationship between teachers and shy children (Nyborg et al., 2022).

The analysis started by identifying how teachers used relational expertise to build common knowledge with the child. This involved them in eliciting and understanding the child's motive orientations and being clear to the child about what mattered to them as teachers. The common knowledge that was then built was used to mediate how the teacher relationally worked with the child in the unfolding of relational agency. Finally, the data were examined to see whether there had been a growth in student agency as a learner over time.

Here is a summary of how a teacher enabled a sixth-grade shy child's motive orientation and engagement and helped her develop as an increasingly agentic learner. It shows how teacher and child used common knowledge, knowledge of what matters to each other, to help shape the child's motive orientation and then give the views of the teacher and child on the growth in child agency over the past year. The quotes are extracted from their interviews.

### *Using Common Knowledge and Relational Expertise in the Unfolding of Relational Agency*

The teacher explained as follows:

> I need to give her confirmation when she has become that confident that she raises her hand. I hug her (and all students), touching her and being near her results in her feeling "I am good enough." I try to build an inner confidence saying "I am good enough." I give her recognition by using looks, that I am interested in her, a question of being seen. We have conversations on a regular basis (once a week) about how she is doing. I often talk about that she has improved in math and ask her what her thoughts are regarding that.

The child explained as follows:

> She looks at me in a certain way; she wants me to say it in a way [...] She is trying to make me say something without getting embarrassed and stuff. Teachers loves hugging and stuff like that, I find it okay. It was fun (teacher touching her hair) and it tickled my hair a bit. It is a bit scary if she suddenly is behind me [...] But it means that I am working well. When my teacher praises me and the class, I feel happy, the others too, I use to pull the arms of my sweater down like this. It is lovely (when her teacher praises her), and very nice to hear [...] it is a bit embarrassing too.

### *A Growth in Student Agency: A Shift in Responsibility from Teacher to Learner Over Time*

The teacher explained as follows:

> It is a major difference in ... from the girl that was by herself when I took over the class. Her mother says it goes much better for her; she has friends. She has said about her own school performance that "I am not good at school" and one of the first things she told me last fall was that "I am terrible in math," but her performance is good now. From being a very quiet girl staring down at her desk, I have now a beautiful girl who looks up, raises her hand, she is active – she was trying to make herself invisible, not being noticed, now she dares (to do things). I can say to her (in class):

What are you doing now? Is that something you should do now? And she says "No" without blushing now. She has become confident in terms of that what she is saying is not always correct.

The child explained as follows:

> It is fun to play with friends – sometimes the others ask first [...]. I like being asked (by the teacher) when I have my hand in the air. (When teacher is correcting her in class): It is a bit of fun, and she helps me to say it right and stuff.

These interviews highlighted the emotional aspects of learning, including acknowledging the importance of peer friendship for a feeling of belonging at school. The teacher had been explicit about what mattered for her including her need to engage all children in an inclusive classroom and the child recognized the teacher's priorities as they related to her. The common knowledge that was built allowed a set of unspoken signs to operate between teacher and child and to give the child the confidence to orient to classroom activities, participate and engage.

The research team found that teachers' attention to the emotional well-being of shy children was also marked during recess. Recess is an important part of the school experience for children, sometimes taking up as much as 25% of the school day (Blatchford & Baines, 2006). During recess, children can act with more freedom than in class and they report that recess offers them time to socialize with peers, choices of activities and opportunities for creativity and personal expression (Blatchford & Baines, 2006). The teachers were therefore concerned that shy children were at risk of missing out on these important opportunities for socio-emotional development during recess, due to their general wariness and dislike of unpredictability.

These analyses of why teachers felt they needed to intervene at recess to support shy children and what they did offer some useful lessons for a relational approach to school inclusion (Nyborg et al., under review). These teachers knew their shy students very well, talking with them regularly about their shyness and how to overcome it. They therefore aimed at understanding experiences of recess from the children's perspectives, not merely describing the children's actions, but also ascribing emotions to them. These emotions were mainly associated with anxiety, creating a motive orientation for the avoidance of contact with peers.

Different teachers talking about different children reported: "[S]he acts this way because she is extremely insecure"; "she is uncomfortable ... I believe she is afraid of big groups"; "they don't have much initiative themselves, often it is not these children who initiate a fabulous game, because they don't dare"; "It is a bit tiring being social when you are not a very social person. It can wear you out, so at the end of the day it's a bit like 'Phew', completely empty"; "If you are very shy ... having your hands full coping outside with others in the class ... there is too much pressure [to play games]."

Armed with these interpretations, they tried strategies that included intervening in games to invite the child in, social training, such as learning to smile at others and approach them. One strategy that had limited success was asking other children to approach and invite shy children to join recess activities. These approaches were frequently rebuffed. However, strategies that involved creating opportunities for shy children to build friendships, through small discussion groups and similar during break times, were successful, with shy students apparently flourishing when playing with children they knew well. We would agree with Nind and Wearmouth (2006) on the importance of peer-to-peer support for inclusion but would go further to suggest that encouraging relational work between children is a key to its success.

## Final Reflections

In this chapter, we have explained what we mean by a relational pedagogy that takes children, their emotions, and their motives seriously, while also engaging them with knowledge recognized by society as powerful. A strong theme through the chapter has been how teachers can support the unfolding of children's agency as learners. We have explained that agency is crucial for the child's creation of their social situation of development. But it is also highly important for their development as moral and mutually responsible citizens, who are able to question the taken for granted and help shape their worlds.

The pedagogies we have discussed all have their early roots in the developmental psychology of Vygotsky. We have shown how researchers and educators from Galperin onward have built on that foundation to offer frameworks for engaging children with conceptual knowledge and ways of representing and testing that knowledge. Edwards' Quadrant Teaching and Learning Sequence (Figure 7.1) owes much to the work of Galperin, but also highlights the shifting role of the teacher in the sequence as children's agentic control over the subject matter knowledge unfolds. We are advocating a very skilled form of teaching, a point we also address in the chapters that follow.

## Final Reflections

The ideas we have put forward in this chapter need to be contextualized and explained with further examples embedded in different practices and with children in different age periods. They are offered here as an introduction to some key pedagogic principles. The dialectical nature of a cultural-historical approach to learning and development calls for detailed attention to actions, in activities, in practices, and the impact of cultural affordances on children and of children on the cultures they inhabit. These topics will be addressed particularly in Chapters 8, 9 and 10.

CHAPTER 8

# The Primary School Age
## Enabling the Agentic Learner

**Introduction**

In this chapter, we discuss primary school-age children, their social situations of development in and out of school and how they can be supported. We recognize that countries differ in how they organize schooling. For example, in the UK, formal schooling starts when children approach their fifth birthday, while in the Nordic countries school starts at age six. In the UK they move to high school at 11 and can then be taught by ten or more teachers in any week; while elsewhere children move from primary school to middle school; where in the Nordic countries they remain primarily with a class teacher and a few subject teachers until they move on to high school at around the age of 15. We therefore emphasize the point we have made in earlier chapters: we are not focusing mainly on the age of a child when discussing their development. Rather we discuss development in relation to their experiences of demands in the practices they inhabit.

The support children receive comes both through how environments are structured and through interactions and relationships which will involve family members, teachers and the other professionals who work with children. How these environments are constructed and sustained, of course, reflects wider cultural influences such as national education policies in schools and cultural priorities at home. Some of the major environmental and interactional demands facing primary school-age children happen at school, but parents and other professionals also benefit from understanding how children make sense of their different worlds and learn to orient to what is important in them.

As we saw in Chapter 6, when starting primary school at the age of five or six children, are moving into a new set of practices. There are established routines to be navigated and new demands to be recognized and responded to. In brief, children's new motive orientations need to be nurtured. Some children will need more help than others to become oriented toward becoming a learner in school. This is particularly so when the emotional experience of life at home is very different from at school.

Relationships are crucial elements in the child–environment developmental dynamic and key to how all children are positioned as learners. Therefore, throughout this chapter we shall discuss how children, between entering school and starting high school, are supported as learners through relationships with others. Key to becoming agentic learners is their use of vital cognitive tools such as literacy and numeracy, which enable them to engage with the knowledge that is valued in formal education. But we shall argue, as we did in Chapters 6 and 7, that assisting the competent use of these tools involves starting with a child's motive orientation and giving care-full relational guidance that enables their confident and agentic use of these resources. As always, we draw on insights from Vygotsky and those who have developed these ideas when considering the developing child as they move into the phase where being a school pupil is a leading activity.

## New Demands in the Transition to School

In one detailed examination of how young children interpret and respond to the demands of school, Hedegaard and Fleer followed young girls and boys in four families. The families were of different socioeconomic status, in Australia and Denmark. In their 2013 book, the focus is four-, five- or six-year-old boys, one from each family, over the first two years at school. Here we discuss Andrew, one of the children from an Australian family on welfare, to show the difficulties he faced with school demands and to point to the longer-term implications for him.

Andrew's family life at home was one of almost constant movement. It is described as follows: "[T]he adults and children rarely sat down – but rather appeared to be moving between rooms and around each other (like a dance)" (Hedegaard & Fleer, 2013, p. 94). The children were also highly aware of what was happening in each room and would gather whenever there was an incident of interest. While at school, Andrew's behavior was, unsurprisingly, marked by constant movement within an activity space, such as the carpet. Recognizing that he could not move freely in school, he scanned the room for activities, limiting his concentration on the demands of the activity he had been allotted. He was regularly told to stop moving. Consequently, he primarily oriented himself to the behavioral rules of being a pupil and keeping out of trouble. These sustained efforts took a lot of energy and were to the detriment of his engaging with the subject matter of the curriculum and developing as an agentic learner. As a result, although he was present in school, he was in some ways also absent. His motive orientation was not toward becoming literate; consequently he was not developing important foundational skills, which in turn impeded his engagement. The detailed observations of Andrew in his first two years of formal schooling point to how rapidly children can become alienated from the pedagogic purposes and practices of school. This is an issue of considerable concern. McDermott and Varenne, for example, alert us to how easily school structures and conditions can create children's learning difficulties, by not working with their strengths and instead focusing on whether they fit into the conventions of schooling (McDermott & Varenne, 1995).

Fisher, studying children's early writing at school in England, observed the beginnings of a pattern of behavior in the approach of two low attaining children that reflects McDermott and Varenne's concern that a focus on fitting in is detrimental to learning. Chloe and Ben, in their first year of school, had tried to work on a quite complicated joint writing task (Fisher, 2011). Like Hedegaard and Fleer, Fisher found that the children were concerned with keeping out of trouble, at the expense of engaging with the demands of the task and accessing the curriculum. Here is an extract from a conversation between the researcher and Chloe after the lesson.

> Researcher: OK what don't you like about writing?
>
> Chloe: I don't like when I get really stuck in my writing, I don't like that bit.
>
> Researcher: What kinds of times do you get stuck, what makes you get stuck?
>
> Chloe: My stuck bit is when I can't think of words to write and I try to think of it.
>
> Researcher: Anything else?
>
> Chloe: Getting into trouble doing writing. (Fisher, 2011, p. 60)

We shall discuss the importance of language and literacy development later in the chapter. At this point we note how the fear of "getting into trouble" can shape a child's motive orientation toward an important area of the curriculum. Fisher concludes that the answer lies in supporting children in their understandings of classroom activities and how they develop motives that enable them to take part in writing activities. We would agree and add that it is crucial that teachers recognize and take seriously the emotional aspects of children's engagement. Not doing so runs the risk of a child

## New Demands in the Transition to School

developing a negative attitude to school because they develop a growing sense of being incompetent, sadly illustrating the force of the argument put forward by McDermott and Varenne (1995).

These studies all show that the route to adolescent dropout can start early. Part of our argument for taking children seriously in a care-full relational approach to supporting their development as learners is that the approach may prevent later alienation. We have explained how motives are developed in the practices we inhabit, and in Chapter 7 we drew on the relational concepts, relational expertise, common knowledge and relational agency to show how practitioners can work relationally with children to elicit their motive orientations and make explicit what matters for them as teachers. This relational work of practitioners helps create a delicate dynamic of child and environment. With that in mind, we can see that children like Andrew present particular challenges and need care-full targeted support. The common strategy of teachers of reception or first classes is to act "as if" the children know the rules and they will come to conform to them. This strategy won't work with all children and therefore doesn't produce inclusive classrooms.

Instead, we suggest that educators need to create classroom architectures, where their expectations for behavior are clearly shared with all children. Also, at the very least, they should try to understand school life from the perspectives of different children and respect the strengths they bring. However, that understanding may not be enough for some children. With children like Andrew, Ben and Chloe, who found it hard to recognize and operate within school expectations, there is a need for skilled relational work.

As we saw with the shy children in Chapter 7, this relational work involves taking the child's perspective and being alongside them to nurture their agency as a learner. It involves building common knowledge, which consists of what matters for the teacher and the child, and then using the common knowledge to mediate an unfolding of relational agency. During that unfolding, the teacher is initially the agentic guide alongside the child, helping them recognize and navigate the social and cognitive demands of school life, but over time the teacher withdraws, enabling the child to move forward in control of their own learning, creating their social situation of development. This is a deeply intensive form of relational work and is not necessary for all children, but for children like Andrew, who find engaging with the curriculum difficult, it is essential if they are to be included in the educational opportunities available.

## Agency, Learning and Development in the Primary School Phase

There is no shortage of accounts of primary school life that claim to draw on Vygotsky's legacy. However, many fail to recognize the dialectical relationship between children and the practices they inhabit, and few start with attention to children and their experiences[1] of school. A focus on children's experiences allows us to examine this mutually shaping dialectical relationship, how children are creating their social situations of development and are making meaning and how school practices enable children's inclusion in the learning opportunities available to them. It gives a rounded view of a child as active agent, with feelings, values and interests, acting in and on an environment. Vygotsky described the importance of examining the child and the environment to capture this breadth and unity in the following way:

> Let us take the development of the personality of the child, the development of the consciousness of the child, the development of relations to the reality that surrounds him; let us see what constitutes the specific role of the environment in the development of the child's personality, his consciousness and his relation to reality. (Vygotsky, 2019, p. 77)

Vygotsky's conception of the developing child is therefore of a complex entity and he entreated us to recognize that complexity. To do that we need to fix our gaze on the relationships between their developing cognitive tools – such as memory, speech, attention, literacy and numeracy – how they connect to how children use concepts and how their development can be supported. These cognitive resources will not develop at an equal rate, but the shifting relationships between these capabilities are what give rise to changes in the consciousness of a child.

For example, for the young child consciousness is dominated by perceptual attention, to what is meaningful to them. In the preschool years, memory and imagination develop, but perceptual attention does not disappear; instead it supports memory. Memory then supports the development of thinking in primary school children. For finely detailed examinations of aspects of these processes, see Chaiklin (2019a) and Friedrich (2021).

---

[1] We use the term experience as both a verb and a noun, recognizing that Vygotsky referred to *perezhivanie* (Vygotsky, Lecture 4 (Kellogg & Veresov eds), 2020). As Kellogg and Veresov observe, the term can be both a verb (to experience) and a concept or a unit of analysis, an experience. *Perezhivanie* also has colloquial meanings in present-day Russian.

Vygotsky also makes a nice distinction between this relationship and how thinking comes to support memory in older children (Vygotsky, 1998).

One way of seeing Vygotsky's view of this complex process of development is as periods of apparent stability where shifts in the relationships between functions are "microscopic." Then what he termed "crises" arise when children meet new demands, such as starting school (Vygotsky, 1998). The shifts in relationships emerge in response to these demands and bring about reconstructions of a child's consciousness. As we discussed in Chapter 6, this reconstruction involves the creation of a new social situation of development, representing a child's new relation to reality.

In Chapter 2, we explained that changes in a child's social situation of development are characterized by what Vygotsky termed *psychological neoformations* (Vygotsky, 1998; 1999). These new configurations of functions are key to the child's relationship with their environment and to their development. They are a way of labeling what leads the development of a child at a point in time and they change when a child's social situation of development changes, for example, when starting formal schooling, or moving to high school. A new central line of development arises, a new relation to reality is created and the previous neoformations become peripheral lines of development.

Vygotsky described becoming a primary school child as a "critical or turning-point period" (1998, p. 289). These turning points or crises can be related to age periods, but this is only in part due to natural maturation processes. As we have already said, the dynamic unity of person and practice is also crucial and new demands from formal schooling give rise to crises. There are also transitions during the primary school phase due to developing literacy and numeracy. Five- or six-year-olds are very different learners from nine- or ten-year-olds. Caring professionals therefore need to be alert to transitions that arise through the growth in independence as a learner, for example, when literacy is mastered and later when the child is able to reflect on their work. But not all children make these transitions with ease.

For example, some children will need more help than others with being freed from a reliance on perception and a focus on the here and now and instead learn how to look forward, imagine and plan. As we explained in Chapter 5, young children's development is rooted in their use of imagination, but for the primary school child, a sense of their own history and change over time is also important. Working relationally with children to discuss shared past events and plan new ones encourages memory and thinking, while also giving children a sense of their own agency and control over what they will orientate to in the future. Visits to the local post office or fire station for younger children are not simply for learning about the community or stimuli for writing activities. The preparation for writing offers opportunities for shared remembering and conversations about the past and possible future events.

But we shouldn't underestimate children. They can very early on build narratives of selves, which arise in the practices they inhabit at home and school, how they are positioned in them and the feedback they get from others. These narratives sustain their identities, how they see themselves, and sense of control over the environment. In Chapter 6, we discussed James, who was one of the children followed by Winther-Lindqvist, as he made the transition from preschool to school (Winther-Lindqvist, 2012). James had a high status at preschool because of his soccer abilities. But the organization of lunches at his new school prevented him from playing soccer. This shattered his sense of his identity as he no longer got the important feedback from friends that he had received at preschool. This lack of feedback created a new identity, which had a low sense of agency and control and impeded his motive orientation toward what was valued by the school. This is an example of a crisis and a conflict between a desire to be agentic at soccer, which was thwarted, and a need to orient toward and unfold agency in the direction of the demands and opportunities of his new school.

In Chapter 5, we discussed how children's play in the preschool period can support the development of imagination, which is itself a foundation for planning and self-control. Over time, primary school children build on this foundation and learn to both plan and to self-regulate. Although planning and self-regulation are largely emergent in the early years of primary school, they needs to be encouraged through, for example, conversations about future events, who will do what and when. According to Vygotsky, the ability to self-regulate arises most clearly in the later years of primary school as it is closely related to the development of thinking using what he termed scientific concepts (Vygotsky, 1989) (see Chapter 6). Let us therefore turn to the changes in children's motive and conceptual development. These developments are of course mediated by education. But a word of caution here; we are not separating cognition and emotion. Their intertwining is at the core of our rationale for care-full pedagogy.

## Children's Development of New Motives and Concepts in Primary School

The development of motives and conceptual understandings arises through the child recognizing and responding to societal expectations. Here we see the importance of the direction of motive orientations: Children recognize and respond to what matters for them, what they see as important. This was clearly illustrated by Andrew, Ben and Chloe who were oriented toward keeping out of trouble to the detriment of engaging with the curriculum. However, when children are oriented to both the behavioral and the subject matter demands of school, they are able to connect curricular demands, such as focusing on the concept of character in a writing task, with processes, such as the cognitive tool of being able to plan.

As we have already seen, the developmental process is complex and the development of the core competence of literacy occurs through the intentional use of signs that are cultural in origin and of which speech is the most prevalent. Vygotsky discussed how speech brings order to our engagement with the world. For example, when describing perception, he noted how speech "leads to thinking about perception, to analysis of reality" (Vygotsky, 1998, p. 88). This analysis enables the child to look back and forward – to a past and future. One of our consistent arguments is that the capacity to look forward and plan is a central element in development as an agentic learner. Caring professionals help by taking a care-full interest in how children interpret their experiences of the past and present and anticipate their futures.

We now turn to how children develop conceptual understandings as they orient to what is important for them. We discussed the emergence of complexes and pre-concepts as the early stages of conceptual development in the preschool child and discussed their engagement with knowledge in Chapter 6. Here we examine how children orient to and make meaning of specific experiences.

Imaginative play prior to school entry will have helped children to detach meaning from objects. For example, when a child rides a stick as if it is a horse, the stick has a pivotal role in helping the child to detach meaning from specific objects and actions and to begin to work with images and symbols. Vygotsky therefore argued that "when the child reaches school age he has comparatively mature forms of attention and memory at his disposal" (Vygotsky, 1987 p. 189). These attributes allow children to develop what he described as "conscious awareness" of phenomena. This conscious awareness frees the child from spontaneous reactions to the here and now and allows for the emergence of concepts that mediate, help them plan and shape, their responses. In brief, speech merges with action, including mental action, and leads to the capacity to plan. Vygotsky explained how speech enhances cognition as follows: "But specifically because of the fact that it [speech] reflects and fixes separate points of practical thinking, it is converted from the reflecting accompanying function into a planning function, shifting to the beginning of the process" (Vygotsky, 1998, p. 114). This development of practical thinking and planning, shaped by a child's motive orientation, is key to development as an agentic learner.

Vygotsky, therefore, paid attention to how children use speech to orient their actions. Like Piaget (1923), he recognized that young children talk to themselves in the presence of others. But whereas Piaget thought that this egocentric speech was a phase that led nowhere, Vygotsky saw it as a step toward thinking. Vygotsky observed the development, from egocentric speech, to internal speech, to thinking, as a process through which children begin to regulate their behavior. He explained this link between speech, action and thinking by describing children's talk about their mark-making or drawing (Vygotsky, 1998, pp. 114–115) (the examples are ours). At first, speech accompanies action; the child talks to themself as they undertake actions, perhaps saying "blue here." But they may not know or be able to label what they are drawing. Over time, the speech that has been used as internal commentary comes to be used to anticipate a future action such as "I need some blue here." Vygotsky explains that this capability takes language use "to a new level." Here the child begins to be freed from being tied to the immediate field of perception, but is looking to the future and using language to do so. Finally, children use language to determine what they will draw or paint, "I'm going to paint the seaside." At this point, language also has a clear external communicative purpose. This communicative effort needs a response, the comments need to be taken seriously and children encouraged to elaborate their plans through a relational exploration of their motive orientations to the activity. These conversations can also encourage the unfolding of children's agency and, along with play, are precursors to self-regulation as learners.

As we explained in Chapter 6, an important distinction, when examining the development and use of concepts, is between everyday or spontaneous concepts that root the child in the immediate present and what Vygotsky termed scientific concepts, those that carry publicly accepted meanings. These scientific concepts allow children to distance themselves from their immediate experiences, to make sense of them, to generalize them and to bring them under control, and language and literacy are again key here.

A Vygotskian view of conceptual development emphasizes the role of teaching in interactions. He explained as follows: "Spontaneous concepts create the potential for the emergence of nonspontaneous concepts in the process of instruction. Instruction is the source of the development of this new type of construct" (Vygotsky, 1987, p. 194). He was clear that conceptual development will not occur without instruction: "Development creates the potentials while instruction realizes them" (1987, p. 195). Of course, the eight-year-old will not use concepts in the same way as an eighteen-year-old; Vygotsky was also clear that what he termed "true concepts" is a feature of adolescence.

In summary, we are stressing the importance of encouraging children to reveal their intentions, their motive orientations, in care-full interactions that take children and their intentions seriously. In this way, children can build a sense of their own agency and responsibility for their own learning and become planful. But what do we know about concepts and conceptual development that will help practitioners support children's learning? Vygotsky explained that concepts mediate our relationship with reality and argued that scientific concepts are connected in a system of concepts. Consequently, instruction needs to both ensure a connection between a scientific concept and concrete reality, and help the child place the concept within a developing conceptual system. In Chapter 7, we discussed how Galperin, Davydov and El'konin developed pedagogies that foregrounded children's command of concepts and their developing conceptual systems. We shall explore the importance of forefronting concepts in pedagogy later when we discuss the Radical-Local approach of Hedegaard and Chaiklin (2005) in Chapter 9.

## Taking the Child's Perspective in Teaching

One of the purposes of education is to enable learners to use powerful resources to orient to, interpret and respond to phenomena in classrooms and beyond, to move forward. We have already emphasized cognitive tools such as literacy and numeracy as well as attention and memory and pointed to how important they are for children's developing conceptual understandings. When Vygotsky emphasized teaching, it was a forward-looking form of teaching that focuses on these cognitive tools and the conceptual understandings they enabled. D.B. El'konin, in his epilogue to Vygotsky's collection of writings on child psychology (El'konin, 1987) explained:

> L.S. Vygotsky ... shows the dependence of the process of development on the character and content of the teaching process itself. ... Vygotsky shows

> that teaching is good that anticipates development and is oriented not towards already completed cycles of development, but towards those that are developing. (El'konin, 1987, p. 308)

This kind of teaching requires practitioners to know the child well, to be alongside them, endeavoring to take their perspective. One teacher cannot be consistently alongside 30 children. But relational expertise can help elicit and identify children's motive orientations so that with the support of their growing literacy children can be guided toward using powerful concepts. In Chapter 7, we mentioned Galperin's emphasis on the orienting basis of an action. We are now suggesting that a relational approach to pedagogy can help guide children toward orienting to, for example, the conceptual demands in a task. This perspective-taking and relational work can enable the unfolding of children's agency as learners. These relationships can position children as active participants in the flow of classroom life. They also position the teacher alongside the child, focusing with them on the task or event, initially guiding them and over time standing back, in the way we explained using the Teaching and Learning Sequence (Figure 7.1) in Chapter 7.

We now offer an example of what teachers can do to assist the unfolding of a child's agency as an engaged learner. The child in question could have become a vulnerable learner with long-term negative implications for them. All too often lack of engagement is put down to a problem in the child; but a Vygotskian view of the unity of child and environment does not allow that to happen. Hedegaard has recently written about the need to instead reframe a child's actions so that they are not seen to be in a *zone of concern*; rather they are in a *zone of development*. She illustrates this distinction with her observation of Lise, a child in the fourth grade in the Danish school system (Hedegaard, 2019a). We present an abridged version of the observation here.

When reading the observation, it is useful to know that Hedegaard worked with a model for consultants' cooperation with teachers that has the following steps (see Figure 8.1): Step I: Problem expansion by clarification of the problem, which involves (a) clarification of the problem of concern; (b) explication of the values connected to children's development; (c) using observation to examine the cooperative actions of the teacher and consultant. Step II: Changing a zone of concern to a developmental zone through the formulation of goals for success and an action plan based on building common knowledge between teacher and consultant (and parents). Step III: Formulating a plan for intervention. Step IV: The teachers have to realize the action plan by using relational expertise and building

# Taking the Child's Perspective in Teaching

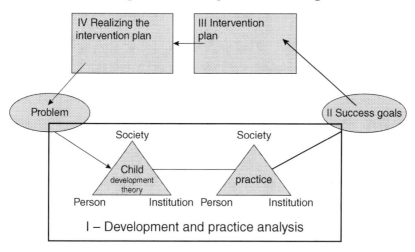

Figure 8.1  A model for how the psychologist consultant can be seen as a participant in developmental psychological practice development for children in a zone of concern (from Hedegaard & Chaiklin, 2011)

common knowledge between the child/children of concern and with children in the classroom in general. The plan should orient them toward what is to be learnt. At this point, the consultant has stepped back and the teacher's role is to relationally support the unfolding agency of the child. This intervention is a process so one should expect that the teacher and consultant need to reanalyze how the intervention is progressing several times, and continuously develop step III.

Lise is in a group of four children.[2] They are soon to visit a museum to examine displays on Stone Age and Iron Age people. In preparation, the teacher has asked them to complete a poster about "what we know" and "what we don't know" about human development in these distant historical periods. (This lesson example is discussed further in Table 9.1.) Lise and her group do not understand the task. When the teacher comes to their table, she tries to help by asking them who the first people were. Annie replies, "Adam and Eve" and Lise says "God." The teacher thinks they are being cheeky. The session lasted three hours and other groups also

---

[2] Lise is in a parallel class to the experimental class described in Hedegaard, 2002. This class participated in the second year of the design experiment described in Chapter 9. This class came into the project after the first year, because the head teacher saw the class as problematic and therefore asked for it to become part of the experimental teaching. Hedegaard in this connection came to act as a consultant.

failed to understand what they should do. Hedegaard noted that Lise's actions were all oriented to the community of children. "She appeared to have problems with the content of teaching because it seemed she was afraid that she was not able to handle it" (Hedegaard, 2019, p. 31). She was unable to create her own goals in relation to the activity; that is, she could not be agentic in relation to learning. Instead, she used jokes to mask her inability to proceed.

Hedegaard, as consultant, helped the teacher to take three actions, based in a reframing of the situation from one of concern to one of development. The three actions were preceded by analyzing the child's social situation of development (Step I), formulating goals of success (Step II)) and considering how practice may be changed (Step III). The changes related to the three actions were: (a) Change the social structure of the classroom through changing the groupings to stop children's off-task interactions; (b) be clearer about the lesson content in the introduction, including task demands; and (c) ensure that students like Lise know what they have to do, including setting clear goals with them. This process included meetings where consultant and teacher analyzed the progression and interventions, using protocols of classroom observations. By the third session after these changes were implemented, Lise was concentrating hard on classroom tasks.

The key points for Hedegaard were: the consultant's reframing of the problem together with the teacher, so that it became a jumping-off point for development; the analysis of Lise's social situation of development; and then creating and agreeing on goals with the teacher so that the teacher took on responsibility for implementing the changes that would lead toward achieving the goals. (For other examples, see Hedegaard & Chaiklin, 2011; Stæhr & Hedegaard, 2019a, b.) This reframing sees children as participants who can act in and on the classroom environment, and it involves taking their emotions, identities and agency seriously.

One theme so far in this chapter is the potential for children to lack confidence, to appear to not know what is required of them as pupils and to fail to orient their participation to what the teacher sees as important. Confidence is another of those words that place the child in the zone of concern with children in difficult situations. Reframing the problem of confidence – that is, as a matter of not knowing the rules of classroom life, or how to approach a task, or lacking literacy skills – is to use a development framing. It involves taking children's perspectives and working relationally with them to support their orientations to what matters and hence their participation as learners.

Of course, many children are, much of the time, confident participants propelling themselves forward with energy and enthusiasm. Yet they may face crises that call for reconfigured developmental pathways. A new member of the family, whether a new sibling or a step-parent, disrupts the networks of relationships that have helped shape a social situation of development, as does family illness, parental unemployment and so on. At any point, a child may unexpectedly become disoriented and vulnerable. Developmental changes in both physical maturity and the onset of puberty and in the development of cognition will also mean that the social situation of development is always under construction, requiring children to negotiate new positions in the dynamics of the practices they inhabit. All of these and similar shifts call for teacher sensitivity. We are not suggesting that teachers become psychotherapists; but we are suggesting that taking children seriously as emotional as well as intellectual beings, starts with care-full listening and observation.

## Challenge and Support for Agentic Learners

Sensitivity does not, however, mean dumbing down to make life easy for children; learning that is ahead of development is not smooth and takes effort. Stimulating emergent neoformations involves challenge, and the challenge needs to be available in the environment and sought by the learner. Claxton's idea of potentiating environments captures what we mean. He uses the slightly vague term "disposition towards" (Carr & Claxton, 2002) rather than Hedegaard's motive orientation, but he shares our concern with how environments limit or enable learning.

Claxton has categorized classroom environments as four "epistemic cultures" (Claxton, 2007). Prohibitive cultures are places where ways of responding are limited. Claxton sees this as typical of traditional "effective classrooms" (Claxton, 2007, p. 124), where possible dispositions are restricted. Affording cultures sound attractive, as children are allowed some freedom of thought, but they are insufficient. Inviting cultures sound even nicer, but they lack challenge and do not stretch children. The culture to aim for is a potentiating one. Claxton (2007) describes it as follows:

> [T]he exercise of learning muscles [is] both appealing and challenging. In a potentiating environment, there are plenty of hard interesting things to do, and it is accepted as normal that everyone regularly gets confused, frustrated and stuck. (p. 125)

Claxton augments potentiating environments with what he calls "split screen thinking" (p. 125). This involves sharing with children not only what is to be learnt, the intended learning outcomes in relation to the curriculum, but also what cognitive tools – what he calls learning capacities – are to be highlighted in the session. This approach reflects our suggestion that, in order to build common knowledge, teachers need to be clear with children about their expectations of what children will orient toward as well as eliciting children's understandings. Importantly, split screen thinking can enhance learner agency by highlighting the development of cognitive tools, such as planning and literacy. To enable this dual focus on both children's capacities with cognitive tools and the conceptual content, teachers need to share with the children the key concept to be tackled, such as measuring area, and the learning capacity to be focused on, such as hypothesizing. Edwards has worked with teacher action researchers who have used split screen thinking in both primary and secondary schools. We suggest that it can be used with children from the age of seven or eight, focusing on cognitive tools such as remembering or planning on one side of the screen. It is easy to imagine how Andrew, Ben and Chloe would have benefitted from such demystification of what was expected of them as they moved through school. The focus on capacities such as remembering or planning helps build children's confidence in themselves as learners, enhancing their motive orientation to curricular demands.

There are several terms that relate to encouraging the development of cognitive tools alongside conceptual development. They include learning strategies and metacognition. These help children to become agentic learners able to orient themselves to what is important. One classic text on learning strategies listed the following actions to be taken by learners:

- Asking questions (defining hypotheses, establishing aims, relating task to previous work, etc.)
- Planning (tactics, timetable, breakdown of task into components, resources, etc.)
- Monitoring (continuously matching progress to initial questions or purposes)
- Checking (preliminary assessment of results)
- Revising (if necessary resetting goals, redrafting plan, etc.)
- Self-testing (final self-assessment of results and performance)

(After Nisbet & Shucksmith, 1986, p. 28)

Nisbet and Shucksmith noted that these strategies "seem to represent higher-order skills which control and regulate the more task-specific or more practical skills" (p. 26). From our perspective, they also offer a blueprint for the actions of an agentic learner. They are well-suited to activities in the Teaching and Learning Sequence presented as Figure 7.1.

All six strategies fit with activities that require children to use target concepts when problem-solving (quadrant 3); while the final assessment of results and performance can be done publicly in the whole class (quadrant 4). Edwards has used these strategies to help children with problem-solving in primary classrooms, and each time she has been struck by how long the children's joint reflections and evaluations (quadrant 4) last and how much learning is evident in them. These processes also connect nicely with Hedegaard's use of the goal-result board in her teaching experiments.

This mutuality between teacher and child and child and child is enhanced by the teacher taking the child seriously as a competent problem-solver. The questions at the start of the process orient children to the task or problem, allowing their perspectives to be foregrounded and their planning gives children control over the process. One of Edwards' examples is from a morning that was part of a sequence of math lessons where ten-year-old children focused on the properties of different shapes. She asked the class to make a box for an egg that her 11-year-old daughter could use on domestic science days as she kept breaking the eggs that she took to school in her cookery basket. The children were looking forward to moving to high school at the age of 11, so were motivated to engage. They worked through the strategies outlined by Nisbet and Shucksmith, including the fun of checking by dropping their boxes with a (boiled) egg in it onto the floor. But their boxes were all different, with different features emphasized. Some were beautifully decorated, and one was even deliberately short-life so that the box would need to be replaced after a few uses and demand sustained! This was clearly a potentiating environment where motive orientations were productively engaged.

## The Double Move and "Radical-Local Teaching and Learning"

We have said little in this chapter about subject matter knowledge and how concepts are acquired and organized in school settings as we discussed these processes in Chapter 6. We agree with Hedegaard and Chaiklin (2005) that Vygotsky's writing paid too little attention to subject matter knowledge and to its relation to children's social lives. We suggested in Chapter 7 that it was left to Galperin, Davydov and El'konin to create the pedagogies that built on his legacy. Hedegaard's analysis of the double move in teaching takes this work further, by attending to children's emotional engagement alongside a focus on conceptual development. A double move is a "process of instruction [that] runs as a double move between the teacher's model of the subject matter concepts of a problem area and the students' everyday cognition and knowledge" (Hedegaard, 2002, p. 78). In doing so it enables children to recognize the relevance of powerful concepts to their own situations and so encourages their motivation to engage with meaningful concepts and what they can do.

The relationship between teacher and child in the double move is explained as follows: Learning at school is: "a spiral of problem solving where, to begin with, the teacher guides the pupils until they become acquainted with a subject domain. Gradually through the process of learning, the pupils take over and guide their own learning processes and, in doing so, find their own problems" (Hedegaard, 2002, p. 78).

For this process to occur, children's motives need to connect meaningfully with an activity from the outset, though their orientations will change as they participate in the activity and learn. For such change to happen, for children to see more in an activity than they did originally, their current way of thinking needs to be challenged and they need to be helped in understanding new key conceptual relations and what such analyses can do. Building on Davydov's highlighting of theoretical knowledge (Davydov, 1977/1990), the double move requires teachers to focus on core conceptual relations, not merely on the concepts in themselves. The teacher guides this process using what is known as a germ-cell model of the central concepts (see Chapter 9). The debt to Davydov can be seen in Hedegaard's focus on using models. Germ-cell models require teachers to have strong understandings of subject matter knowledge as well as expertise in working relationally with children

At the start of the process, the teacher engages children in research tasks that are oriented to a topic within the subject matter area and build on the children's questioning about the topic. The learners, through their questioning and researching, create their own models of the connections between elements in the topic. These are material representations of what they see as the core conceptual relations in the area. These first models are used as objects for collective reflections in class discussions. In Hedegaard's work with children, these models were quite often figurative diagrams drawn by a child or group of children that showed the relationships. The models gradually became extended and refined through new research tasks (see Chapter 9).

Hedegaard and Chaiklin provide a rich example of how the development of Vygotsky's ideas to place more emphasis on knowledge and connections between concepts can get played out in elementary schools (Hedegaard & Chaiklin, 2005). Their Radical-Local initiative, which is discussed in Chapter 9, was with children of Puerto Rican heritage in East

Harlem in Manhattan and the curriculum area was social studies. Their starting point echoed Vygotsky's view that education enables people to improve their life conditions and ethically all children should be able to access and use conceptual tools as they act in and on their worlds.

The initiative expected children to act as researchers in order to recognize specific conceptual relations when they analyzed their concrete and historical living conditions. The conceptual relations that guided the construction of teaching tasks were family life, living conditions, resources and work. The initiative was a form of design experiment in which the teacher collaborated with the researchers before each session to plan the new themes related to the core model guiding the teaching. The planning was informed by observations made of children's activities from the previous session.

The topics for the research activities were meaningful for the children. They were Puerto Rican life in the early twentieth century; living conditions for Puerto Rican immigrants to New York in the same period; and current living conditions for Puerto Rican families in East Harlem. The aim was to give children a sense of their history alongside understandings of how to research topics that were both objectively meaningful and personally engaging.

Its success lay in giving equal status to the unfolding of children's agency as learners alongside their access to the powerful ways of theoretical thinking that gave them some insights into the conditions of their lives. There have been other successful larger-scale responses that have much in common with this initiative. They include "Authentic Education" in the US (Newmann & Associates, 1996) and the "Queensland School Reform Longitudinal Study" (QSRLS) in Australia (Queensland Department of Education, 2001). Both aimed at equity through enhancing pedagogies so that they increased the intellectual demands on children and connected with their lives outside school. The Radical-Local initiative was, however, particularly noteworthy because of the detail of the pedagogic interventions, based in Davydov's developments of Vygotsky's thinking. But as the QSRLS showed, wider success very much depends on engaging educational policymakers as well as teachers and children.

## Creating Challenge and Reflective Awareness through Assessment for Learning

Policymakers globally are certainly concerned with Education, usually aiming to control it with legislation. These legislative demands are often not based strongly in understandings of society, pedagogy or curriculum, but are short-term responses to, for example, competition in international tests. These quickfire responses are all the more alarming as evidence, from, for example, the OECD (The Organisation for Economic Co-operation and Development) shows that what helps good student outcomes is that teachers feel well-supported in their schools and there is teacher development through professional collaborations in and across schools (Schleicher, 2019).

One consequence of legislative demands is that schools, exhaustedly, may respond to such demands through performing the changes, rather than engaging with them in the critical depth needed to identify what is worth working with. One example of where performance has limited the impact of changes that have the potential to be worthwhile is the use of Assessment for Learning (AfL). We regard AfL as a pedagogic tool with massive potential for enhancing learning and learners' agentic engagement.

A frequently used definition of AfL, originating with the UK Assessment Reform Group, reads: "Assessment for learning is any assessment for which the first priority in its design and practice is to serve the purpose of promoting pupils' learning. It thus differs from assessment designed primarily to serve the purposes of accountability, or of ranking, or of certifying competence" (Flórez & Sammons, 2013, p. 3).

Unfortunately, teachers' attempts at AfL all too often become performative rather than formative. Desmond Tan's study at Oxford examined the purposes of classroom assessment in schools where student teachers were being trained. He found that the majority of teachers who were supervising the student teachers in his study were employing Assessment of Learning (AoL), rather than AfL and were not using their assessments of students responsively to guide the students toward better understandings (Edwards et al., 2019; Tan, 2017). The reason appeared to be the emphasis on teacher performance by national school inspectors when they observed and judged lessons.

We discussed responsive teacher assessment as a process of formative assessment in all four of the learning-oriented activities in the Teaching and Learning sequence shown in Figure 7.1. These activities were: introduction of key concepts and creating engagement, giving structured tasks, supporting learners to use key concepts in problem-solving tasks and demonstration of key concepts and ways of inquiring. These activities formed a sequence described in detail in Chapter 7. Teachers need to assess where children are in their grasp of concepts and methods of working and relationally support them as they move forward. Assessment here is not a matter of testing; rather, it is at the core of a responsive pedagogy.

School practices are, however, notoriously difficult to change. We see practices as "knowledge-laden, imbued with cultural values and emotionally freighted by the motives of those who already act in them" (Edwards, 2010, p. 5). In short, they are historically constructed to support current actions, and current actions reflect the affordances of these historic constructions. It is therefore important to recognize that tools, such as AfL, are not simply procedures, rather, understanding how and why the tools are used is crucial. From a cultural-historical perspective, their uses, the actions taken with them and the motives for doing so are shaped by the practices in which they are located.

One way of achieving change is to totally disrupt a practice to create new spaces for innovation; but schools need stability if social order is to be sustained. Another solution is to question and develop the narratives of good practice. Bruner (1990) has usefully explained how narratives work as tools that help organize how we are positioned in activities, what we are able to do, with what resources and what matters in our actions. In brief, narratives are what sustain our practices and can help to take them forward. A study of how teachers in Norwegian schools dealt with new policy emphases on AfL has shown the importance of what Hermansen and Nerland have called teachers' knowledge work, the backstage discussions about how AfL could enrich those aspects of practice that mattered most to them, such as talking with parents (Hermansen & Nerland, 2014). The teachers' discussions revealed new motives that were woven into narratives that explained and validated the new way of assessing. The study reflects the OECD observation about teacher collaboration and shows how important motives, captured in talk, are for shaping cultures and therefore how tools are used.

Here we highlight just one aspect of AfL, children's self-assessment, and link it to metacognition and their development as agentic learners, who can propel themselves forward. This movement forward, creating their social situation of development, is made easier for children if they are adept at evaluating their own progress. We mentioned in Chapter 7 that a person is agentic when they not only set their own goals; but are also able to evaluate whether they have accomplished them.

In one example, Hedegaard' design experiments, that will be presented in Chapter 9 based in the work of Davydov, self-evaluation was a phase in the teaching and learning process. In these studies, the intention was that children would understand the relationship between the formulation of the problem, its themes and intermediate goals through self-checking at regular intervals. They were given the opportunity to look back at the start of each teaching session in order to remedy limitations in their previous understandings of the themes and the subject matter. As a final phase, the students were set assignments in which they evaluated what they had learnt and what else they would like to learn (Hedegaard, 1988, 2003a).

We would agree with Brown and Harris (2014) that seeing self-assessment as a form of self-regulation or metacognition clarifies its relevance for children's learning. Drawing on Zimmerman (2001), they define self-regulation as "self-directive and self-generated metacognitive, motivational, and behavioral processes through which individuals transform personal abilities into control of outcomes in a variety of contexts" (p. 24), a definition that has much in common with our concerns. Also, despite the heavy focus on the individual in this definition, Brown and Harris go on to emphasize children's feedback from their child peers and justifying their own self-assessments to their peers, all of which, as we discussed earlier in this chapter, are features of a demonstration of a grasp of key concepts and ways of enquiring as depicted in quadrant 4 in Figure 7.1. But self-assessment cannot float free of the curriculum and the subject matter knowledge it carries. Vygotsky was clear that reflection and the grasp of concepts support each other, saying: "[R]eflective consciousness comes to the child through the portals of scientific concepts" (Vygotsky, 1986, p. 171). We return, as we have throughout this chapter, to the importance of demystifying classroom demands and processes for children and finding ways of engaging them as active participants shaping their own learning and contributing in important ways to the classroom environment.

## Digital Resources and Agentic Learners

The pedagogic potential of digital tools took some time to be recognized by teachers. This was partly because they initially tended to see the computer as simply another resource, an electronic work card or worse. Chaiklin et al., writing in 1990 about how this new technology could be used productively with minority culture children, observed that it had largely been used "as instructional delivery systems to provide drill and practice programs" (Chaiklin et al., 1990, p. 270). The alternative taken forward in the Radical-Local initiative was to see computers as tools for children's investigations, problem-solving and communication, directly related to the subject matter knowledge being worked on. In brief, ICT (information and communications technology) was incorporated there into a well-designed pedagogic initiative. The problem for most primary school teachers, however, was that the ICT programs available to them were often not shaped by pedagogic principles and therefore tended not to provoke new ways of thinking about pedagogy (Scrimshaw, 1997). Additionally, there were also often very few computers in a classroom (Wegerif & Scrimshaw, 1997). Though, this gap led to an important series of studies focusing on children's talk around computers (Wegerif, 2010).

The problem of a lack of pedagogic underpinnings of ICT in schools has persisted. More recently Laurillard observed that education should be driving the use of technology, but, she argued, discussions of pedagogy in relation to the opportunities offered by technology are thin on the ground (Laurillard, 2013). We suggest that a relational pedagogy that aims at releasing children's agency is a valid response to Laurillard. This is of course a challenge for program designers and not only for teachers.

One way forward within classroom settings is to, as Omland and Rødnes (2020) suggest, focus on how technology can support learners' agency. In their study, they found that how teachers interacted with primary school-age children, who were using digital resources, could position children as competent participants in classroom life. Key teacher strategies when interacting with groups included taking up children's contributions by revoicing them, thereby respecting their motive orientations and taking them seriously as contributors and allowing their ideas to be expanded on by others; by responding with 'mhm mhm' to give children time to think; and by eliciting responses from quieter children. Omland and Rødnes argued that these simple strategies positioned children so that they had "the power to influence and partly to choose the direction of the classroom conversation" (p. 8). Teachers in the study also used *Talkwall* technology as a device that could reveal all the children's contributions, again showing that they were valued and could be discussed by other children.

Making knowledge-building visible through devices such as *Talkwall* is part of the legacy of Scardamalia and Bereiter's earlier work on CSILE (Computer Supported Intentional Learning Environments), which they developed with Toronto teachers (Scardamalia et al., 1992). They too were driven by the problems of using technology to reinvent the familiar (Scardamalia & Bereiter, 1993–1994) and their, then breakthrough, work had a Vygotskian framing, what they called sociocultural. CSILE seized the opportunities for rethinking pedagogy offered by advances in technology, including the Internet. The aim was to create classrooms as knowledge-building communities where the teacher was decentered, the children's knowledge-building was open and visible using different media, and knowledge-building became a collective enterprise. They connected their encouragement of children's visible contributions using computers with the need to engage and motivate learners and they talked of recognizing and respecting different contributions, in ways that chime with our concern with recognizing motive orientations and taking children seriously (Scardamalia & Bereiter, 1993–1994). They also saw how ICT-mediated networks allowed children to engage with knowledge communities beyond school boundaries.

Stenild and Iversen's e-bag project (Stenild & Iverson, 2012) offered another way of using technology to motivate children. Drawing on Hedegaard's work on the double move in teaching, the researchers used children's motives for using their cell phones, which most schools had forbidden during classroom hours, as a tool for combining their everyday activity and knowledge from outside school with classroom activity and subject matter teaching. Children's motives for using their phones were expected to engage them with subject matter knowledge when the phone was used as a tool in math and language teaching. The project was run in grades 2–9 in four schools, where students were guided to use cell phones in subject matter teaching sessions.

The intervention was successful in classroom settings, to the extent that children used their phones to search for material. But another aim of the study, to link school experiences with those outside school, was less successful. For example, children did not send material from their lives outside school to the school white boards. This intervention, nonetheless, shows how Hedegaard's double move approach (Hedegaard, 1990, 2002) should be seen as a double move from what matters for students toward creating new motives as well as a double move from everyday knowledge to subject matter knowledge.

Wegerif has also focused on the exciting advances offered by the digital resources of the internet age as they enable children to look outward, beyond the school walls. Wegerif (2013), for example, has detailed how children are helping each other to solve problems encountered in computer games. Edwards' autistic grandson, while in primary school, had over 1,000 followers of his YouTube site on animations; while it is commonplace for primary school children to visit YouTube to support their project work. These opportunities can challenge the authority of schools and teachers in shaping children's developmental pathways. What then becomes crucial is children's capacity to find and use sites productively.

We therefore return to children's agency and a capacity for reflection to support the early development of metacognition. We need to take children seriously as agents of their own learning and help equip them to engage with knowledge. We follow Scardamalia and Bereiter in arguing that positioning them as participants who contribute to as well as learn from classroom discourses is good preparation and support for their critical engagement with extra-mural sources. Our starting point is to recognize that digital media are cultural forms that operate across all the domains of a child's life and that even primary school students can be digitally literate. This observation leads us to suggest that because emotion plays a large part in children's engagement with media outside school, a focus simply on, for example, developing reasoning without care-full attention to motives is too narrow.

A large-scale study in Hong Kong directed by Nancy Law has a direct focus on digital literacy and citizenship. It has explored the digital competence of primary and secondary phase children, to reveal their extensive experience of on-line resources from YouTube to TikTok (Reichert et al., 2020) and is designing activities to develop responsible citizenship in children. The study takes digital citizenship to be: "The competence, rights and responsibility to engage and participate in a globally networked world for personal and social wellness" (communication from Law to the Hong Kong Research Grants Council). It is more than digital competence; it involves an engaged and responsible agency with attention to personal and societal well-being. It also suggests that being a responsible agentic learner involves connecting to the well-being of others and this is unlikely to happen if they are not in classrooms where these aims also shape the discourse and their responsibility is encouraged. Again, we return to the learning sequence in Figure 7.1 to point out that these concerns should inform digitally based problem-solving activities in quadrant 3 and evaluation activities in quadrant 4.

The focus on digital literacy emphasizes the responsibility of learners and raises questions about the role of the teacher. There is much talk in the ICT literature about decentering the teacher. Our view of a relational pedagogy can help to unpack what decentering means here. We have been arguing that digital technologies can allow the unfolding agency of children as they make decisions and follow fresh leads. But the capacity to do so, to engage with subject knowledge in productive ways and to be safe, needs to be nurtured by teachers. This nurturing involves, not only agreeing and sustaining ground rules for interactions with digital resources, it also involves working relationally with children. A shared focus on a screen decenters the adult as they work alongside children, eliciting children's interpretations of the content and modeling ways of making sense and responding. In this way, common knowledge, knowledge of what matters to everyone in relation to the content, is made visible. That knowledge can then mediate children's responses to the tasks or problems that are presented by the software. The term decentering is therefore perhaps a little misleading. The teacher's role remains crucial.

Recognizing the digital literacy of school-age children takes us to how schools can support children's development as responsible and agentic digital citizens within and beyond school. One approach has been to connect the growing makerspace movement with the idea of responsible engaged participation in collective efforts for community well-being. A makerspace brings together art, technology, and collaboration with a focus on learning. It allows participants to explore problems together and collaborate in building solutions. 'Maker Spaces in the Early Years' project was an international collaboration where makerspaces for young children were set up in educational and community settings (Marsh et al., 2018). In a case study in Finland with children in the pre-primary class, the focus was the forest in Finland. This class is where children begin to see themselves as school children, but are not yet recruited to a curriculum, a point we illustrated with the example of Emil in Chapter 5.

The children's processes of research and design were digitally supported and led to them creating material artifacts that eventually formed an exhibition at the local library. The motivation and collective agency were high and boundaries between school and the world beyond were breached, a teacher explained:

> The best part with this project has been how active the children have been, and how this nature theme has been a part of our preprimary school activities for many months. The parents have also been active, sharing ideas and materials with us. The children have been very excited about this since the beginning, which made it so much fun for us as well. (Marsh et al., 2018, p. 11)

The three-month project engaged children with the natural environment, encouraged critical thinking and emphasized collaborative planning and decision-making. Marsh et al. therefore argued that: "The maker project demonstrates how the status of these children was transformed from mere socialisation towards active agency and creative citizenship" (p. 11). Importantly, and in line with the aims of the Radical-Local intervention we have been discussing, the authors comment on the need for practitioners to be alert to contentious local topics that are reflected in children's everyday lives and to involve them in researching and addressing them.

Makerspaces aim at releasing the creativity of students while they engage with challenges that will promote their development, their emotional well-being alongside engagement with knowledge. They can therefore be directly connected to curricula and are ideally suited to the quadrant 3 open problem-solving tasks in Figure 7.1. Kumpulainen et al. (2019) describe these spaces as: "a powerful context to foster students' agency, persistence, creative problem-solving, digital literacy, science, technology, engineering and mathematics learning and twenty-first-century skills important for workforce development and overall functioning in the contemporary knowledge society" (p. 186). The analysis we draw on here is from their study of a digital makerspace, the FUSE studio, located in a Finnish lower secondary school.

While in the makerspace, the middle-school children worked individually or in small groups with tools such as 3D printers, computers and materials for other kinds of making, including craft. They photographed or videoed and documented their own progress in tackling their challenges. The learning process was child-led, while the challenges were embedded within the FUSE website, with video tutorials and instructions. The 'kit' that was needed to tackle a specific challenge was also supplied. Importantly, however, students were able to create novel solutions to the challenges. One might therefore expect children's agency as engaged actors would be enhanced as their orientation was, in Galperin's terms, complete but constructed by the learner.

The research team tracked a form of agency which they described as a "reframing process evidenced in young people's initiative and commitment to transform their activity and its context(s) for personal and/or academic ends" (Kajamaa & Kumpulainen, 2019, p. 268). To a large extent, this definition fits Figure 7.1 quadrant 3 open task problem-solving activities, but the purpose of makerspace activity is not simply an opportunity to agentically externalize what has been learnt. Rather, the research team argued that it involves the generation of transformative agency, which connects individual agency with the collective so that the activity is transformed. The process the team tracked with one group involved initial conflicts and breakdowns in children's collaboration, which led to them eventually deviating from their usual dependency on teachers. Over time, the children become increasingly independent of the teachers, switching roles among themselves to help each other make progress. They finally moved from an activity that was instruction-based to one that reflected their own interests and which they could collectively reshape. The authors recognize that transformative agency is usually thought of in terms of an intervention at the level of a system (Sannino, 2015) but they make the case that the concept also captures the jointly made creative shifts they observed in makerspace group activities.

Kumpulainen et al. (2019) have described these moves as a motive-demand dynamic as children's motive orientations shifted as they made the transition into more open-ended activities. Interestingly, these activities, by invoking their creative responses also led children to both resist and contribute to features of the makerspace environment. Kajamaa and Kumpulainen (2019) described how the children extended their roles as students by teaching their peers and helping their teachers. There is more work to be done in this area, not least in reducing reliance on existing digital programs and connecting experiences more securely with curricula. But it does seem that the material configurations of the digitally enhanced makerspace, by decentering the teachers, enabled the unfolding of a creative agency among the children.

### Developing Self-Awareness in Primary Age Children

Our focus on agency in the social situation of development connects with the growing self-awareness of children. Their sense of who they are is constructed in interactions in practices. A study by Edwards, using repertory grids, showed that children as young as four years of age were aware that they felt and behaved differently in different situations in different practices (Edwards, 1984, 1988). Unsurprisingly, "playing out with friends" was somewhere where they were most at ease. Each practice makes different demands on children and so contributes to the development of their sense of self in a practice, as the baby of the family, as the class clown, as a good football player and so on. These situated selves are negotiated within practices and contribute to a sense of their competences, such as *I am good at reading and not good at running*. These judgments about themselves, of course, impact on their motive orientations.

Motive orientations are crucial. William James in 1890 argued that self-esteem, how we value ourselves in different contexts, can be explained by the fraction – success over pretensions. If a child's pretensions are low, "girls don't do technology," then the girl in question is unlikely to aim for success in working with technology. The key to supporting children as learners is therefore to raise pretensions, or in our terms nurture their motive orientations.

We will say more about gender and racial identities in relation to children's identities when we discuss adolescence in Chapter 10. But a considerable amount of research reminds us that both gender and racial identities begin to be formed from a very early age and can contribute to how motive orientations are formed. One way of reading the Radical-Local program implemented by Hedegaard and Chaiklin is in terms of identity. Looking back to their families' origins in Puerto Rica and then to their current lives, the East Harlem children were able to develop as learners alongside a growing awareness of their heritage and their identities as Puerto Rican Americans. Gender and racial identities can also impact on difficulties in accessing opportunities for learning and development; Edwards' then 12-year-old daughter, who was an accomplished young artist, was told she couldn't study design and technology at school as "she would be the only girl taking the subject." However, the biggest contribution to a lack of access to learning opportunities is poverty. We therefore turn to the broad topic of social inclusion.

## Supporting Inclusion and Nurturing Resilience

We start by distinguishing between inclusive schools with associated school inclusion, which most education systems aim at, and the wider concept of social inclusion, which attempts to address how children and families are able to access and contribute what society offers its citizens. However, they are closely linked concepts, and we shall argue that approaches to school inclusion have much to learn from how social inclusion is being tackled.

Schools are all too often caught in a market economy, forcing them to pursue short-term externally imposed indicators of success, which don't encourage shifts in practices to reflect the challenges of the different contexts schools find themselves in. Inclusion and equity are areas that have not always fared well for this reason. The ills of society, poverty, racism, disability, class and so on are thrown into sharp relief in schools and creating inclusive schools has been the headline response. Yet national Education policies, driven by OECD League Tables and national systems for monitoring schools, are not always compatible with school inclusion. The increasing off-rolling of poorly performing students in England is just one sign of the impact of these policies on schools. Indeed, inclusion is often reduced to a performance (Allan, 2003). Allan's way forward is compatible with ours and includes the need to create environments that include all children and to listen to children and their families about what school inclusion means for them.

A series of research projects undertaken by Edwards in the first ten or so years of this century all showed clearly that schools in England and elsewhere were tightly boundaried with limited links with their communities and other services supporting children and families (Edwards et al.,

2006, 2009). Indeed, schools frequently described themselves as havens, leaving children with the huge challenge of negotiating their developmental pathways with inconsistent support as they moved between school practices and those of other aspects of their lives. Our position is that a child-focused approach to inclusion cannot separate school inclusion from social inclusion, or more precisely the prevention of social exclusion.

Social exclusion became a policy focus in the 1990s and as we explained in Chapter 3 was described by Room (1995) as being detached from the communities that comprise society and from the rights and responsibilities involved. Preventing such detachment then became a policy priority across the EU and elsewhere (Edwards & Downes, 2013) and called on universal services, such as schools, to recognize their role in preventing the escalation of problems for children (Treasury-DfES, 2007). However, there has been little attention to the child's perspective as they managed to orient toward different expectations in different sets of practices. Not recognizing children as active participants in school and with lives outside had led to practitioners objectifying children as problems and discussing them as, for example, "a school uniform problem" and talking of handing on "bits of the child" to other services (Edwards et al., 2009). Our argument is that taking children seriously means recognizing the efforts they may need to make as they navigate the boundary crossing between home, school and other activities.

Being resilient helps with these efforts to deal with disruptions and frustrations. Practitioners who work with children therefore need an understanding of how resilience can be nurtured. It is a concept that has undergone some changes. At one point, resilience was mainly described as a capacity for adaptation to appropriate developmental pathways despite disruptions such as family crises, and the best predictors of resilience were relationships with "caring prosocial adults" and "good intellectual functioning" (Masten & Coatsworth, 1998). Others have emphasized contexts alongside relationships (Luthar, 1993), and resilience is now recognized as a dynamic process of interaction between sociocultural contexts and developing individuals (Howard et al., 1999). Jack has also argued for far more attention to the area and community components of children's well-being (Jack, 2006).

In Chapter 3, we discussed interprofessional work and showed how the three relational concepts, relational expertise, common knowledge and relational agency, can lead to sustained and consistent support for children across different practices. We now discuss how these concepts can help with the development of resilience (Edwards & Apostolov, 2007).

To illustrate our argument, we draw on a national evaluation of an English initiative 'The Children's Fund,' which aimed at (i) preventing the social exclusion of children aged 8–13 years through partnerships between locally based providers of services for children and (ii) encouraging the participation of children and their families in shaping these services (Edwards et al., 2006). Involvement in developing services was key to the unfolding of children's agency. There were many examples of the impact of that involvement on children's sense of their own agency and well-being (Evans et al., 2006). Simply asking children for their ideas for the services being provided and, importantly, putting their suggestions into action, enhanced children's confidence and their further engagement.

The services were almost all run by voluntary agencies and therefore not restricted by the demands that shape practices in schools and statutory agencies such as social work. This difference allowed practitioners to interact with children by listening to them and consequently treating them with respect. Evans et al. reported that children and their families explained that workers didn't "walk off" when children talked with them, the children were given "more leeway" than in school and were "not bossed around." But more than this, practitioners acted on what they heard, "giving us [the children] a say in what they do, they're not just telling us what to do." The ideas could be very simple, such as when a child said: "The coffee morning was my idea." Or "I don't want to be big-headed, but I came up with the idea of the conference!"

The participation aims of the initiative focused on developing services; but the researchers also observed how practitioners, once they had shown that they would listen respectfully, negotiated new developmental pathways with children and families. A practitioner explained: "[T]he main participation is in the individual packages we do with families, which are very much family-led really. It's around their description of the understanding of their needs – the targets that we all agree to work towards, and their evaluations of the things at the end really." This point about their evaluations is key. It returns us to Taylor's definition of individual agency (Taylor, 1977), which proposes that one is only truly agentic when one not only sets one's own goals but is able to evaluate that one has achieved them.

Children and parents also reported how being taken seriously by adults gave the children life skills such as communication. In summarizing the findings, the research team concluded that it could see a link between participation and resilience, being taken seriously was very important for the children (Evans et al., 2006). Here is a practitioner describing her participation work: "It's about building them up, about having a voice, having confidence, building self-esteem, being part of a democracy and buying into things and having ownership of where they live and what they do." The research team also noted how the children, who had been helped through strong and trusting relationships with practitioners, then helped other children. For example, children with refugee backgrounds or with disabilities who had experience of support from projects then helped children with similar needs. These relationships all exemplified relational agency in action.

These observations led Edwards to expand her view of resilience (Edwards, 2007; Edwards & Apostolov, 2007). Her suggestion was that the concept of resilience should be extended so that it includes a capacity to work with others to shape and reshape one's own conditions of development and to be an active agent in shaping one's own developmental pathway. She drew on Vygotsky's notion of the social situation of development and his view that learning is evidenced in the actions people take in and on their worlds. She noted that much of the national policy discourse around building resilience simply encouraged caring and clear communication. She hoped that this cultural-historical version of resilience gave space for recognizing the agency of children in shaping their own futures. She concluded: "Shifts in practice to include parents, caregivers and children as partners who can negotiate pathways and can act on their worlds to shape not only their trajectories but also the 'social situation of development' have long term implications for society." (Edwards & Apostolov, 2007, p. 82)

In Chapter 7, we discussed decentering the teacher to create new pedagogical relationships where the child's motive orientations are taken seriously. In this chapter, we have examined how digital environments can help to connect schools to their wider communities and nurture responsible citizenship. The cultural-historical view of resilience that forefronts children's responsible actions on their worlds, offers an enriched version of school inclusion in line with Allan's (2003) advice that schools should listen to children and their families about what school inclusion means for them.

## Final Reflections

This chapter has shown what tremendous changes take place for children during the primary school years. It has also indicated what the adults in their lives can do to assist their participation in the practices they inhabit, being shaped by and shaping those practices. We have been concerned

## Final Reflections

throughout, that children can all too easily find themselves on pathways that lead to alienation from schooling and toward social exclusion. Taking children seriously, seeking and working with their motive orientations is one way of preventing such outcomes.

We have presented examples from practice, from our own and others' research to illustrate what we mean by the relational pedagogy we outlined in Chapter 7. How the agency of children as learners unfolds and is supported in that unfolding has been the key theme. We have noted that the delicate process of guiding that agency toward productive engagement with the demands of practices is highly skilled work for both family carers and caring professionals.

The care-full pedagogy we are advocating recognizes that not only should children's motives in school be taken seriously; children should also be seen as rounded human beings who have lives beyond school. Practitioners therefore need to help children to look outward to connect what they learn in school with wider reality. Doing this serves at least two purposes: it helps to make the subject matter knowledge of school increasingly meaningful, and it helps children to ask critical questions of aspects of wider society.

Taking children seriously means recognizing that they are involved in a process of making their future selves and these future selves should be able to impact on the conditions they inhabit, the communities of which they are part. The agency we are advocating is therefore not individualistic, rather it involves a capacity for working with others in ways that are shaped by ethics and community values. Practitioners who work with each other and children in the relational way we are suggesting are likely to be excellent role models for that endeavor.

CHAPTER 9

# *Developmental Teaching as a Double Move between Subject Knowledge and Children's Appropriation of Personal Knowledge*

## Introduction

The societal and historical aspects of knowledge and its situated and distributed character are formed in everyday practices and are the foundation for the communicative and argumentative character of an individual's thinking (Billig, 1998). Importantly, engagement in societal practices precedes an individual's societal knowledge (Jensen, 1986; Wartofsky, 1979). Consequently, knowledge can never simply be knowledge of "essence," which is independent of societal practice. Our argument, therefore, is that thinking and personal knowledge should be seen as a personally acquired capacity to engage in the processes of cultural and social activities. A child's knowledge acquisition and concept formation, therefore, need to be recognized as occurring through their participation in collective cultural activities and through instructional guidance. This personal knowledge should become a tool that children use to orient, act, and create their everyday life worlds (Wartofsky, 1979).

In this chapter, we will discuss the importance of recognizing different societal knowledge forms for subject matter teaching and argue for the importance of guiding children to acquire theoretical knowledge. In this we draw on Hedegaard's experimental teaching projects in Denmark within the subject areas of biology, geography, and history in grades 3–5 (Hedegaard, 1988, 1990, 1995, 1996, 2002, 2020; Hedegaard et al., 1985). Hedegaard's teaching project entitled *The Double Move* is built on Vygotsky's (1987) ideas on how teaching in school has to relate to children's everyday knowledge in order to be meaningful and motivate children to learn scientific knowledge. In her double move pedagogy, Hedegaard (1999a) extended Davydov's *Developmental Teaching and Learning* approach – (Aidarova, 1982; Davydov, 1988–1989; Davydov & Markova, 1983) – to encompass children's emotional engagement.

The double move was introduced in Chapter 7 as a process of instruction where the teacher guides the children's learning activity both from the perspective of the general concepts and methods of a subject matter area and from the perspective of engaging students in situated problems that are meaningful for them. The problems engage children in relation to their life situations and developmental age period (Hedegaard, 2002). It is a relational form of teaching, where the teacher may use common knowledge to mediate their interactions with children. Together with Chaiklin, Hedegaard also worked with the process of the double move in the formative experiment of *Radical-Local Teaching and Learning*, run in East Harlem, New York (Hedegaard & Chaiklin, 2005), as introduced in Chapter 8. In the final part of this chapter, we will present a questionnaire as a system developed by Hedegaard and Bang for a dialogical way to evaluate children' emotional situations in school, thereby creating common knowledge of what matters in school and about how what they learn becomes relevant outside school.

## Different Collective Knowledge Forms in School Teaching

The idea of knowledge forms in relation to teaching needs elaborating. This involves examining the relation within a subject matter area between valued societally shared collective knowledge, and personal knowledge based on individual concrete life experiences. Therefore, a conception of collective knowledge that can be the foundation for school teaching and vocational training is called for.

Our point of departure for this analysis is Jensen's (1986) description of how societal knowledge has evolved through creating procedures for solving important societal problems in different historical periods. This starting point connects teaching and learning to the historical evolution of human activity. Jensen uses medicine as a prime example and shows how different conceptualizations of an illness, such as diabetes, have changed over time, both how diabetes is characterized and how different remedies have been developed and used. Information science and computer technology are examples of more recent societal problem areas where knowledge and procedures have evolved rapidly. The procedures for solving problems in areas such as health and information science become formalized through the evolution of processes in these practices and have become knowledge forms. These knowledge forms reflect what is valued in the institutional practices, including ways of communicating. At the same time, the knowledge remains open to changes that arise through responding to new challenges, such as a pandemic, and the availability of new resources such as YouTube and Twitter.

However, over time, strategies and procedures that have developed in practices in societal problem areas become divorced from the original problem and become fossilized. Procedures for undertaking scientific investigations have been incooperated in educational practice. This fossilization has led to an overdependence on a relatively static form of *empirical/categorial knowledge*, which is ubiquitous in school curricula and in everyday public knowledge. This kind of empirical knowledge used in teaching is characterized as a process of abstracting aspects of an area of knowledge and generalizing from the abstraction to form categories, without connecting the categories to everyday life. We are not dismissing empirical knowledge but argue that it needs to be seen as a societal knowledge form among others that may organize children's experiences.

Both Davydov (1977/1990) and Bruner (1986) have written critiques of how empirical knowledge based on formal logic dominates school teaching at the expense of other forms of knowledge. Similarly, what concerns us is that this kind of empirical knowledge, based in formal logic, is seen as independent of societal practice and historical time periods. As an alternative form of knowledge, Bruner (1986) has pointed to *narrative knowledge*. Narrative knowledge is oriented toward situated content and is represented in accounts and conversational flows that enable the development of shared meanings: The relational is important here. Its processes and methods are connected to the challenge of giving meaning to emotional experiences. Bruner explains the procedures associated with narrative knowledge as: (a) changeability in intentions, (b) possible mutable perspectives and goals that interact, and (c) the involvement of feelings and emotions. As we see it, narrative knowledge characterizes the communicative activity in children's daily activity settings at home, in the community, and in school, when interacting with other children in learning activities.

Empirical and narrative knowledge are valid and important knowledge forms both in and out of school. Empirical knowledge that is constantly reality tested helps in transcending concrete events and seeing them in a general context, allowing them to be organized into hierarchical systems. This process usefully reduces information load. Narrative knowledge is important in discussions and in group work where children learn to cooperate, respect each other's views and build common knowledge. In this way it may also help with developing moral relationships with others and with nature. Hedegaard argues that in subject matter teaching both empirical and narrative knowledge should be put into a frame of theoretical knowledge (2002). Doing so allows children to make connections between abstract knowledge and emotional experiences.

*Theoretical knowledge* is a dialectically connected system of categories that has evolved through a historical process of constructing specific practice-related methods. Knowledge formation in both science and handicraft are examples of this. Collective theoretical knowledge within a practice area evolves through a historical process of experimentation with methods and strategies for solving problems and contradictions central to society. Revealing the primary relations or germ cell in a subject area is key to this process. The germ cell depicts the dialectical relation between the core categories of the subject area, categories that can only be understood in relation to each other, such as, individual and society, animal and ecology. Through continued use in practice, the germ cell evolves and changes and, in that way, conceptual knowledge in the subject area increases. The primary relation and how it evolves within a subject area may be represented in the form of graphic models as illustrated in Figure 9.1.

Theoretical knowledge is not self-evident, nor can it be discerned and acquired by one person simply observing another. Therefore, education is at the core of its acquisition. Stenild and Iversen (2012), for example, argued in their introduction of information science and computer technology into teaching, that one can teach young children to use a camera or a computer by encouraging their imitation of the actions of others. Yet while kindergarten children can carry out procedures for using these objects, they do not know how the objects work. That knowledge demands much more than knowledge of procedures, and ways of acting. To get this kind of knowledge, they need to understand the principles of how the different central features within a problem area interact. They need to recognize that when one aspect changes, other features will be impacted. This form of knowledge is complicated and cannot be accessed through observation. Instead, it is built through experimentation within a practice area. One consequence of this view is that teaching should be structured around initial relations. For example, when the theory of evolution is taught, teaching should be structured around the core concepts of animal life forms, population and habitat (see Figure 9.2). In that way, the new understanding becomes a tool for children to use to organize factual knowledge and personal experiences into general conceptual understandings. Later in this chapter, we will illustrate this process in a discussion of teaching biology, where children aged nine and ten learn about

**a: Problem area model: the evolution of animal species**

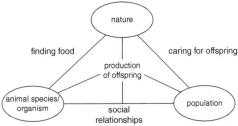

**b: Problem area model: the origins of man**

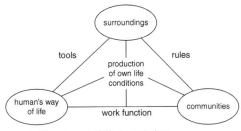

**c: Problem area model: change of different ways of life through time**

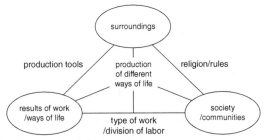

**d: Final model for historical changes in societies through time**
Rules, work functions/the division of labor and production tools become the deciding factors.

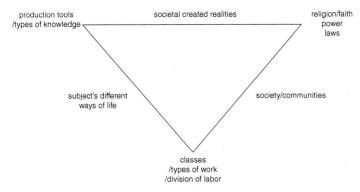

Figure 9.1   Models for subject-related content

# Different Collective Knowledge Forms in School Teaching 207

**Step I. The primary relation between a species and its habitat**

**Step II. Model for animals species' adaption to their environment**

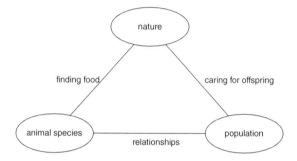

**Step III. Model for evolution of animals species**

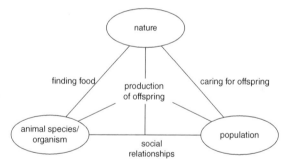

Figure 9.2   Models for how the primary relation in evolution of species became extended

animals' adaptation and evolution using the germ cell of the relation between species, population and habitat. The example will also show how the germ cell may become extended and changed.

Through theoretical knowledge, the specific and unique situations of children's experiences are related to general concepts. Hence, the epistemological procedures of theoretical knowledge relate to both concrete instances and general ideas. In this way, children can come to understand the generalities in their concrete experiences (Davydov, 1988–1989,

2008). We are therefore arguing that acquiring general concepts is not a goal in itself. Rather, concepts are resources to be used to analyze and understand the complexity of unique situations. The strategies of working with theoretical knowledge in this way have been characterized as ascending from the abstract to the concrete (Lompscher, 1999). We are suggesting that theoretical knowledge is central to school teaching because it creates possibilities for combining children's learning of general principles with the familiar cultural practices of their everyday lives.

## The Appropriation of Personal Knowledge in School

Children's learning is not based on their direct experiences of the world; it is always mediated in interactions with others. In school, teaching that guides learners through their systematic organization of concepts in different subject areas, is the main form of academic mediation. Children also learn in other contexts, but how they are educated changes when they enter school. In school, activities have explicit learning objectives and are planned and orchestrated by teachers. While the logic of the subject to be learned gives direction to children's engagement as learners as they move forward and acquire conceptual competence.

Vygotsky (1998, 2021), writing about young people's conceptual acquisition, explained that the main way they systematize their conceptual understandings is through a reciprocal system of interdependent relationship between the concepts in a practice area and its personal meaning for the learner. In this way, young people acquire conceptual systems that relate to the social, societal and political aspects of life. Consequently, young people become aware of societal ideologies and values and of themselves as people in society, and their self-consciousness develops.

But an extensive cultural-historical explanation of conceptual systems in subject matter knowledge was not produced until Davydov's contribution. His formulation of the characteristics of theoretical knowledge based on dialectic logic was key here. Dialectics are central to an understanding of the mechanisms of human mental activity. As we have already explained, the logic of subject areas and cognition are in a dialectical relationship with the societal problems they address. This relationship leads to the historical formation of scientific thought. It also can explain how children come to make sense of their worlds, building and testing theoretical knowledge in their engagement with their worlds.

Our focus is children's engagement and acquisition of knowledge. As we have explained in earlier chapters, we are guided by Vygotsky's (1998) paradigmatic view, that knowledge must be discovered by children as they take forward their social situations of development, where the teacher's task is to create the conditions for children's learning. By this statement we are not making a case for a laissez-faire form of discovery learning; rather, our approach is highly structured. This approach to learning and instruction was developed by Galperin (1969) with his focus on phases in children learning (see Chapter 7). Davydov (Aidarova, 1982; Davydov, 1982, 1988, 2008) took this pedagogic line further by formulating the Developmental Teaching approach as a continuation of both Vygotsky's paradigm and Galperin's conception of phases.[1]

Davydov (1999) argued that only by understanding learning in school as an object-related learning activity, is it possible to teach in ways that develop children's capacities. Although children learn in other settings, teaching in schools is always oriented to learning goals that should lead to specific outcomes in the form of object-related knowledge and skills. He explained:

> One important characteristic feature of activity is that it is always, whether explicitly or implicitly, object-related. This implies that all its components have some object-related contents and that the activity itself is necessarily directed toward creation of some material or spiritual product. (Davydov, 1999, p. 124)

Even when learning activities take place in classroom collectives, they entail individual motivation to engage and involve some creative action as children appropriate new understandings, connecting them to what they already know. Davydov outlined the process:

> Children can only appropriate knowledge and skills through learning activity when they have an internal need and motivation to do so. Learning activity involves transformation of the material to be appropriated and implies, that some new mental product, i.e., knowledge is received. . . . It is through experimentation and exploration that children obtain knowledge of general aspects of an object that is theoretical knowledge through experimentation and exploration. (Davydov, 1999, p. 125)

The following four principles (Table 9.1) build on the idea of ascending from the abstract to the concrete and are central to organizing students' learning activity in classrooms (Aidarova, 1982; Davydov, 1999). In this activity, a germ-cell model guides the teacher's construction of activities and, when students have formulated their versions, it guides their activity.

---

[1] Other cultural-historical researchers in Russia have followed Davydov-El'konin's Developmental Teaching approach that now is formulated in programs for teaching in public schools in Moscow (Zukerman, 2011).

Table 9.1 *Principles for Developmental Teaching*

- Concepts cannot be given as ready-made knowledge but have to be acquired by the students through their own research, guided toward conceptual relations.
- Acquisition of general knowledge in the form of core relations has to come before specific and concrete knowledge.
- Through key examples, children should be led to construe the primary relations (the core relations) that determine the content and structure of the subject matter area.
- The primary relations should be depicted in graphic models or schematic drawings that give a description of their relations in their pure form.

Teaching that builds on the principles in Table 9.1 is based on the idea that concepts in a subject matter area are connected with people's collective interaction in concrete practices. Vygotsky indicates the dialectics in this process when discussing children's development of word meanings, a topic we addressed in Chapter 5. He explained: "Social interaction presupposes generalization and the development of verbal meaning, generalization becomes possible only with the development of social interaction" (Vygotsky, 1987, p. 48).

The Developmental Teaching approach started with experiments in math teaching (Davydov, 1990, 1999) and literacy (Aidarova, 1982; Markova, 1978–1979), where they focused on how specific subjects contributed to children's appropriation of core conceptual relations within a subject area and their reflections on their own capacities. Davydov's approach to enabling children's appropriation of personal knowledge was: (a) to design tasks so that children come to deduce the primary relations within a subject area; (b) to design assignments where children are able to explore the relationship in various instances within the thematic area in its diversity and (c) to give children tasks that require them to take a critical standpoint in relation to both their own competences and to the conceptual relationship they have been examining. He related these steps to the following phases in children's learning: (a) the goal formation phase, (b) formulating core relations within a subject area and (c) evaluation of their own learning (Hedegaard, 2002, p. 89). Davydov's conception of theoretical knowledge with its focus on germ-cell concepts is central in this approach.

In the following section, we return to how children's concept formation occurs through connecting emotional experiences with subject matter concepts. Hedegaard introduced this idea into the Developmental Teaching approach as the double move between theoretical knowledge and concrete emotional imaginations and conceptualized it as a movement that went both ways. "In the double move approach teaching and learning in school is not conceptualized as a straightforward process, but rather as a spiral of problem solving, where, to begin with, the teacher guides the pupils until they become acquainted with a subject domain. Gradually, through the process of learning, the pupil takes over and guide their own learning process and, in doing so, finds their own problems." (Hedegaard, 2002, p. 78)

This approach to teaching and learning shows how teaching should start with children's everyday knowledge and engagements and, through guided activities such as tasks and assignments, relate these to core concepts and procedures in subject matter knowledge. Then, when working with these tasks, the skills and knowledge children acquire work back on children's everyday concepts and motives.

## The Double Move Approach: Using Germ-Cell Models

In cooperation with teachers in two Danish public schools and with subject matter specialists in biology history and geography, Hedegaard ran a series of teaching experiments inspired by Davydov's conception of theoretical thinking and knowledge. In the teaching experiments, the three subject areas were integrated into three related problem areas (see Figure 9.1): the evolution of species, the origin of humans and the historical change of societies. The historical change of societies had two steps. The first encompassed the production of different ways of life and the second encompassed change in societies through time, by focusing on rules, divisions of labor and the production of tools as core relations. In the experimental approach these problems were guided by the models shown in Figure 9.1. These should be seen as evolved from each other (see Hedegaard, 2002, pp. 84–85).

The models in Figure 9.1 guided the experimental teaching by giving teachers tools for their design of teaching activities and enabled the cooperation between researcher and teachers. The research and teacher team worked together the following way:

(A) There was an initial period of the formulation of a general plan for the entire school year, containing goals for the subject area of instruction, and discussion of the conceptual models as well as phases in children learning activities;[2]
(B) Over the whole teaching period, in order to concretize and regulate the plan and structure phases in the teaching, the researcher, student observers, supporting specialists and teachers met weekly for two

---

[2] These were (1) goal formulation, (2) exploration activity and (3) evaluation of their own activities.

hours to plan each three-hour teaching session. In each meeting, the research team discussed the observations of the previous lessons, and the suggestions for the next period. That lead to a plan for each session including the aim, concepts, materials, teaching acts and students' learning acts.

An overview of plans for teaching the evolution of species can be found in Hedegaard (1988, pp. 250–263). This overview should only be seen as a source for inspiration. The idea with the double move is that, when planning teaching, one should always take into consideration both the subject matter and students' social situations of development, including their understanding and engagement in the previous session. Through these meetings of the research team and teachers, common knowledge was being built by the participants, including the students. This common knowledge mediated the long-term collaboration.

The teaching aimed at promoting children's acquisition of theoretical thinking and knowledge by engaging them in cooperative activities and discussions and in creating their own models. This was accomplished by using a research procedure to engage students in exploration and reflection (see Table 9.2). The reflecting enabled them to organize their knowledge into models that contained the core relations, the germ cell. Their understanding of the germ cell was then a tool for their further investigations in the subject areas (Figures 9.4 and 9.5).

The experimental teaching took place between 1983 and 1989, in grades 3–5, as three separate experiments. The first was as a pilot study of teaching *the origin of man* over three months in grade 3 (Hedegaard, 1984). The second was a one-year teaching experiment of *the evolution of species*, again to children in grade 3 (Hedegaard, 1988, 1990, 1996). The third phase was a three-year initiative that covered all three areas, *evolution of species, the origin of man and the historical change of societies* (Hedegaard, 1995, 1997, 2002).

Here we draw from the one-year formative experiment of the evolution of species, to illustrate the double move approach to classroom teaching.

Table 9.2 *The Goal-Result-Research Procedure*

1. Who is investigating?
2. What do we want to research? (What questions are being investigated?)
3. What do we know?
4. What don't we know about what we investigate?
5. How can we express what we know and don't know in goal-result models?
6. How are we going to explore our questions further?

We focus on the germ-cell model of the evolution of species and its transformations as the core of students' learning.

### The Germ-Cell Model of the Evolution of Species Guiding the Teaching Activity

The teaching was centered around the students' formation of a germ-cell model based on a neo-Darwinian theory of evolution (Gould, 1992; Jensen & Harré, 1981; Mayr, 1976, 1980).[3] The teaching of the conceptual relationships within the theory of evolution of animal species was based on three successive steps to formulate the germ-cell model (see Figure 9.2).

> *Step I* depicts the primary relationship between animal species and their environmental conditions, where different animal species have adapted to characteristic of a particular biotope.
> *Step II* depicts whether an animal species adapts to environmental changes. A species will survive if members of the population can adapt to change in their living conditions (habitat).
> *Step III* depicts changes in a species. New species will evolve under the following circumstances: (a) segregation and isolation of part of a population that entails change in the biotope, which involves change in ways of living; (b) variation in the genetic material both through mutation and gene combination; (c) selection of offspring.

### How to Create a Motive for Engagement with Subject Matter

Teaching needs to be tailored to the age periods of learners, both to what is their leading higher psychic functions, and to their motive orientations. In Chapter 5, we explained how, in modern societies, imagination dominates kindergarten children's thinking when they start school and in their first years in school, while at the same time their capacity for thinking and reflection emerges. Children in the first years in school still have questions about the world around them of the kind Piaget has described (Piaget, 1923). These questions might be: Where the sun is when it is dark? Where does the Earth end? This kind of questioning was what Hedegaard et al. used when designing the initial teaching about evolution. The specific questions were: Have there always been the same animals on Earth? Have they always

---

[3] Natural selection is still the primary explanatory principle, but it is not thought to be directly connected to the organic characteristics of species. Rather selection refers to the population's adaption to changes in the biotope. Change in a gene pool interacts with change in the environment. The way of living is the criterion for selection of new organic traits. Evolution is thereby conceptualized as a gradual process in which ways of living are decisive factors in directing the evolution of species.

looked the same? The team hoped that such questions would lead to children's imagining and wondering together with the teacher. The teacher could then follow this up with the question: How can we find out about this?

Hedegaard (1988) named this way of starting teaching, using children's wondering about the world, to create *the initial motive* for classroom activity for subject matter learning. It is called the initial motive because it is a stimulating motive for starting the learning activity but cannot motivate children throughout the whole planned course. Older children in later grades have to be motivated by other types of question to create an initial motive, but for nine-year-old children, their wondering is still related to the world around them.

The initial motive for class activity should be connected with the double move of engaging children. That this was the case in the experiment was illustrated by children bringing into the classroom objects, pictures, books, drawings and letters they wrote that were related to the subject matter themes (Hedegaard, 1988, pp. 152–155). When this initial motive is created, the second requirement is to ensure that what is discussed in the classroom relates to the general teaching objectives, and at the same time stays meaningful for children. In the concrete case to accomplish this, the team used a research procedure, a set of questions (see Table 9.1) as a tool for starting each teaching session with a teacher-guided discussion.[4] The discussion was structured by the questions that were gradually introduced. The first two sessions started with the first question so that the children came to accept that they were the ones who investigated and explored. The fifth and sixth questions were introduced later after the teacher had led children through tasks where they identified the primary relation that explained why and how animals have changed over time.

### *Organization of Classroom Teaching*

In the teaching experiments, the rule was that the teachers never lectured but brought material and tasks that engaged children. This was done through film, pictures, objects, museum visits and short written texts, which underpinned the research activities of the children. Consequently, the children used their classroom time to complete tasks or group projects or engage in class discussions to analyze 'what we know' and 'what we don't know' in relation to proposed activities.

---

[4] Through the first two years in the experimental teaching (grades 3 and 4), this dialogue was teacher-guided; later in the third year (grade 5) students took turns guiding the class dialogue.

## The Double Move Approach: Using Germ-Cell Models 215

The way of teaching was a double move from the abstract to the concrete and from the concrete to the abstract, working with oppositions, using children's everyday knowledge and questions to create their motivation for exploration. The teachers' tasks and guidance took as their point of departure the three steps in the germ-cell model (Figure 9.2). This guidance aimed at children's creation of coherence among the different themes brought into the class, and at the same time was oriented to what engaged them. The children learned through explorative activity in teacher-prepared tasks that demanded analyses of concrete matters introduced via museum visits, film presentations and photographs.

The teaching was highly relational, oriented to children's cooperation on tasks and projects and classroom discussions that were designed to connect to children's motives and knowledge. But learning in groups or group work is not something that children can do without guidance. Therefore, the children had to learn to work in groups that were directed toward a shared objective, as well as how to function in the classroom collective. Children's group work was organized so they had different roles in a group such as: a group leader, who kept the goal of the group activity in focus; a note writer and a presenter of shared solutions in the class discussion hour. The students took turns in these roles in each group.

This way of teaching does not require children to remember what the teacher has told them. Instead, they have to be aware of the research questions introduced and shaped in class discussions and the implications for their explorations of the germ-cell relations, as well as formulating results.

The teaching was based on three steps that organized the content of the subject matter (see Figure 9.2).

*Step I* depicted the relationship between an animal species and its environmental conditions. Here the two first sessions were oriented to the students' understanding of the objective of the biology teaching: to learn about animals' adaption and evolution. The leading questions that would guide the class activities over the whole year were:[5] *Have the same animals always lived on Earth? And have they always looked the same?*

The teacher started the first session by presenting the goal for the year's teaching and then read three different descriptions of how animals evolved. He then asked the children to discuss what they thought was the right description and ended the discussion without reaching a conclusion. In the second session, the teacher brought in a surprise. Before he presented it, he started a discussion about how children imagined what a researcher did, as

---

[5] There were 29 periods in the teaching period of one year, each with three class hours.

illustrated in the extract below. They were then given the task of drawing a picture of what they thought they could explore if they were researchers. An example of a child's drawing can be seen in Figure 9.3. In the third session, they visited a museum of natural history with an exhibition of prehistoric animals and got tasks in relation to this visit.

Figure 9.3  A child's drawing of what can be researched in biology, from the second teaching period

## Extract from the 2nd teaching period about how scientists work

The teacher (T) brought into the classroom a box covered with a cloth. The children are excited but become quiet when he withdraws the cloth and shows them the content. They are now really quiet. Each gets something from the box to look at.

T: What are these?

Birger: Prehistorical animals.

Heidi has also brought some stones with marks from fossils into the class.

T: Yes, but are these the animals?

Palle: No, these are stones.

Heidi: These are fossils.

T asks if they know who has found out about fossilizations.

Bo: It is scientists.

T: I have been thinking that we should work as scientists.

Palle: But then we need a laboratory.

T: Yes, you say something important; we will wait with this for a while, but not forget it.

Now bring out your sketchbooks, and in the middle draw a scientist.

T: Who should be the scientist?

Bo: Me.

T: Yes! You and you and you (pointing at the different children). You should draw the scientist in the middle of the page but not too big.

The children seem happy.

Some draw a head, others a child. The teacher moves around to look.

T: What was it then that the scientist could research? It was fossils. Can they research anything else?

Martin: He could research bones.

Hanne: Mice.

Hans: TV.

T: Palle, you told us that a scientist had a laboratory. What could he explore there?

Palle: Small animals.

Other children mention animals, humans, dogs, crows, hamsters

T: Now we have mentioned many animals. Can they also research stones, or stars?

Children: Yes

What did we start with?

Children: Bones.

T: Yes, fossilized bones.

They all draw in their sketchbooks, and the teacher draws on the blackboard.

We talked about how a scientist could explore other things.

Now we write biology. What did we say earlier that this was about?

Children: Humans, animals, plants, the Earth, prehistory?

Can you draw what biology can be about?

Hans: Can it be about blood?

T. Yes but this is difficult to draw.

Hans: No, you just have to draw some drops and color them red?

The children are eagerly drawing.

In the fourth session, the children started to identify what they knew about different animals' habitats. Each child created a first step in the germ-cell model of the primary relation by drawing connections between living animals and their habitat, as illustrated in Figure 9.4. One child suggested that a single animal would be lonely. Consequently, a new category was introduced, fellow animals, which the children used for the concept of population.

The teacher's use of the opening question in the fourth teaching session resulted in a *goal-result* drawing on the black board as a summary of the children's discussion of their research and drawings related to the questions in Table 9.1 (i.e., what we want to research, what do we know, what don't we know, etc.). The primary relations were not presented to the children but were constructed by them through the tasks they were given. One example of a task was to identify the living conditions for polar bears in the Artic after viewing a film about polar bears in Greenland (see Figure 9.4). Another was about living conditions for different animals in African deserts. These tasks were followed by a class discussion about what would happen to the animals from Greenland if they were moved to Africa, and vice versa. From that discussion, it was possible to conclude that animal and habitat were connected.

## The Double Move Approach: Using Germ-Cell Models 219

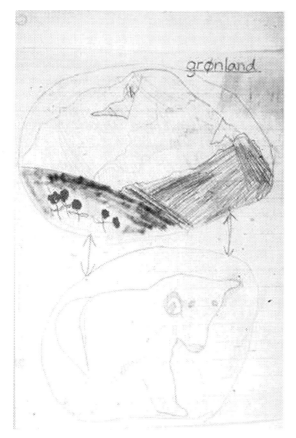

Figure 9.4  A child's drawing of how animals and nature belong together in Greenland, from the fourth teaching period

A class library with many relevant books for this age group, with lots of pictures, was available in the classroom. The children used these books to solve problems; they were not used as textbooks, but could also be used as relaxation when a child had finished a task.

*Step II* depicted whether a species adapts to environmental changes. A species will survive if members of the population can adapt to change in their living conditions. In the 10th teaching-session they discussed why polar hares changed when moving to the Faroe Islands. In this way they progressed to Step II in Figure 9.2. The outcomes of the discussions were generalized to different animals. This generalization was represented in children's drawings of the relation between ways of living together, finding food, cooperation and breeding; some children drew relations between formulating the relations in language, others in drawings (see Figure 9.5).

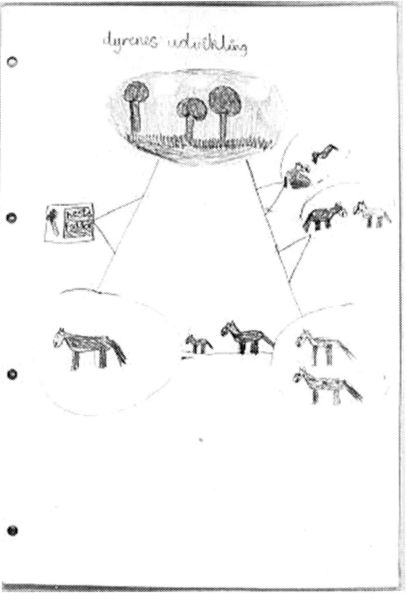

Figure 9.5  A child's model of how animals live together, from the 10th teaching period

## The Development of Children's Conceptions in Relation to the Evolution of Animals

The children in the teaching experiment were all interviewed at the start of grade 4[6] about their understanding of evolution, together with a parallel control class at the same school (Hedegaard, 1996). All children, both in the experimental and in the control class, had some knowledge of evolution. The difference was that children in the experimental class had some kind of explanation of evolution; this varied from a general explanation of evolution of animals through their offspring to a more specific explanation of evolutions exemplified by variation in and the adaption of offspring to change in habitat.[7] How a 10-year-old child may give a general explanation of evolution can be seen in Cecile's description.

> Cecile: (In a continuation of her reply to the question, whether animals we know today have already existed.) No. They certainly have not. They look completely different, e.g., a giraffe – I don't quite remember what it looked like, but it had a really peculiar look. I read about that in a book. They looked completely different. For instance, a sabre-tooth cat, and the leopard, a lot of other animals looked different.
>
> I: In your opinion, why did the animals change?
>
> Cecilie: Because so many years have passed. That is, if there isn't sufficient food in one place, they have to move on to another place with possibly another climate, and then they simply have to change. So, if they mate, their children may have changed slightly, and then the children grow up and mate, then their children will have changed, and so on.

Not all children in this first experiment came to formulate ideas of Step III on the topic of evolution, but they came to understand that there is a relation between species, population and nature (Hedegaard, 1996).

Children in the following three-year experimental double move approach to teaching were supported to continue to draw models (Hedegaard, 1995, 2002). In the second year, they made four posters for the goal-result board, based on the questions in Table 9.1. The posters were hung in the classroom, each with its specific model, respectively of evolution of animals, the origin of man, the formation of society and the historical change of societies. The

---

[6] Children in the one-year experimental teaching project and in the following three years project were interviewed.

[7] Both from the task-solving and the interviews, it can be concluded that all children reached Step II, which is not the case for any child in a control class who was not taught about adaptation and evolution.

children were very proud of these posters, so much so that when the Librarian asked if they would hang them in the School Library, they voted no, because other children would not take care of them and they were afraid their posters would be spoiled.

### Related Experimental Teaching Projects

In 1966, Bruner outlined the important design experiment *Man a course of study* (Bruner, 1966b, 1970) Hedegaard did not know about this teaching experiment when starting the double move projects, we have just described, but they are in several ways very close in both content and pedagogy. In Hedegaard's projects the content was designed to guide children's agentive exploration in their learning activity. Children's agentive exploration was also stressed in *Man a course of study*. The content of "The evolution of animals, the origin of Man, and the historical change of societies" are in line with those Bruner et al. chose as themes in their project. Their themes were structured around three questions "What is human about human beings? How did they get that way? How can they be made more so?" (Bruner, 1966b, p. 74). This project worked with five knowledge areas. These were the five great humanizing forces: "tool making, language and social organization, the management of man's prolonged childhood, and man's urge to explain the world" (p. 75).

However, the way the teaching material in Hedegaard's projects was organized went a step further than the material in *Man a course of study* by using germ-cell models and the goal-result research procedure. The models and procedure were used by the teacher to guide their planning and task design and by the students as they integrated the different concepts they came to understand through their exploration. The germ-cell models were never presented by the teacher. Rather, the students built them through teacher-guided tasks and discussions. In this way, they transformed and extended their concepts throughout the teaching period when new thematic areas were introduced.

Orientation to everyday meaningful activities was also evident in Lave's research criticizing math teaching in the US (Lave, 1988) leading to the introduction of apprenticeship learning (Lave & Wenger, 1992), though not in school contexts. Nonetheless, both the idea of meaningfulness in teaching and apprenticeship learning got footholds in later projects and theoretical discussions. Brown, Collins, Duguid and Newman were members of a research group that initiated an apprenticeship learning into debates about schooling, through their action research (Brown et al.,

1989a, b, Collins et al., 1989). Their teaching program built on the preconception that knowledge can be compared to a set of tools, and that practice in the intellectual use of tools promotes cognition. Academic disciplines, professional and manual trades were seen as communities of cultures, and to learn how to use tools as practitioners use them, a child in school, like an apprentice, must enter that community and its culture. This research group also stressed that learning in the school system must be located in situations that are meaningful to the children, through their working together with competent people. They define teaching as a process of enculturation, which must be supported through social interaction. Activities in school have to be authentic, meaning that they have to be oriented toward real problems and then approached through group problem-solving activities with the participants in different roles. The teacher is seen as a master who has the task of confronting the children – the apprentices – with effective strategies that can be used in practical ways.

Palinscar (1989) and Wineburg (1989) both made pertinent critiques of Brown et al.'s rather one-sided focus on everyday practice in apprenticeship teaching. They agreed that teaching should be meaningful for children, but at the same time pointed to the importance of integrating and generalizing the learned skills and knowledge into the more general goals of schooling. They argued that Brown and her research group neglected the societal perspective on school, which is about children learning subject matter content and so gaining qualifications. Wineburg (1989) also criticized the apprenticeship approach for ignoring the fact that teaching children in a classroom is different from teaching in the workplace.

Although apprenticeship as a model for learning in school can be criticized, it is important also to recognize that Brown et al. point to a crucial aspect of school pedagogy; namely, that children should be given opportunities to experience learning as a meaningful activity in relation to practices outside school. In the double move approach, the meaningful aspect connects to children's everyday knowledge and what is to be learnt may be seen as situated and anchored in the local community. The Hedegaard and Chaiklin Radical-Local initiative in East Harlem, New York City, which was introduced in Chapter 8, extended the Danish Double Move experiments (Hedegaard & Chaiklin, 2005). Working with children from Puerto Rican families they introduced a new theoretical dimension to Hedegaard's approach to helping children's learning. This was their focus on the relation between school and the local community and its culture and traditions.

Chaiklin has argued (e-mail, 2021) that "local themes" is a "tough" problem because it is too easy to approach "local" in terms of "immediately visible" (i.e., superficial). (See, e.g., how "multicultural" is often addressed through folk dances and food.) But "local" (for those who are planning teaching) must also be understood theoretically, which requires knowledge of societal conditions and societal practices. Paolo Freire's work (e.g., in *The Pedagogy of the Oppressed*) describes the efforts of the team of anthropologists and sociologists called "investigators" who investigated local life and introduced the idea of generative themes, which opened up exciting possibilities for further discussion and explorations.

None of this is a solution to or a definition of "local." Chaiklin continues, "I find that when I read what Freire was trying to do, it raises consideration of what one wants "local" to mean. In other words, do not assume that "local" is a well-defined box where one can go around collecting up some examples to drop into the box. Rather it is a theoretical challenge about understanding what content is significant in the lifeworld of pupils. From that point of view, Freire describes one way that they are approaching the problem (but remember they are working with the problem of trying to introduce literacy (reading and writing) to illiterate adults), which might give inspiration for thinking about how to approach the problem of local for children who are living in more or less functional families."

## Culturally Sensitive Teaching

The double move projects were background for Hedegaard and Chaiklin's (2005) Radical-Local approach in an after-school project with Puerto Rican children in New York City in 1989.[8] The aspect in the Radical-Local approach that extends the double move is the introduction of core models that include community practice. So, it is not only what matters for children here and now but a more encompassing approach where their community is included. Hedegaard and Chaiklin found that this became important for the children, engaging them in the project. They also found that including community could also overcome children's negative view of their minority status in relation to the majority culture.

Children from either refugee or immigrant or other kind of minority families may have to relate to different traditions and values in the country

---

[8] The project was connected to Puerto Rican Studies at Hunter College, City University of New York, and done in cooperation with Pedro Pedraza.

## Culturally Sensitive Teaching

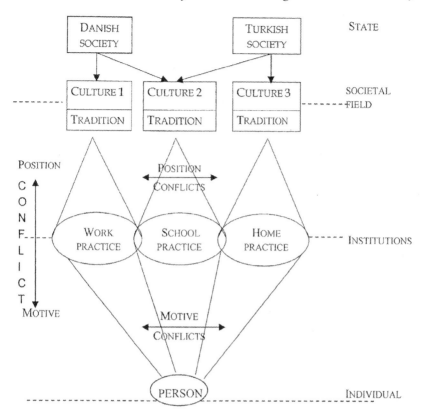

Figure 9.6 The double society model

they came from and the country they now live in, respectively, as can be seen in the model in Figure 9.6.

The model in Figure 9.6 shows that people moving to another country as either immigrants or refugees may, in their families, relate to the country they have left, with the traditions and values they learned there. They may also continue with the traditions in the new country in their home practices, and this may come to characterize the local community. Outside home and community, children meet institutional practices and values in school or after-school programs that are dominated by the receiving country. So, children entering school may have to orient to different values of how to act in everyday settings, they then have to orient to both values from home and school. This is also the case for children from local families when entering school, but school values usually more or less reflect their families' values. Children from immigrant families may come to experience conflicts, identity confusion and sometimes low self-evaluation (Hedegaard, 2003a). We return to this point in Chapter 10.

The Radical-Local after-school project was created because Puerto Rican children in New York did not manage school well.[9] Instead of becoming simply an after-school training activity to nurture literacy and math, the activities in the initiative were related to activities in the local community and to children's history as children of families coming from Puerto Rico. The objective of the Radical-Local formative teaching experiment had several levels. Because the after-school program was given a donation of computers, on a formal level the aim was to support children's acquisition of literacy skills facilitated by computer use. This aim became embedded in a social science teaching and learning project because the functioning aim was to create motivation and self-respect among the children as both children from Puerto Rican families and as Americans. This aim was realized by having students explore the positive aspects and potentials of their own community, by acquiring knowledge of their own history. These new understandings were used as foundations for learning to read and write using the computers. By learning to appreciate their family and community culture, while still functioning in a society with a different dominant culture, it may be easier for them to become motivated for learning. In an interview project with immigrant children from Turkish families, discussed in Chapter 10, the problem for many children throughout school was the split between how they should relate to their own families' values and those of school (Hedegaard, 2003a, 2005).

In the project with children from Puerto Rican communities, as in the Danish Double Move project, children started by identifying themselves as researchers. Hedegaard and Chaiklin wanted the students to understand that neither their own community nor the families in Puerto Rico always have looked the same. Rather, they have changed, and will continue to change in the future and these changes should be understood in relation to core aspects such as resources and living conditions as depicted in the relations in the core models (see Figure 9.7).

The teaching comprised three procedures related to the different themes arising in the teaching. The first procedure aimed at connecting what children already knew with the new tasks or problems and positioning them as active participants in the processes of the initiative. It involved recalling what was researched last time; identifying what had been learned

---

[9] The project ran two afternoons every week for a year. The children's age varied from 8 to 12 years.

# Culturally Sensitive Teaching

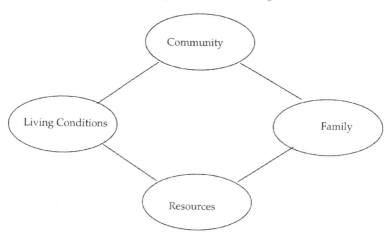

Figure 9.7 The core model that guides the teacher's activities and the students had to understand (From Hedegaard & Chaiklin, 2005)

and what is still not known; and reflection on what had been learnt and depicted in their drawings and modeling. This led to formulating the goal for the day; and deciding on the activities and tasks. This procedure took the form of a class discussion at the beginning of most sessions, creating an agenda of tasks for the day (see Table 9.2). The second procedure involved the teacher in giving tasks that involved the children in using computers. For example, they may prepare interview questions for interviewing an elderly citizen and later for writing the answers into the computer. They also might take an excursion to a museum or their local community with research tasks related to theme. The third procedure was again class discussion reflecting on the activities connected to identifying core relations between ideas that could be visualized and written into a goal-result board to extend already drawn models, using the computers. When possible, the computers were used by the children on these tasks either working as a pair or individually.

How children built knowledge using the third procedure is exemplified by how the core relations of family life and living conditions were connected and modeled by the children. This knowledge-building involved them in solving tasks related to how material conditions differed between Puerto Rico and New York City at the beginning of the twentieth century and contemporary New York City. How this started to become conceptualized by a child can be seen in Figure 9.8. The child's understandings

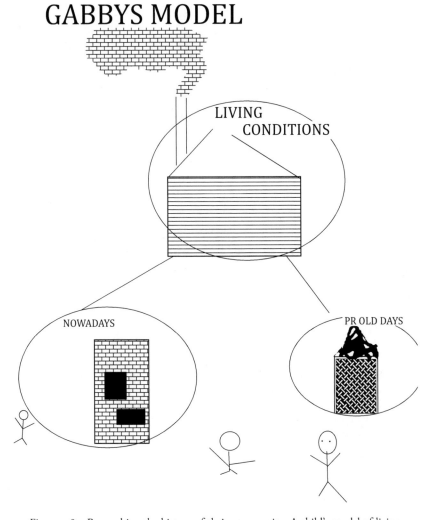

Figure 9.8  Researching the history of their community. A child's model of living conditions

grew through their research about the division of work in families as exemplified by living conditions in the historical periods. Through class discussion the children recognized that family life and living conditions were connected. This initial groundwork could then be further developed

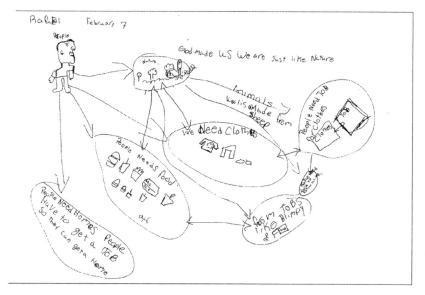

Figure 9.9  Model for what a family needs living in a community

into later models when they researched the history of their city (see Figure 9.9).

There are other experimental projects drawing on Vygotsky's theoretical legacy that are oriented to teaching cultural minority children. Tharp and Gallimore (1988) with their project *Rousing minds to life* have played central roles. The project started in Hawaii but has been developed elsewhere (Vogt et al., 1993; Tharp et al., 2000). These projects have aimed at enhancing children's literacy and have taken into consideration how traditions for ways of interaction and communicating support children's literacy learning. Another related focus is found in Moll's projects about *Funds of Knowledge.* Moll (Moll & Greenberg, 1990; Moll et al., 1992; Moll & Diaz, 1993) has pointed to the importance of drawing on minority communities' funds of knowledge to support children from minority families' learning in school. These funds of knowledge include both what families have brought with them from their cultures of origin and what has evolved through surviving in the new conditions. To draw on minority families' funds of knowledge in teaching may be seen as in line with Vygotsky theory of using children's everyday knowledge about their community to support their learning in reading and writing in school.

Hedegaard and Chaiklin had close contact with Moll during the 1989 period when the Radical-Local project was run in East Harlem and the Funds of Knowledge project was underway in Tucson, Arizona. Hedegaard visited Moll's project and followed class teaching, and Moll visited the research group in New York City, and all went together to a conference in Puerto Rico to present their work.

What was central in Moll et al.'s project was that it not only involved knowledge, but also invited family members into the projects, to support children's learning. Hedegaard used this idea later in her involvement of family members in a project for creating a school for young people from minority families from Middle Eastern countries in Denmark, who had a history of being expelled from public schools (Hedegaard, 2003; Hedegaard et al., 2004). Minority families who do not engage with schools may also inhibit their children's engagement (Hedegaard, 1999b; Kohl, 1991; Willis, 1977).

There are differences between the approach found in the Funds of Knowledge and that of the Radical-Local project, despite the shared focus on the local knowledge and the close contact between the projects. A crucial difference is the central role of theoretical knowledge in the Radical-Local project, using core models as guide for the teacher's activity and for the students' learning as this became expressed in students' discussions and drawings. They thereby qualified everyday knowledge, moving from the general to the concrete in understanding the conditions in their own community. These aspects were not a part of the Fund of Knowledge approach; there the local was used to exemplify the relevance of math and literacy, and not to move back to connect the concrete and the general. The Radical-Local initiative has subsequently been used as a process in history and literacy teaching/learning in Denmark (Hedegaard et al., 2004) in math teaching/learning in Ghana (Davis & Chaiklin, 2015) and in math teaching and learning in South Africa (Hardman & Teschmacher, 2019).

## Addressing Assessment Challenges through a Double Move Approach

National education policies reflect the cultural, political and economic development in a country. In Denmark, the school has for many years been based on traditional social democratic values of equality through education as well as educating for democracy. The Ministry of Education explicitly stresses values, like preparing students for future participation in a society with freedom and democracy. Also, the expectation is that schools should develop children's desire for learning and being sensitive to one's own and other cultures. These values were stressed in Hedegaard's Double Move teaching project in grades 3–5 in public school in Denmark. At the time that the project was run, the Danish Ministry of Education had announced the creation of the wholeness school (Undervisningsministeriet, 1998) with no exams before grade 8. Teachers had freedom to choose their curriculum and that made it easy to run the project in a public school. As there were no exams, the outcomes of the teaching were assessed through portfolios.

After 2000 curriculum goals became more central in education policy with clear goals in different subjects. Evaluation of courses and goals in Middle School became oriented toward standardized tests at a national level (inspired by international testing comparisons). To counter this tendency in primary schools, Hedegaard and Bang created another way to assess children, that was more in line with the Double Move project. This resulted in a questionnaire to evaluate children's well-being and learning. respectively, in grades 3 and 4 and in grades 5 and 6 through expression of desires and self-evaluations of competences (Hedegaard et al., 2007; Bang & Hedegaard, 2008).

Hedegaard and Bang wanted to find a way to assess children's social situations of development, where the child's perspective becomes more explicit and at the same time the subject goals are central. The intention was that the assessment could be used as a tool for dialogue between children, parents and teachers at the yearly teacher–parent meeting about the child's progress and well-being in school. They also wanted the tool to be used by professionals to explore and improve their local practice. This would be accomplished through using the assessment tool as the basis for a dialogue with students, to acquire mutual understanding and formulate mutual planning in situations of concern. To take forward these aims they constructed a questionnaire. The questionnaire needed to give children an opportunity to express themselves in relation to activities and social relations both in and outside school and reveal developmental possibilities.

A questionnaire that addresses the child's social situation of development, which captures the child's perspective on her participation in a practice, should reflect: (a) how an individual child participates in institutionally valued activities; (b) the relation between the child and other children; (c) the relations between the child and significant others (pedagogues, teachers, parents); and (d) how the child thinks and feels about her own participation. A questionnaire should reflect the national values, and

Table 9.3 *Example from the questionnaire of Mathematics in Grade 3 related to the Ministry of Education's Common Goals*

|  |  | Many ways of learning |  |  |
|---|---|---|---|---|
|  |  | Mostly in class | Mostly at home | Mostly at afterschool care or other places |
|  | Ministry of Education's Common Goals. |  |  |  |
| *How an individual child participates in institutional valued activities* | Do you play games where you count and add up? |  |  |  |
|  | Do you sometimes measure something and work out its size? |  |  |  |

|  |  | Desire to learn |  |  |
|---|---|---|---|---|
|  |  | Often | In between | Seldom |
| *How an individual child participates in institutional valued activities* | Do you enjoy doing math? |  |  |  |
|  | Do you enjoy doing math homework? |  |  |  |

|  |  | Learning together with others |  |  |
|---|---|---|---|---|
|  |  | Often | Sometimes | Seldom |
| *The relation between the child and other children* | I like to do math projects with others. |  |  |  |
|  | I like to sit by myself when I do math. |  |  |  |

|  |  | Learning together with others |  |  |
|---|---|---|---|---|
|  |  | Often | Sometimes | Seldom |
| *How the child thinks and feels about their own participation* | When the teacher asks a question in a math lesson, do you give your opinion? |  |  |  |
| *The relation between the child and significant others* | When you have math lessons, do you feel sad? |  |  |  |

*Source*: From Bang and Hedegaard (2008).
The right hand columns show the researcher's theoretical consideration.

the curriculum outlines for specific subject areas when oriented to the child's social situation and concerns in school. Hedegaard and Bang focused on subjects of Danish language and math. In 2007, when the questionnaire was constructed the Danish Ministry of Education had created a guide called 'Common Goals' for all subject areas and each teacher was expected to teach with reference to these national goals. The goals in the guide emphasized the value of viewing learning and personal development as an integrated and inseparable unit. Those values were specified in three integrated domains:

- Many ways of learning
- Desire to learn
- Learning together with others

Using a questionnaire for accessing children's participation in math activities or other subject matter activities may give information about what children engage in and outside school; how they relate to other students; and engage with school in general. It can be a tool that teachers use to help them to include children in classroom life. It should not be seen as a summative evaluation tool but as formative tool to guide teachers to find ways to support children's motive development and help them to see the relevance of what is being taught to their everyday activities. The questionnaire was designed in relation to literacy and math in the Danish school system and cannot be copied directly to other school systems. But it may inspire others to find questions relevant to everyday activities in other countries. In 2015, it was revised to reflect how teaching in these subjects changed over the years in Denmark.

## Final Reflections

> Not all learning is developmental. But sometimes, through educational activities, persons acquire particular intellectual functions (e.g., thinking with theoretical concepts) or conceptual models (e.g., learning about ecosystems), which engender qualitative changes in a person's relation to their social environment, and would be considered development in this theoretical perspective. (Chaiklin, 2022 in press)

Developmental teaching has a long history starting with Vygotsky's ideas of teaching reaching into the zone of proximal development, an accomplishment that is only possible with the help of qualified teachers. Developmental teaching is oriented to (a) children's acquisition of competence and their formation as people able to undertake theoretical thinking and (b) motive orientation. Central ideas in developmental teaching were that general knowledge in the form of core relations should be taught before specific and concrete knowledge, and that children through agentic but also teacher-guided exploration should be able to recognize and work with these conceptual relations. These ideas have been extended with ideas of the double move in teaching and learning that Hedegaard developed and took forward in projects focusing on the subjects of biology, human geography and history. This approach is a relational approach in which children's everyday concepts and motive orientation are stressed as a point of departure for teaching and for children's learning. In this approach, teaching always needs to start with teachers reaching out to understand children's everyday concepts and motive orientation, creating common knowledge orienting children to subject matter concepts and at the same time being aware that subject matter concepts have to transcend and qualify children's everyday concepts. This qualifying should lead to children acquiring competence to use their concepts as tools to ascend to the concrete, to better understand their everyday life activities and events.

The concepts children meet in school may take different forms depending on the logic that dominates the subject area; here we distinguished between empirical knowledge, narrative knowledge and theoretical knowledge[10] In this chapter, we have argued that theoretical knowledge should dominate teaching in school, to support children's acquisition of the subject matter knowledge that may qualify their personal experiences and knowledge. The aim is that they become able to use their conceptual knowledge as tools in their understanding and acting in everyday activities. The foundational subjects in school we see as literacy and math. These become tools for the acquisition of other forms of subject knowledge, theoretical knowledge both as content and methods are important when children have to learn and acquire these tools. Both empirical and narrative knowledge should be seen as support systems in this process. This was illustrated with children in Aidarova's research (1982) on teaching the concept of communication as the core in children's literacy learning. In Hedegaard's example of teaching biology that is presented in this chapter, we showed that both narrative and empirical knowledge are needed to

---

[10] Other forms of knowledge may also be found in a society, such as theological knowledge and mythical knowledge.

recognize the theoretical core relations in evolution, so that these relations too become tools for children's further analyses. In this process, teaching is a double move from the abstract to the concrete and from the concrete to the abstract, working with oppositions, using children's everyday knowledge and questions to create their activities and motivation for exploration.

When children become oriented to core knowledge within in a subject area, their knowledge of the relations can support the development of their theoretical thinking as a higher psychic function. This development is evident when children are able to move between imagination related to everyday activities and general understandings in a subject area.

In 1989, when Hedegaard, together with Chaiklin, engaged in the Radical-Local initiative, the double move in teaching and learning was combined with the ideas of including students' community in developmental teaching and learning. The importance of relating to children's community becomes particularly striking when teaching has to include students from minority families. In Chapter 10, we examine cultural identity and the importance of teachers working relationally with children to ensure their inclusion in what schools can offer.

CHAPTER 10

# *Adolescence and Transitions into Early Adulthood*

## Introduction

All too often, discussions of adolescence focus on problem behavior such as drug-taking, gang membership, or early-age drinking. Yet much of this kind of activity is simply experimentation, which is not always as dangerous as it appears to be, and most adolescents become good and productive citizens. Steinberg and Morris, in their 2001 review of research on adolescent development, suggested that because of the focus on deviance there is a gap in our understandings of what might be called normal development in adolescence. The gap, they argued, was because the available analyses of adolescent development offered by Erikson, Freud and Piaget had declined in influence and nothing had yet taken their place.

For us, the omission of Vygotsky's work on adolescence as a viable approach to understanding adolescent development is an oversight that we attempt to address in the early parts of this chapter. Though, our cultural-historical approach means that we offer ways of understanding relationships between the developing young person and the societal conditions they inhabit, rather than a blueprint for normal development. In the later sections we focus on how young people can be helped as learners during the high school period and their transitions to work. There we make connections with the pedagogical perspectives outlined in Chapter 7.

Adolescence is a period of turbulence in which young people try to find their own ways forward, searching for meaning in the transitions they experience. Their imaginations of possible futures give shape to their decisions and actions and are imbued with emotions as they picture possible future identities. The adults who are important to them can help by trying to understand their dreams of their futures and support their activities in their social situations of development as they move toward adulthood.

The relationship between intellect and emotion in children and young people's development is complex, containing within it the contradictions that allow for change and growth. Vygotsky used the term *Perezhivanie* to capture its complexity. Often translated as experience, the term is intended to embrace a unity of social conditions, the developing person, together with intellectual development and emotion. We use the term emotional experience to reflect these elements and processes.

## Understanding Adolescent Development

Vygotsky saw adolescence as a cultural construction and a phase not to be found in all cultures (Vygotsky, 2021); consequently, different cultures offer different affordances. Pedersen's study of the lives of six Danish young people in their daily activities after they made the transition into four different high schools reveals the diversity of pathways to early adulthood, even within one national culture (Pedersen, 2022). Her work reveals how the ecological or cultural settings of each high school offered different opportunities for development. Her analysis shows the interdependence of the young peoples' emotional experiences and their environments as they worked on their identities within what Pedersen termed eco-niches. For Pedersen an eco-niche comprises "collective processes of production and reproduction of meaning to which a person actively contributes" (p. 51). This meaning relates to both the individual and to collective meaning-making over time.

Pedersen's study also nicely shows how adolescent identity is always in the making. Lisa, one of the participants in the study, carried with her a vest that had the following inscribed on its back: "Under construction – beware of danger," when asked what it meant she said: "[T]hat is just how we are – under construction" (Pedersen, 2022, p. 1). Here is sixteen-year-old Lisa being interviewed by Pedersen. Lisa attends Southside High, a private school located in Copenhagen in an area historically known as the cradle of autonomous and radical groups.

> Lisa: All of my childhood, I was like: 'Okay, I'm here, and I'm a human being.
>
> And I am me', right. And I didn't really feel the need to have more answers than that, you know. But then when you become more aware – and I think you do in your teenage-years – then something happens where you start to question: 'Who am I? Who is the'me'? what exactly is this me-

thing really?' [...] In a way, I think people really want to be put in boxes all the time, right. It is a human need. One hundred percent. And for me, I really needed to know how and who I was.

Me: But how do you know, when you've found out?

Lisa: I don't know... and I actually don't think one ever finds out. (Pedersen, 2022, p. 223)

Pedersen's work is interesting because it brings attention to material and social values within eco-niches into her conversation with the cultural-historical approach we are taking. Pedersen shows how the ecological settings in the four high schools revealed considerable variability in materiality and ideology in the lives of young people and how this interacted with their emotional experiences and confusions about who they were. The concept of eco-niche helps us recognize the variations in the pathways created by young people. Pedersen particularly refers to Hedegaard in her discussions and we see how the line she is taking nicely nuances differences in different life pathways.

Adolescence is a period of heightened experiences of change, not least because of physical and sexual maturation but also because of societal expectations of personal responsibility. These changes sit alongside the young person's future-making efforts. Their social situations of development and relations to the world therefore undergo continuous changes as they meet and make new demands in their environments. Vygotsky described the nature of these shifts as follows. "In the structure of the personality of the adolescent there is nothing stable, final and immovable. Everything is in *transition, everything is flux*" (Vygotsky, 1998, p. 184 italics in the original translation). Yet he does help us find a way through this potential turmoil, by recognizing how conceptual thinking is a key marker of adolescent development. This is not simply the formal logic that Piaget centered on. Rather, it is a way of thinking that accommodates judgment, values, emotion and a form of imagination that is shaped by the adolescents' capacity for abstract thought, the future-oriented "what ifs" that have galvanized the recent political activities of teenagers from Sweden to Chile. These and other adolescent activities are often collective, with social relationships giving adolescents a sense of belonging and reassuring feedback in a time of flux, while identities are tried out and shaped.

Vygotsky was clear that becoming an adolescent and developing toward adulthood during adolescence was not a matter of simply building on previous developmental states. Instead, the dynamics of the development of higher psychic functions, which we have outlined in previous chapters, continue to shape adolescent development. He argued that toward the end of formal schooling a new wave in the development of concept formation emerges. This development is marked by their organizing concepts into systems related to practice (Vygotsky, 2021). We note that Vygotsky was writing in the context of Russia in the early decades of the twentieth century. We therefore observe that Davydov's later work with the conceptual germ cell to be found in subject matter knowledge (e.g., Davydov, 1990), and discussed in Chapter 9, shows that this organizing can and should start earlier. But much of course depends on whether teaching aims at such development.

Importantly, Vygotsky identified a lengthy transitional period within adolescence where neoformations emerge. In this transitional period, the personality, in the sense of a partially defined structure of consciousness, arises through the relation between reality and the developing self. This transitional period of adolescence can last several years. The early part of this period is marked by a dual developmental process. Vygotsky observed a critically negative phase and a general transitional phase running in parallel in the first part of the transitional period, which may last a year or more. This period will be all too familiar with those who work with teenagers. He characterized the two processes as follows:

> as crises of a transitional age in two senses: first of all, the critical phase which distinguishes the transitional age from school age, and, secondly, the whole of the transitional age in the sense of its relation to the state of [the age of] maturity, a transition to what should be regarded as a certain parallel age, during which the child goes through a mutable age. (Vygotsky, 2021, p. 293)

It may be of some comfort to practitioners working with adolescents that Vygotsky saw the critical phase as particularly important for adolescents' concept formation. The process arises from the adolescents' contrasting emotional experiences that imply a kind of dissociation of consciousness. Vygotsky explained: "I have in mind unceasing indications of a 'schizothymic' character in the adolescent, the similarities between the schizoid temperament and the temperament of the adolescent, etc." (Vygotsky, 2021, p. 301).

The presence of negative symptoms indicates the emergence of a series of differentiated emotional experiences, relatively separated from each other, which have not yet been brought into a new unity. He explained: "Consequently, in my opinion, the link between dissociation and the function of concept formation which has been experimentally confirmed constitutes, to my eyes, one of the most compelling indications or arguments in favour of the schism, or dissociation as the central neoformation of this phase" (Vygotsky, 2021, p. 312). This dissociation may lead the young person to an understanding of the oppositions and connections that are the core in dialectical thinking. Over time, these contrasting emotions may become transformed into a unity at a new level of complexity, that is, dialectical conceptual thinking.

Because of how social conditions and emotional histories are reflected in what concepts are developed and how they are used, there is considerable variation in capacities for conceptual thinking within adolescent age cohorts. Here we emphasize that emotion is a key element in that variation. One UK study of students' conceptual thinking in science found that the concepts in high school science curricula were not being grasped by a significant proportion of students, a problem they argued that was hidden by emphases on rote learning. That finding led to a program designed to accelerate "cognitive thinking" (Shayer & Adey, 1993), which reported some mixed success. When reviewing the program, Leo and Galloway (1996) found that that student motivation distinguished between those who benefitted from the program and those who didn't.

Conceptual thinking, in science and elsewhere, is vital because it allows close analyses of current realities. Vygotsky explained that being able to use concepts helps adolescents to understand their worlds, to see connections they had not previously recognized, to be able to grapple with complexities, to make judgments. These capabilities also allow them to look beyond their immediate surroundings and become actively responsible citizens. Conceptual thinking therefore needs nurturing in environments that present meaningful challenges, offer the resources that can help young people tackle them and recognize the role of emotion in conceptual development.

## Identity Construction in Adolescence

Throughout this book, we are arguing for analyses that capture the interweaving of person and practice and the importance of emotion to what children orient their actions toward and how and why they take actions. We continue to do so, while noting that when studying or supporting adolescents, their interpretations of others' expectations of them together with their future imaginings, add new dimensions to the challenge of taking the child's perspective.

## Identity Construction in Adolescence

Pedersen's (2022) analyses of six 16-year-old students' everyday lives give an account of the importance of social relationships, within the material conditions of local communities, to the future-making of adolescents. These material and social conditions combined to form eco-niches that reflected school priorities, such as academic achievement and competition, but also included out-of-school activities with their peers, such as partying and beer-drinking. The students entered these niches with their own histories, motive orientations and imagined futures. There was also noticeable variation in material and social opportunities and expectations embedded in the new-to-them practices of high school. These expectations varied across schools and peer groups, setting standards for behavior, and shaping the different eco-niches.

> Here is Lisa again talking with Pedersen about the expectations of her city-centre school and peer group.
>
> Lisa: There is so much to live up to. Also, for instance some of the things that we have an active stance on here at Southside High, like grades etc. I mean, this is a pressure that one has to live up to at many other places, and we also have that going here (at Southside High). And even though we don't get many grades, we still get some and we also receive written feedback, and either you get a good or a bad feedback, right.
>
> Me: So, what you're saying is that there is still a lot of comparisons. . .? And perhaps there is something about being governed without being aware of it
>
> Lisa: Very much so! The worst part is actually when being aware of being governed but still doing it (conducting one's everyday life accordingly).
>
> Me: Yeah, can you elaborate on that?
>
> Lisa: Sure! I mean, we're fucking controlled by beauty ideals, food ideals and all sorts of measurements, like BMI etc., telling you how to be or how to look. (Pedersen, 2022, p. 82)

El'konin (1972/1999) has described how adolescent friendships and the mutual judging that goes on within them is a key element in adolescent development. He argued that the intimate friendships expand young people's understandings of life and possible futures. While in judging others, they also make judgments about themselves, thus increasing their self-consciousness (Zanelato & Urt, 2021).

Eco-niches in Petersen's study were in part discursively constructed by school staff and students in relation to schoolwork and between peers outside school. Participants in other schools, in the suburbs or in rural areas, were governed by different sets of expectations, all influencing their future-making. In each case, the adolescent's agency could be seen as they negotiated their ways forward, but Pedersen reminds us that the affordances of the material and social conditions in the practices they inhabited were also key.

The students' reflections on different institutional and societal demands relate to Hedegaard's Wholeness Approach as well as to Pedersen's work on eco-niches. Both forms of analyses employ the concept of activity settings as a central tool for analysing concrete social situations of development. Hedegaard's analyses offer the concepts of demands and dynamics from society, institution and activity settings (see Table 2.1), while Pedersen's analyses, in a complementary way, focus on the affordances of the material and social aspects of community life including friendship groups.

Another Nordic study tracked children and young people to investigate the transitions in their lives and their emergent identities. The *Learning Lives* study was based in one suburb in Oslo and involved observing and interviewing 5–6-year-olds, 15–16-year-olds and 18–19-year-olds (Erstad et al., 2016). One of their aims was to capture how participants' agency enabled them to mobilize the resources available to them within different cultural settings and learn. When working with the 15–16-year-olds, the team examined the young people's intellectual development and emotional experiences together with their efforts at constructing their future selves. Erstad and Silseth (2019) explained the process of making a future as "primarily a narrative process of justifying, rationalizing, and selecting evidence to support an emerging story about the self" (p. 311). These young people took control of their learning pathways over time, and their motives in relation to their identity formation were central to those pathways.

Erstad and Silseth discussed the example of Ugur, who was of Turkish origin, comparing his disengagement with math at lower secondary school, with his engagement with the subject at a cultural center in the local community, where he worked with college students on math and robotics. The meaningfulness of these activities for Ugur was more than successful problem-solving, he explained: "It is nice when people applaud your work. You get attention, you get respect ... I became very happy. You know? People begin to say hello to you. You get new friends. This does something with your self-esteem, you know?" (Erstad & Silseth, 2019, p. 318) When he moved on to upper secondary school, he brought the knowledge gained at the cultural center into play with considerable success. Recognizing the emotional experiences of young people as learners engaged in identity creation is a key to motivating students.

Ugur also planned to move back to Turkey as an adult and start a business there; this too informed his motivation as a student. We have highlighted the role of imagination and its relationship with thinking with younger children in previous chapters. In adolescence, imagination plays another important role, allowing the young person to consider possible futures and their identities within them. Vygotsky described this process as fantasizing "building castles in the air" (Vygotsky, 1998, p. 158) and explained that for the adolescent, it takes the place of the play that absorbs younger children. As the adolescent develops, their imagining becomes increasingly abstract, less connected with material objects in the present and can be highly creative. Vygotsky observed that in fantasy, "the adolescent gropes for the first time for his life plan" (1998, p. 165).

A growing capacity for conceptual thinking is central to this kind of development. It frees adolescents from the concrete and the here and now and allows them to imagine other possibilities in what Vygotsky saw as their secret fantasies. Vygotsky described the relationship between fantasy and emotion as "extremely significant" (Vygotsky, 1998, p. 164), as fantasy allows young people to create, explore and find ways of controlling their emotional lives. This is because fantasies give them the opportunity to experience their feelings and impetuosity, without acting out in the real world. Here we can also see the development of an increasingly reflective self, the emergence of the self-conscious teenager, often an uncomfortable phase. Nonetheless, it is an important element in the search for identity, which can be reflected in the kinds of experimentation we mentioned earlier and also in the accounts of young people like Ugur.

Another case example offered by Erstad and Silseth (2019) similarly reveals how future-making connects with motivation to learn. Lien was born in Norway of Vietnamese parents and was tracked from lower secondary school into upper secondary school. She described herself as "not caring much about what happens around me" (p. 316) and had instead become engrossed by Korean culture as a result of watching Korean popular entertainment online. That fascination meant that when in upper high school she chose to study the Korean language, even though that meant a long journey to the only school in Oslo that offered it. At the time of the interview, only ten students from the original 30 remained in this challenging course and Lien reflected on what that said about her ability: "[M]aybe I am clever if I take Korean and all that" (Erstad & Silseth, 2019, p. 317).

The examples of both Ugur and Lien reveal how they were taking control over their own pathways as they moved toward adulthood, drawing on the resources offered in their wider communities and various media. These resources were employed as they oriented toward what was meaningful for them in their identity construction. In brief, their motives were oriented toward those aspects of activities that they saw as relevant for their emergent identities and future-making.

## Cultural Practices and Identity

Cultural identity has become a widely discussed concept within the social sciences (Friedman, 1996; Giddens, 1991; Holland & Lave, 2001; Holland et al., 2001). Identity is now seen as a cultural self-conception created by people through their activities. Hedegaard (1999b, 2003a, b, 2005) has, in her studies of children from immigrant families, examined cultural identity and its connection to traditions and values in different practices. Her premise was that when families move to live in another country, the country of origin remains an influence on their values as an imagined community (Anderson, 1991). How this may influence their practices is depicted in Figure 9.6.

These families bring with them their valued traditions and may form cultural enclaves that sustain them in their new country. But they also face demands from the institutions, such as school or work, that comprise the receiving country and which have been constructed through different values and traditions.

Hedegaard's study (2003, 2005) of 20 children from immigrant Turkish families reveals how different cultural environments offered by home and school were experienced by young people and how they found ways of combining these values and traditions. The young people were interviewed immediately after leaving 10th grade to gather their impressions of their experiences throughout their school lives from class zero onward. The analyses showed that these young people wanted to acquire the competences necessary to get on in the Danish educational system. They expressed disappointment when they felt that the school had not demanded enough of them intellectually and had restricted the acquisition of competences that would allow them to flourish educationally. Several also explained how they made efforts to overcome difficulties to get the qualifications they needed.

They also described the challenges for them in being in the Danish school system while relating to their Turkish family and community traditions. For some it had been directly conflictual, and they explained how they had developed strategies for handling these conflicts. These strategies differed depending on the kind of conflicts they experienced between school and home. Importantly, while at school they became aware of their cultural background and whether they could move easily between the two cultures, with a double cultural identity, depended a great deal on their peer relations.

Three types of conflict were apparent, and they led to three different types of strategy. These were conflicts between: (i) a *student's motives*; (ii) *value positions in home and school*; and (ii) *parents' value positions and the student's motives*.

*Conflicts between students' motives* led to strategy of active pattern breaking. This conflict arose when students were torn between defending themselves while being put down by their teachers or classmates, and their motive to progress through the education system. Hedegaard found that these types of conflicts may lead some students to explode in the form of fights and anger. Alper's story illustrates this angry reaction and how he overcame this by breaking his pattern of angry explosions.

> Interviewer: How did you get along with your schoolmates in 9th grade?
>
> Alper: Well, you see, my schoolmates were okay; actually, I don't know, I have no comparison because this is the only class I know ... but, you see, I think it was okay – no big fights or anything like that. So, I was content because in 7th grade my teacher told me that – you know. At that time I got into fights with the older pupils – and then my teacher told me that if I managed to finish 7th grade without fighting, I would do fine. Or, that is, later I learned that if I had continued to fight they would have expelled me from school.
>
> I: Your teacher told you that?
>
> A: Yes, my physics teacher told me so.
>
> I: I see. They would expel you from school?
>
> A: Well, it wasn't really a warning. She just told me to watch my step, you see, because they might expel me because of it. And then ... well, I promised myself not to fight anymore. And for the last couple of years I haven't heard anything. That is, they haven't told me anything like that.
>
> I: So, you haven't started a fight since 7th grade?
>
> A: Practically no [*chuckles*] – well, perhaps I have once in a while! But not like when I was younger and did it a lot. I would beat them and kick them ... So, in 8th and 9th grade it was more like discussing matters, that is, I would say something, answer back. Well, if they said anything – I didn't go for it. But one has to defend oneself; one has to, right?
>
> I: After 7th grade you would defend yourself by means of words, right?

A: Yes, instead of fighting ...

I: All right. Ahem, did anything upset you in 9th grade?

A: No, not in 9th grade. That was earlier, particularly in 7th grade.

I: In 7th grade?

A: Yes, in 7th grade – I remember that – I believe it was in 8th grade – I was sitting in class and had just come down from the school kitchen – I was crying because, you see, when you start to, it's ... I couldn't bring myself to beat and kick.

Alper explained that he owed it to his parents to graduate and that their attitude toward his future had helped him to overcome the very troubling grade 7 period of being teased by schoolmates. In grade 8, all students had to undergo formal assessments. Yet in grade 8, although other children again gave him a hard time, he didn't retaliate; instead he made even greater efforts to gain high marks, and succeeded in moving to a competitive-entry upper secondary school. Breaking the pattern of angry reaction to teasing required great effort.

*Conflicts between value positions at home and at school* were resolved by some students with a strategy of alternating between being Danish and Turkish. This strategy was used if the children were not expected to bring the value positions of their parents to school, or if they were not expected to bring the school's values into their life at home.

*Conflicts between parents' positions and the student's motives* led to a strategy of silence and withdrawal. Here there are also differences between home and school value positions; however, there is no mutual tolerance for the two sets of values, respectively, in school and at home. The young person has to act on and defend the demands of their parents in school, whether they want to or not. This led to a strategy of becoming quiet and withdrawn, a strategy followed by Halime.

Halime described how she had to relay to the school her parents' opinions about what girls can and cannot do. She was caught between respecting her parents' positions and meeting demands from her teachers and schoolmates, demands that reflected her own wishes. But because she could not follow these motives, her feeling of who she was and her general attitude to others were influenced. In hindsight, she regretted that the pressure of these conflicting demands had made her withdrawn at school. Her case does raise questions for school inclusion, as the social conditions for participating in school practice left her with little opportunity for action and for expressing her own value positions.

Hedegaard's study has shown the challenging strategies employed by children who find themselves needing to inhabit very different practices at home and school. It also points to how the demands made by both families and schools can ease the constructions of dual identities and reveals the importance of good peer group relations for these adolescents. These cultural differences between home and school are not limited to children of minority ethnic backgrounds. As we shall see, gender and class can also play a part.

## Working Relationally for Adolescent Future-Making

For some young people, their experiences of resources and social practices have created identities marked by disengagement from what society offers. Their futures are of social exclusion and all the difficulties that go with it. This problem has been tackled by Vadeboncoeur and her colleagues. with their idea of moral imaginings (Vadeboncoeur & Vellos, 2016; Vadeboncoeur et al., 2021). Much of their research on this topic was carried out in alternative school provision in Australia and Canada where they observed how practitioners helped young people who had been excluded from mainstream schools to reshape their life pathways after experiences of schooling where they had been labeled in stereotypical ways based often on race, gender and social class. The students therefore entered the alternative provision with a sense of injustice or of low self-worth.

The responses from practitioners that made a difference for the young people were based in moral imaginings and have much in common with the relational pedagogy we discussed in Chapter 7. Vadeboncoeur et al. (2021) describe moral imagining as "a quality of student–teacher relationships that enabled participants to create new social futures as a function of their relatedness" (p. 4). They outline a three-stage process that is based on the premise of what they called "accept and build." The first step is an acceptance of *what is*, what the young person presents as their own narrative with all their felt inequities. This ensures that she or he is no longer invisible behind some category label and, reflecting the title of this book, is taken seriously. The next step is exploration of *what if and what could be* alongside practitioners, where the usual relational distance found between teacher and student is absent. Instead, young people work with practitioners towards the third stage where *what should be* is decided upon and the young person and practitioner jointly build possible futures for the young person, including identifying communities they could connect with and become part of.

Vadeboncoeur et al. (2021) summarize the processes in these stages in ways that reflect our relational emphasis on building common knowledge, knowledge of what matters to each other, their motive orientations, as a resource to mediate the unfolding of relational agency as practitioners and children work together on a problem. In this case the problem space, what is being worked on, is a young person's future-making.

> Given the range of experiences that students have prior to arriving at alternative programs – including experiences disproportionately marked by racism and social inequities both in and out of schools, as well as the process of school exclusion itself – inquiring into how re-engaging is mediated may help to make visible both what matters to students and teachers in relationships and the potential of relationships to overcome relational distance created and perpetuated by social inequities, including those institutionalized in school systems. (p. 10)

We suggest that moral imagining as described by Vadeboncoeur et al. has much to offer mainstream schooling as the following analysis starkly reveals. Research by Callanan et al. (2009) on the disengagement of young people from education in England found four types of engaged or disengaged pupils in their Year 9 (age 14) sample.

- 'Engaged' young people who represented 40 percent
- 'Engaged with school not higher education' who represented 25 percent
- 'Disengaged from school not education' who represented 23 percent
- 'Disengaged' who represented 12 percent

The last two groups totaled around one-third of the age cohort. Students who were disengaged from school not education were generally negative toward school, they faced challenges with school discipline and were likely to play truant. They were less likely to have positive relationships with their teachers and more likely to misbehave and report problems with the school rules. Disengaged students did not want to continue with education; they displayed poor behavior at school and were very likely to play truant. Their attitude toward school was particularly negative and one-third reported that relationships with teachers had broken down. They were likely to have limited sense of control over their future, preferring not to think about it, but rather wait and see.

The importance of relationships with adults as part of future-making was also evident in a study undertaken by Honess and Edwards in the UK in the 1980s. It examined the identities over time among young people in South Wales who were leaving school with little or no formal qualifications, at a period when youth unemployment in these previously industrial areas was high. They were interviewed in their last year at school and in their first year at work or unemployment (Honess, 1989; Honess & Edwards, 1986, 1990).

One analysis centered on situations where the young people felt that their agency could either unfold or was restricted or even absent (Honess & Edwards, 1986, 1990). In every case, being with their friends was conducive to the unfolding of their agency; but there was much more variability when at school or with their parents. In both of those situations, adults could be the problem in different ways. Some of the young people discussed the frustrations of adults having too much control over them and inhibiting their actions. When discussing examples of this phenomenon, they often named a teacher or their father. But an equally debilitating problem in their relationships with adults was an adult's lack of interest in them and therefore no meaningful connection with them, again a teacher or their father were most often named. What they needed in order for their agency to unfold was a relationship where they were recognized and taken seriously as actors, something that some teachers and parents were able to do. For example, teachers in practical workshop activities were often named as good to be with, as they worked alongside the students in lessons. Today we would refer to this kind of teacher–student relationship as enabling the unfolding of relational agency in ways that ultimately enhanced the agency of learners. Honess and Edwards observed, for example, that those young people who enjoyed these relationships presented a stronger sense of who they were and where they were going.

The Honess and Edwards study also revealed the importance of parents to adolescents in other ways. Adolescence is marked by changes in young people's relationships with their parents, but that does not mean that parents do not have roles to play in supporting them as they move through school and on to work or higher education. The research team found that parents were particularly important in helping the young people find work or make choices about what work they could do (Honess & Edwards, 1986), so much so that Edwards fed back to the schools where the young people had been students that working with parents as students approached school-leaving age would be a useful thing to do. A study some 30 years later in England offered more detail on how important parents were when their children were making their life choices, such as what public exams to enter.

The study (Alexander et al., 2014) examined how Year 9 students who were not entirely certain about whether to progress to higher education imagined their futures. These students were seen by their schools as capable of entering university but were unsure about whether it was the right pathway for them. The study aimed at providing information for university outreach systems to help them attract a socially broader range of students. These were the 25 percent of students identified by Callanan et al. (2009) as engaged with school, but not higher education.

UK government policy at the time focused on what they called poverty of aspiration among such students. The research team found no poverty of aspiration; neither did it find unrealistic imagined futures that centered on celebrity culture. The young people had clear ideas about where they might be heading and that university might be a possible step, but most had no idea about how to get there, the means to realize their ambitions. As part of the study, the research team explored their life trajectories: past, present and imagined future. It, unsurprisingly, became clear that the young people were navigating the parallel practices of family, school and friends and that for the most part, schools had assumed that families would be where discussions of higher education occurred. But that was rarely discussed there and when it was, it was often in terms of the negative experiences of other family members.

The research team argued that schools should take the long view and build, over time, common knowledge with parents and young people about possible futures, with the aim of demystifying pathways to alternative futures. These pathways are waymarked by key choices and activities, which young people need help in orienting their motivation toward. Back in 1970, Bernstein wrote of how education cannot compensate for society. Here we suggest that, nonetheless, more can be done so that schools and families build common knowledge to understand each other better when children are approaching significant transitions.

### Engaging Adolescents with Curricula

It is a given that schools for adolescents are required to guide students toward successful engagement with standardized curricula, where success is gauged by examination performance. If the knowledge embedded in curricula is to stick, however, it needs to be meaningful for students. We know from the Callanan et al. (2009) study that student disengagement with school and its purposes is a problem; while the Alexander et al. (2014) report found that a liking for a curriculum subject was barely mentioned by young people when discussing their life choices. This problem has been examined by Shires who worked with expert secondary school teachers in a curriculum development project.

Shires' project was informed by the double move in teaching explained by Hedegaard (2002) as a move between students' everyday concepts together with their motive orientation to the subject matter and the aim of the teaching episode, moving back again to qualify and shape students' understandings and engagement with the subject (see Chapter 9). Shires and the teachers focused on forms of task design that engaged students with subject knowledge and drew on the Teaching and Learning Sequence presented in Chapter 7, and shown in Figure 7.1 (Edwards, 2014).

Unsurprisingly, Shires found that "[d]uring the project, the relevance of a cultural-historical analysis and its focus on meaning-making grew in significance as it became clear that one of the teachers' drivers was not activity *per se*, but how [student] meaning was developed through activity" (Shires & Hunter, 2020, p. 3). The teachers' aim was that students would become agentic in the subject area, able to make informed decisions in relation to the subject. The teachers shared the values that motivated them and their love of the subject with students and saw their role as relational, enacting knowledge in their interactions with the students. They planned lessons for student understanding rather than recall, where understanding was described as an internalizing of the subject matter in ways that informed students' identities, for example, as emergent historians, that would impact on the adults they might become.

Edwards has also worked alongside several group action research projects with English secondary school teachers, which have also captured key aspects of meaningful engagement with the subject matter knowledge carried in curricula. The projects also used the Teaching and Learning Sequence (Figure 7.1), where the aim was for the students to be able to use the concepts introduced in the curriculum in ways that were meaningful for them as they worked on real-world open-ended tasks in quadrant 3 of the sequence. We share just two examples to reveal the slightly different emphases that were possible within this framing, with one focusing overtly on using concepts in problem-solving and the other emphasizing the affective aspects of facing such challenges as learners. They are also both outlined in Edwards (2014).

In the first example, John[1] and Joe, teachers of religious studies, observed that although their Year 9 students were successful in examinations, they lacked a deep understanding of the crucial concepts in the

---

[1] Not their correct names.

subject area and were not the motivated self-directed learners that they would need to be as they moved on to university. In their action research study, the two teachers worked through quadrants 1, 2 and 4 of the Teaching and Learning Sequence in several cycles with their classes. In brief, this cycle involved introducing key concepts and ways of representing subject knowledge, giving tightly structured group or paired tasks for students to begin to use the ideas and checking students' emergent understandings in plenary discussion sessions. After several cycles through these activities, they created a list of "big questions" from which the students could choose to work on over a few weeks. The questions included: "Can Buddhists who follow *ahimsa* (the principle of nonviolence) fight in a war?" Or "Is there any justification for the Hindu caste system?"

The students were guided toward planning and continuous self-evaluation against their plans. Consequently, they were consciously using the learning strategies outlined in Chapter 7 and were exercising metacognitive awareness as they took agentic control over their use of key concepts. The approach involved John and Joe in careful planning and resourcing prior to sessions. But during these open activity (quadrant 3) lessons, they stood back and were simply resources who responded to students' questions and worked relationally with them, while the students made meaning through wrestling with these challenging questions. John and Joe also reported that they felt that in these sessions they were really teaching rather than delivering. Seeing the success of this approach, they used it with more senior classes and began to observe how students' in-depth understandings increased and, interestingly, that students were moving faster through the curriculum, allowing John and Joe to cover more ground in the time available. Although their previous students had gained strong examination results, results were even better in the year that followed.

Ellie and Enid, in the same school as John and Joe, were teaching modern languages, and dance and drama, respectively. Both subject areas involved student performance to different degrees and both teachers were concerned about the anxiety that arose for students as a result. Their concerns were therefore different from those of John and Joe, as they were clearly focused on students' emotional engagement. They worked through the quadrants and found them helpful and observed that as students became more agentically in control of their own learning pathways, they began to be more open about their anxieties about performance. Ellie and Enid started to listen more carefully to the students as they voiced their fears. As a result, they began to adjust their own language to show they were taking students' fears seriously. They also introduced the young people to strategies, such as ways of revising, that allowed them to take control of aspects of learning that they thought were beyond their control. Interestingly, the students themselves became more collegial, aware of how fellow students were feeling, and supported each other. Ellie and Enid reported that the students were becoming much more self-organizing, less teacher-dependent and generally thriving.

These are small-scale examples, but they are located within an English education system that emphasizes individual achievement and competition. All four teachers were carving out safe spaces within such a system, where ideas could be tested and self-evaluated, where emotion was recognized as a key to engagement and anxiety is not a product of the person, but of the social practices in which they are obliged to act. In line with this view, writing about student anxiety about mathematics, Roth and Walshaw (2015) argue, "Anxiety, then, no longer can be the reflection of an individual, as traditional approaches determine it to be, but is a reflection of society and the social relations of which the individual is a constitutive part" (p. 229).

In the next two sections, we discuss how relatively new sets of affordances are reshaping pedagogic practices by decentering teachers, positioning them as not leading the session, to offer scope for the unfolding of student agency as learners. They also remind us that different motive orientations lead to different forms of engagement with these affordances.

## How Information Technology Can Support Learning in and out of School

It has taken a long time for information and communication technology (ICT) to be integrated into classroom pedagogies and shift pedagogic discourses in a marked way. In part, this is because the technology design processes have not always been driven by pedagogical understandings and in part due to an early tendency for teachers to use technology as just another classroom resource, without considering how it might change how they are positioned in classrooms in relation to their students. Time has passed, but understandings of how ICT can be a tool or resource for enhancing students' conceptual development remain limited. We now suggest that approaches to pedagogy, which built on Vygotsky's work and were presented in Chapter 7, can help with recognizing how ICT can be deployed to support learning for students in high school.

Engeness has drawn on Galperin's framings to explain how students engage with digital resources to support their learning. One study examined processes in play while Norwegian adolescents worked with a digital resource aimed at supporting science learning (Engeness & Edwards, 2017) and another that assisted learners' essay writing in English (Engeness & Mørch, 2016). In both cases, the teacher was decentered, but still had a role. Engeness found that this role was to set up the initial learning situation, to engage the adolescents' general motivation, before they moved into small groups to interact with the digital resources. In an analysis of that process with the science resource, Engeness and Edwards noted that the digital resource was one element in a mix of pedagogic tools available to the teacher. These tools included asking students to draw their own representations of what was happening and to discuss these representations, and task sheets, where students were required to answer a sequence of questions, assisted by the content of the digital resource. In Galperin's terms (see Chapter 7), materialized action together with communicated and dialogical thinking were occurring throughout the process. Engeness and Edwards made the point that these digital resources disrupted the linearity of Galperin's framework explained in Chapter 7, but the framing still held good as it pointed to the need for flexibility in teachers' responses.

The students' discussions with working with the digital resource in science lessons were informed by both the digital program and teacher interventions, which centered on orienting the students to key aspects of the digital content. In that way, the resource became the focus for both the children and the teacher, while the children's agency was engaged as they orientated to tasks in a manner that was, in Galperin's terms, complete but jointly constructed by them. As the students continued with the tasks, their communicated thinking became increasingly informed by the resource and their capacity to identify and discuss what was crucial in relation to the tasks.

Over time, the teacher's role therefore moved from helping students' orientations to, instead, a monitoring one where students' models, written answers and discussions revealed their developing conceptual understanding. For the students, the centrality of the digital resource meant that their discussions were oriented toward jointly interpreting the images and other stimuli presented by the program on the screen. As they moved between materialized actions, communicative and dialogical thinking, they used exploratory talk (Mercer et al., 1999), tried out ideas, held them up to the scrutiny of others and learnt.

But a danger with digital resources is that they can simply focus on completing a given task, without addressing the conceptual development of learners. An analysis of how a teacher used a digital tool aimed at supporting essay writing revealed what could go wrong. The task was to write an essay that was assessed on the complexity of the argument being made, focusing on the number of sub-themes presented to support the argument (Engeness & Mørch, 2016). The digital resource was meant to involve the adolescents in group discussions, and it provided tailored feedback to them on their individual writing. Engeness's observations revealed how the teacher depended on the digital program when giving their own feedback, to the extent that the adolescents' initial orientation to the task, in Galperin's terms, was complete but was not being constructed by the learners. In our terms, their agency as learners was not engaged during the orientation phase. The group that used the tool did produce essays with more sub-themes than those of the control group. However, the control group, where the teacher introduced the task by identifying the demands and key features of the task and students used strategies based on the formative assessment process of assessment for learning, showed a greater conceptual grasp of how to approach this kind of essay.

But we cannot discuss adolescents and ICT without considering the impact of out-of-school use of digital technologies on identity and learning. Brevik, researching L2 (English) reading among Norwegian high school students, has undertaken a series of studies prompted by what seemed an anomalous finding in her analyses of national data on reading comprehension in L1 (Norwegian) and L2 (English): that some, mainly male, students were poor readers in Norwegian, but good readers in English (Brevik & Hellekjaer, 2018). These outliers scored less than 20 percent on Norwegian reading comprehension tests and over 60 percent on English reading tests.

In one follow-up study, Brevik (2019) tracked 21 grade 11 outlier students over six months. She found three types of leisure time L2 users: gamers, who gamed around eight hours daily, surfers and social media users. The two former groups were all boys and the latter group all girls. Interest, context and motivation were key to their engagement with the L2.

This finding led to an intervention study with one teacher who was working on a vocational course (Brevik & Holm, 2022). The intervention drew on Gee's notion of an affinity spaces as a place where people of similar interests can gather (Gee, 2017). The teacher created an affinity space in school where the adolescents could draw on their out-of-school interests in, for example, gaming, as part of the L2 language course. The study revealed that their use of English was stronger in the affinity space than in other school contexts where English was used. Throughout this strand of her work, Brevik emphasizes the importance of motivation to reading in another language.

The studies of both Engeness and Brevik return us to key themes in this book. First is the connection between agency and motive orientation and the part they play in student learning. Both are essential if children are to create their social situations of development and propel themselves forward in engaging with powerful knowledge. This theme connects directly to the need to take children seriously as agentic decision-makers in control of their learning pathways. For adolescents in particular, their emergent identities give shape to and are reinforced by how and why they engage with that knowledge.

## Transitions toward Adulthood

We have discussed several transitions in earlier chapters, explaining that moving between practices requires children to attune themselves to the demands of each practice and develop motive orientations toward what is considered important in each practice. In adolescence, these transitions between practices coincide with physical transitions, from childhood through puberty to adulthood, and emotional shifts, which presage their independence from parents and other carers.

Adolescence is a time of quite major transitions between practices, from middle school to high school, from high school to sixth form college, from school further to higher education and from education to work. In these transitions the expectation is that the adolescent is approaching adulthood, or if they are aged 18, has reached it. Society expects adults to be independent and personally responsible; consequently, help to ease transitions, particularly toward the end of compulsory schooling, is often very limited.

The first example of how young people can be supported in this transition is the third space. This is a discursive space in which adolescents can rethink who they are in order to anticipate possible futures. The idea of a third space arose initially as a response to how teachers' monological discourse limited opportunities for dialogue and engagement with adolescents' scripts. The adolescents' scripts, in those circumstances, centered on noncompliance with what teachers demanded of them (Gutierrez et al., 1995). The third space was offered by the researchers as a place where these two scripts can meet, and shared understandings develop. The research team did not use the terms relational expertise, common knowledge and relational agency; the ideas were still under development in the 1990s. The team did, however, talk of teachers' discursive construction of power in classrooms and therefore the need to counter this through intersubjectivity and "the potential for shared understanding" across the scripts (Gutierrez et al., 1995, p. 445), so that the intersection of these discourses can lead to "more authentic interaction" (p. 446). Like us, Gutierrez et al. were concerned about the need to take young people seriously and the lack of agency afforded the adolescents due to the controlling monologic talk of teachers. Given what little agency high school teachers have in contexts of strong state control over the profession, it was unsurprising that one of the team's initial 1995 attempts at creating a third space in a classroom had little traction.

Over the years, Gutierrez has, nonetheless, implemented these proposals through the Migrant Student Leadership Institute (MSLI) at the University of California, Los Angeles (Gutierrez, 2008). The four-week summer residential program for adolescents from migrant farmworker backgrounds at MSLI has been designed as a learning ecology to enable participants to develop competences in critical literacy practices and prepare themselves for future accomplishments, both academically and socially. Gutierrez described the underpinning philosophy of these environments in ways that resonate strongly with our concerns. They are "characterized by the ideals and practices of a shared humanity, a profound obligation to others, boundary crossing, and intercultural exchange in which difference is celebrated without being romanticized" (p. 149).

Importantly, MSLI is not simply a space where difference is celebrated. Rather it is a transformative space where different sets of social practices are brought together and interrogated, through critical literacy practices, to create an enriched understanding of how these practices may constrain academic and social learning. The ambition is bold, not merely to enable adolescents to transform their positioning in practices, but to transform broader educational practices. This ambition is laid out in Gutierrez's 2011 AERA Presidential Address where she offers the idea of "resilient ecologies" as a way of intervening in the academic trajectories of adolescents and of reimagining what education for vulnerable children and young people might be. In brief, that they may "become agents of newly imagined futures" (p. 187) or in our terms, develop new motive orientations.

While it seems that this broader ambition is currently thwarted by market-driven models of education and outmoded state-enforced pedagogies in so many places, the concept of a third space, at the boundaries of institutions, where different scripts can intersect, and complexities of different interpretations can be explored holds good as a model for transforming how adolescents position themselves. We suggest that as a model it is central to so many of the examples of adolescent pedagogy we have described in this chapter.

Transitions are particularly marked for adolescents with special educational needs, who have until now been in environments that have been configured to enable their participation. Bøttcher (2019), for example, has examined how societal expectations for 18-year-olds clashed with the ongoing needs and capabilities of adolescents with severe cerebral palsy. One outcome of the mismatch is that the mediating support of parents becomes discounted. Bøttcher notes, for example, when children reach the age of 18, the Danish system stops the payments to parents that were meant to compensate them for lost earnings due to their enhanced caring responsibilities.

Like other adolescents, the case study children followed by Bøttcher imagined themselves into possible futures, but feared or experienced obstacles that might prevent their accomplishing them because wider society felt unable to offer the necessary support (Bøttcher, 2019; 2021). In her 2021 article, Bøttcher explains how a mother of one of the adolescents, Emilia, supported and encouraged her daughter through her own imaginings of possible futures for Emilia. There, Bøttcher makes a link between imagining and agency and the potential for development that exists within the relationship between mother and daughter. In our terms, a form of relational agency was in play in the way that her mother's imaginings of the future meshed with those of Emilia to help Emilia to move forward. Indeed, Bøttcher has argued that transitions to adulthood for these adolescents require the exercise of relational expertise by parents and professionals to create an enriched understanding of how these adolescents can be supported (Bøttcher, 2019).

One important lesson from Bøttcher's studies is that we should be thinking in terms of interdependence rather than independence as part of the process of becoming adult. Of course, the need for interdependence is clearer among those with special needs as another study, on autism and transitions, illustrates.

Autism presents itself in many forms and is best seen as a profile of strengths and difficulties. It has been increasingly recognized as a learning difficulty, with UK estimates of its prevalence at 1 in 100 children (Baird et al., 2006) and US estimates at 1 in 68 (Chen et al., 2015). It is also noted that the anxiety associated with autism increases during adolescence (Chen et al., 2015). This anxiety is understandable, not least because of the major transition from a safe and supportive school environment to college or the world of work. Shepherd's UK study revealed the challenges of moving into further (post-school) education (Shepherd, 2015); while a UK report on autism and transitions into work (Wittemeyer et al., 2011) revealed that only 17 percent of adolescents with autism had the support they needed in getting a job and only 15 percent had the support they needed in staying in a job. Though pointing toward the benefits of interdependence, 53 percent reported that other people's understandings helped them.

Concerned about this transition, Edwards and Fay undertook a small-scale study of the moves into further education or work of adolescents with autism. The aim was to inform the design of a cell phone app that might support these transitions and increase mutual understandings (Edwards, & Fay, 2019). We interviewed three schoolteachers and one college lecturer who worked with autistic learners, four autistic adolescents who were about to leave school, three parents of autistic adolescents about to make the transition, five employers who worked with autistic young people, and two autistic young men who were currently in full-time employment.

The study was framed by our concern that autistic adolescents could find it difficult to orient toward what mattered in college or in the workplace and that they were in danger of orienting toward aspects of the workplace that were not important. The app was intended to capture and make visible their changing motive orientations and their needs for support; while at the same time making visible what tutors or employers saw as the key demands to be faced by the young person. In relational terms, the app was holding the common knowledge that was being built between the adolescent and the tutor or employer. That common knowledge, knowledge of each other's motive orientation, would mediate face-to-face interactions.

The app was to be updated with new information weekly and the parents were to be involved in the updating process. The app is yet to be built, but the interviews offered some interesting insights into autistic adolescence and what might be of help. First, like their peers in mainstream education, they imagined their futures as a hairdresser or mechanic but, also like some of their peers, could not see how they might get to that point. Once in the new environment, the tutors' or employers' contributions to the material held on the app would help address that problem. Second, echoing Bøttcher's studies, interdependence with parents was crucial and involving them in helping to populate the app alongside their child was seen as useful. Third, using technology to mediate interactions gives the adolescent an opportunity to take some control and orientate toward the demands that matter in their new environment, while at the same time providing the assurance of interdependence with those in the new setting and their own families. Finally, the young people at work and at school all wanted the app to capture what they liked doing and what they were good at. They were not simply a disability; rather they were adolescents for whom some things, such as playing football or cooking, mattered a lot. They wanted to be taken seriously.

Both pieces of work, with adolescents with cerebral palsy or with autism, indicate clearly that emphasis needs to be placed on interdependence during and after this major transition. The stress here is on 'inter.' It is not denying an adolescent's responsibility to self or others; instead it emphasizes the relational aspects of adulthood. This suggestion is not only relevant to children with special needs. The Honess and Edwards study we discussed earlier (Honess, 1989; Honess & Edwards, 1986, 1990) showed how adolescents' agency unfolded when they were in environments where they were taken seriously and that relationships with parents, as well as those with friends, were important parts of that environment.

## Final Reflections

We started by suggesting that a Vygotskian framing of adolescence can remedy what has been seen as a recent dearth of useful work on adolescent development. Drawing on Vygotsky and others who build on his ideas, we have presented an account that recognizes adolescence as a state of flux. It is where self-consciousness emerges; cognitive development becomes increasingly complex, allowing young people to use new conceptual framing to question what they had previously taken for granted, and possible futures are imagined and worked toward. During this turbulent period, the agency and emotional orientations of adolescents remain a central concern. As 16-year-old Lisa earlier in this chapter observed, adolescents are "under construction".

We have indicated the diverse pathways that different adolescents create through the possibilities for action available to them. As Pedersen (2022) showed, their development is not context-dependent, but environments can limit and enable their becoming. Pedersen's study is one of several mentioned in this chapter that point to the importance of the peer group in the construction of identities during the transition to adulthood. But we have also stressed the importance of the role of caring adults.

The way we have discussed the development of young people in this chapter has emphasized their agentic interdependence as they begin to construct their futures. One of Hedegaard's studies revealed some of the conflicts experienced and worked through by immigrant children (Hedegaard, 2003b, 2005). Their agency, when it came into play, was laudable, but we also noted that their pathways may have been eased by a more relational approach from the adults in their worlds. The analyses of Vadeboncoeur et al. on the moral imaginings of students who had been failed by their schools (Vadeboncoeur & Vellos, 2016; Vadeboncoeur et al., 2021) provided a nice example of how relational support can be accomplished, while Gutierrez' work on the third space (2008, 2011) also shows how young people can be helped relationally to work their way through some of these challenges.

Nonetheless, while there is an important role for adults in the lives of young people, attention needs to be paid to how adults position themselves. We would suggest that the idea of relational agency, of adults supporting the unfolding of adolescent agency, describes this interdependence. This point is also relevant in formal school settings. We saw in Engeness's accounts of students working with ICT (Engeness & Edwards, 2017; Engeness & Mørch, 2016), how some digital resources had the potential to decenter teachers and enable agentic responses from students.

When discussing transitions to adulthood, we drew on studies of young people with special needs to emphasize the enormity of that move from adolescence to adulthood. But we could see from other examples throughout the chapter that part of the turbulence and tensions of adolescence arises from both the excitement and fear associated with such a massive change in societal expectations. The fear arises in part because of the self-consciousness and reflective self-evaluations that become features in the lives of young people. Adults can help, we suggest, by building common knowledge (knowledge of what matters, their motive orientations) with young people and using that as a resource to mediate how they support the construction of pathways to adulthood. These processes were explained in Chapter 7 in relation to pedagogy and are also relevant to helping young people through these challenging transitions.

CHAPTER 11

# A Caring Relational Approach to Education
## Implications for Practice and Policy

**Introduction**

Our aim has been to reveal the important but different roles families and practitioners play in children's learning and development. We have argued that caring emotional support is crucial for development throughout childhood, from infancy to adolescence. For example, Lisina's (1985) research demonstrates that from the first days of life, social relations with caregivers are the central force in infants' development. Our starting point therefore is that children's development springs from the emotional relation between child and caregivers. It is from this relationship that children's intention, agency, will and motives develop as neoformations in a child's consciousness. This emphasis on care and emotion is, we believe, one of the major contributions made by the book.

Care that is sensitive to children's emotions depends on reciprocity between child and caregiver. Therefore, throughout the book we have shown what can be learnt by taking the child's perspective as they make sense of the practices and activity settings they inhabit and negotiate their way through the demands they encounter. Here the three relational concepts – relational expertise, common knowledge and relational agency – can help explain what is involved in care-full relationships, which take children and their intentions seriously. Employing these concepts, we have been able to explain the unfolding of children's agency as learners who are able to benefit from what society has to offer and to contribute to the development of practices and the well-being of others. These concepts also reveal for practitioners what is involved in a care-full professional work with both children and adults.

Our concern with children's agency and social relations has stressed that adults need to take seriously children's intentions, meaning-making and motive orientations, recognizing that emotional engagement is key to meaningful actions by children and young people. We have argued that adults should also be clear to children about what matters to them. Common knowledge in a care-full relational pedagogy consists of the motive orientations of both children and adults. Building it therefore involves demystifying what matters for the adult in an activity setting. We have argued that this demystification particularly helps more disadvantaged children.

While we make the case that care can lead to developmental changes, we emphasize that care also needs to change in relation to a child's developmental shifts. We have also noted that children and young people experience several different practices in their everyday lives. For example, in early childhood, children may move between different forms of childcare, such as home and nursery. They may then find that family and nursery caregivers have different views on how to interact with young children. We therefore recognize that institutional practices and care for children may differ in different developmental periods, but may also vary across different practices, even within the same society. Additionally, different societies have different cultural traditions for play and learning activities. We have argued that, across these diversities, play and more formal learning experiences are tool-mediated and that new tools can lead to new activities and thereby a restructuring of children's mind and hence development.

We have also shown how a child's social situation of development changes when the practice which they are part of changes, or they move to a new practice. One major change, much discussed in this book, is the move to formal education settings and the need to engage with subject matter knowledge and theoretical generalizations. Our dialectical understanding of development has meant that we have indicated some of the implications for the adults in these transitions and later. We have discussed how they should observe children, while care-fully trying to access their sense-making. They should build common knowledge with children and use that common knowledge as a resource when relationally supporting the unfolding of children's agency as learners.

We have explained that concepts are tools and that mediation of conceptual tools occurs in conversations and shared activities with material tools, recognizing that conceptual and material tools are interdependent. Consequently, how adults engage with children in mediating this dialectical relationship between child and culture is crucially important. Taking children seriously therefore involves supporting them as they propel themselves forward in their social situations of development. These situations are seen from a wholeness perspective of action in activity settings in shared practices and hold the potential for children's development; what adults do to help development in those situations is crucial.

In this chapter, we consider the implications for practitioners in more detail and point to what this could mean for the policies that create the possibilities for action that are offered to adults who work with children.

## The Importance of Knowledgeable Practitioners

Throughout this book, we have indicated challenges for professionals, not least by questioning how they are positioned in relation to children. Questions of power, status and knowledge are relevant for all practitioners who work pedagogically with children and families and focus on children's emotional well-being. The result is that we are advocating a highly skilled and knowledgeable form of professional action that relies not on status, but on an ability to engage with, guide and support the considered meaning-making of children and young people.

Members of the caring professions need to work pedagogically to support children, young people and their families as they construct their own pathways to becoming responsible citizens, able to both question the taken-for-granted and support others. We have discussed three types of knowledge in this book, and all inform the work of caring professionals. These are knowledge of: (i) child and adolescent development; (ii) subject matter in schools, and for other caring professionals their core professional knowledge, such as legal responsibilities for social workers; and (iii) pedagogy. When working with children and young people, these three knowledges are intertwined and if used in isolation of each other are insufficient. What connects all three is the emotional engagement of children, and here the skill of successful practitioners can be seen. We now summarize the three types of knowledge and their implications for practice.

Our cultural-historical approach to development talks of age periods, but not in the sense of a natural unfolding of maturity. Age periods in our approach are related to the demands in the institutional practices that children participate in. They are cultural constructions, but nonetheless real. They involve children in distinct transitions between practices, such as from preschool to school and call for the nurturing of motive orientations that enable children's engagement with what is offered in new settings. Because learning is the foundation for development, practitioners need to be aware of a child's capabilities. But this awareness is not a matter of waiting for readiness to learn so that adults can match the task to the child, as so many child-led developmentally based curricula required. Rather it gives adults much more active roles, for example, creating learning environments and connecting children with the conceptual and material resources that help them take forward their social situations of development.

This kind of subtle work requires a strong grasp of the knowledge that underpins professional actions. Although we have talked of care-full practitioners, we are adamant that care alone is not enough. Teachers, including those in elementary schools, need wide-ranging understandings of the key concepts and ways of knowing in different subject areas. We recognize that in most jurisdictions, teachers have little choice over curriculum content. But our hope is that the examples we have offered: from the detailed phases of Galperin's framework, through the ground-breaking pedagogy of Davydov and his work on the germ cell, to Hedegaard's formative experiments based on Davydov's work, including the Radical-Local initiative and Edwards' Teaching and Learning Sequence, all explain why teachers' knowledge of subject matter is crucial. Equally, practitioners in other professions that work with children need to be confident in their own specialist professional knowledge if they are to contribute to efforts with other practitioners and families to ensure the well-being of children.

Knowledge of pedagogy weaves its way through the previous two types of knowledge, whether it is part of working with children, with families or with other professionals. It is central to Hedegaard's development of the double move: a move between students' everyday concepts together with their motive orientation to the target subject matter and a move back again to refine and shape students' understandings and engagement with the subject. But as Hedegaard's work shows, it calls for a close understanding of how children are moving forward as learners. We have been advocating a caring relational pedagogy as a way of achieving this mutual understanding. The intended outcome of these relational approaches is the emergence of agentic learners who are socially oriented, able to move themselves forward, tackling demands in practices as well as acting on and questioning those practices. Key to that outcome is building common knowledge, knowledge of each other's motive orientations, which then mediates the collaborative work that strengthens agency.

We therefore do not underplay the challenges facing practitioners who value knowledge, wish to engage children and young people with powerful knowledge and encourage them to work agentically with these understandings. In brief, agentic learners need the support of agentic practitioners, who find support for themselves in their own working conditions. We therefore expand slightly the Wholeness Approach that has been such an important part of Hedegaard's contributions to the cultural-historical field, by using it to reflect on how practitioners are supported in the reciprocal work we are advocating.

## Creating Knowledgeable Practitioners

We have argued that the main objective of formal education should be to develop theoretical thinking as part of forming children's personalities in relation to their lifeworlds. This approach is exemplified in the Radical Local initiative discussed in Chapter 9. We have also advocated Hedegaard's double move as a strategy for supporting children's theoretical thinking. This move, between children's engagement and motive orientation and the learning goals and values of education, changes as children take part in different practices over time.

We have therefore explained why, in early childhood, practitioners should promote activities that support the development of psychological functions that are relevant for subsequent theoretical thinking and where emotion is seen as a psychological function. When children enter formal schooling, the goals of practice include promoting theoretical knowledge in all subject areas. This means that children's everyday concepts have to be connected to key concepts in different subject matter so that they become tools for children to understand phenomena and act in new ways. We have characterized theoretical knowledge as powerful knowledge. Hedegaard's program based on the germ cell and discussed in Chapter 9, has, for example, shown how, through the generalization of content, children can come to combine their knowledge of science with societal practice in everyday life to analyze concrete events. These informed analyses of societal events should enable children to become future citizens able to support sustainable relations between the natural world and society. Here there are so many possible ways in which teachers can collaborate with other professionals and with primary caregivers. We suggest that the relational approaches to interprofessional collaboration and working with families, discussed in Chapter 3, may be particularly relevant.

But knowledge is a political matter and in so many countries teachers are restricted in what they are allowed to do. Unfortunately, the origins of state education in most countries have meant that Education has been regarded by policymakers as a means of sustaining control over its citizens. In England and Wales, for example, the 1867 expansion of the male franchise was followed rapidly by the 1870 Education Act, which required all children between five and twelve to attend school. The rationale for the Act was made clear in the comment of one member of the UK House of

Lords: "[N]ow we must educate our masters." The education that was offered, involved rote learning of facts and tight monitoring by government inspectors. Educating for the release of student agency and the capacity to approach new challenges was certainly not on the agenda. Recent Government-ordained changes in curricula in English schools show that this rationale still pertains.

The professional interactions with children, families and other practitioners that we are advocating can be summarized as reciprocal. This is not simply a matter of being responsive, it involves ongoing mutual engagement, where power differences are played down. Much therefore depends on how institutional leaders mediate government policies, whether in Education or Welfare. In Chapter 8, we discussed a Norwegian study of how shy children are supported as learners by their teachers. As part of that study, the research team examined how the teachers, all of whom were working reciprocally and successfully with shy students, were supported by their leadership teams (Solberg et al., 2020a,b). In every case, the leadership teams worked relationally with the class-teachers, taking seriously their concerns and offering support in pedagogic ways, giving the teachers freedom of movement in how they worked with the students and providing support when it was needed. These successful teachers were clearly agentic in the reciprocal ways they were able to support the unfolding student agency within a broad framing of the national policy for school inclusion.

The relational aspects of leadership were also evident in a study of how successful leaders of children's services mediated policy demands during a period of change in the configuration of services in England (Daniels & Edwards, 2012; Edwards, 2012). Daniels and Edwards analyzed how the successful leaders helped their teams adjust to and develop the new system. The leaders' accounts were deeply pedagogic and involved listening to what mattered for their junior colleagues and being clear about what mattered for them as leaders. They frequently embedded that common knowledge in narratives about the future of their services and over time empowered colleagues to make decisions that would enrich and support that narrative. The leaders were agentic and enabled the unfolding of the agency of their teams within a broad values-laden framing. Their mediation was aimed at enabling frontline practitioners to work in reciprocal ways with children and families; whereas the unsuccessful leaders tended to simply dictate what needed to be done and monitor compliance.

Creating and sustaining agentic practitioners is a leadership responsibility. This responsibility involves a focus on professional learning and being explicit about the values that underpin professional practice. Orton and Weick, in their seminal 1990 paper on organizational cultures, argued that successful educational organizations are what they termed loosely coupled, giving a degree of freedom of movement to practitioners. Their organizations are not bound together by tight regulation, but by attention to shared values that play out in everyday actions in institutional activities. A study of the implementation of an educational reform aimed at supporting troubled children in four high schools in Chile (Edwards & Montecinos, 2017) corroborated this analysis. It showed how important shared values were for enabling the professional agency of school-based psychologists, social workers and teachers when working with these children.

Our plea to policymakers in many jurisdictions therefore is to focus on the professionalism of practitioners, the knowledge and values that underpin their professional work. We are not suggesting blind trust but suggest that closer relationally oriented collaboration between professional bodies and policy communities can only benefit policymaking in many countries.

## Moving Forward

We have drawn on the work of Vygotsky who was writing in the early decades of the last century and shown how his legacy has been taken forward over the last 90 or so years. We have looked back at previous research in order to look forward. In every example, the researchers' intentions have been to contribute toward constructing an inclusive society, where power differences are eroded and knowledge is both respected and questioned. Our focus on the agency and social orientation of children and young people as knowledgeable contributors to shaping society has reflected a cultural-historical concern that by understanding the world, people can reflect on it and help shape it. This is a forward-facing societally oriented approach to development. Vygotsky explained: "Life then discloses itself as a system of creation, of constant straining and transcendence, of constant invention and the creation of new forms of behavior. Thus every one of our thoughts, every one of our movements, and all of our experience constitutes a striving toward the creation of a new reality, a breakthrough to something new" (Vygotsky, 1926/1997, p. 350).

We have also drawn extensively on our own work and given greater emphasis to emotion, care and well-being than was always evident in the work of Vygotsky and his earlier descendants. We first met 20 or so years ago. We had much in common, including a rejection of our experiences in mainstream psychology and working in early years' research and on pedagogy. We had also been keen horse riders when younger, had children the same age and agreed on politics. But we have had different research trajectories, both too long to go into detail. Hedegaard's has been largely focused on child development and an experimental approach to formative change in education, while Edwards describes herself as an educational researcher with a background in child development.

Writing this book has allowed us to see much more clearly the commonalities across our research, both that undertaken recently and before we met. Examples include how Edwards' concern with disposition and agency has been refined by Hedegaard's work on motive orientation, which has also informed the definition of common knowledge. Common knowledge is now seen to comprise the motive orientations of each participant. Hedegaard has reinterpreted her earlier work on pedagogy by employing Edwards' relational concepts and particularly the building and using of common knowledge. We have both worked on the identity of children and young people. Hedegaard has particularly focused on cultural identity and its impact on children's developmental pathways, while Edwards' focus has been more on self and agency in relation to learning and inclusion. Hedegaard's methodological focus has largely been on children and their perspective, while Edwards has tended to concentrate on the work and workplaces of practitioners. However, we both believed strongly that knowledge had been underplayed in most accounts of pedagogy. In short, we have learned a great deal from each other over the two years of writing this book.

We have also learned so much from collaborating with colleagues worldwide, from conversations and from reading their work. Please accept our thanks; we hope we have done justice to your ideas. Our doctoral students have also promoted our learning by regularly challenging our thinking. Many of them are now having their own impact on the field, as their contributions to our arguments in this book make clear. The field is therefore thriving, and we hope that this book is a useful contribution to it. But more than that, we hope that the ideas we have presented offer a pathway forward where children's well-being and mental health is addressed through ways of working that offer care and support that are sensitive to children's emotions. The pathway encourages creative imagining, critical thinking, informed reflection and mutual support: ways of being that are essential if we are to address current societal problems.

Here questions of values arise, and we conclude by addressing them. In earlier chapters, drawing on Zaporozhets (2002), we discussed how children develop a sense of what is morally right and learn to control their actions, we have also pointed to how children pick up on the value positions of the adults who mediate what is important in a practice. The care-full relational pedagogy we have been advocating models mutual respect and taking seriously what matters to others. The agency that emerges arises in relationships of reciprocity and is therefore connected to societal priorities and the well-being of others. This does not lead to mere compliance, but to a constant questioning of practices so that what is mediated within them orients participants toward the common good. This is no small challenge. Benhabib captured its relational essence in her 1992 work on communicative ethics: "What I propose is ... the model of a moral conversation in which the capacity to reverse perspectives, that is the willingness to reason from the others' point of view, and the sensitivity to hear their voice is paramount " (p. 8).

# References

Afwedson, G. B., & Afwedson, G. (1995). *Normer och mål i skola och undervisning (Norms and goal in school and teaching)*. Stockholm: Liber.

Aidarova, L. (1982). *Child development and education*. Moscow: Progress.

Alexander, P., Edwards, A., Fancourt, N., & Menter, I. (2014). *Raising and sustaining aspirations in city schools*. Oxford: Oxford University Department of Education.

Allan, J. (2003). Productive pedagogies and the challenge of inclusion. *British Journal of Special Education, 30*(4), 175–179.

Anderson, B. (1991). *Imagined communities: Reflections on the origin and spread of nationalism*. London: Verso.

Anning, A., & Edwards, A. (1999). *Promoting learning from birth to five: Developing professional practice in the pre-school*. Buckingham: Open University Press.

Ariès, A. (1962). *Centuries of childhood: A social history of family life*. London: Jonathan Cape.

Arievitch, A. (2003). A potential for an integrated view of development and learning: Galperin's contribution to sociocultural psychology. *Mind, Culture, and Activity, 10*(4), 278–288.

Arievitch, I., & Haenen, J. (2005). Connecting sociocultural theory and educational practice: Galperin's approach. *Educational Psychologist, 40*(3), 155–165.

Aronsson, K. (2018). Daily practices and the time policy of family life. In M. Hedegaard, K. Aronsson, C. Højholt, & O. S. Ulvik (Eds.), *Children, childhood and everyday life* (75–90, 2nd ed). Charlotte, NC: Information Age Publishing.

Aronsson, K., & Gottzén, L. (2011). Generational positions at a family dinner: Food morality and social order. *Language in Society, 40*, 1–22.

Baird, G., Simonoff, E., Pickles, A. et al. (2006). Prevalence of disorders of the autism spectrum in a population cohort of children in South Thames: The Special Needs and Autism Project (SNAP). *The Lancet, 368*(9531), 210–215.

Bang, J. & Hedegaard, M. (2008). The questionnaire as a tool for researching children's perspective in institutional practices. In M. Hedegaard, &

M. Fleer (Eds.), *Studying children: A cultural historical approach* (157–180). Aarhus University Press.

Bantawa, B. (2017). Designing the epistemic architecture for Galaxy Zoo: The case study of relational expertise in citizen science. In A. Edwards (Ed.), *Working relationally in and across practices* (283–296). New York: Cambridge University Press (1998).

Barker, R. G., & Wright, H. F. (1954). *One boy's day: A specimen record of behavior.* New York: Harper.

 (1971). *Midwest and its children: The psychological ecology of an American Town.* North Haven, CT : Archon Books.

Benhabib, S. (1992). *Situating the self: Gender, community, and postmodernism in contemporary ethics.* Bristol: Polity Press.

Bernstein, B. (1970). Education cannot compensate for society. *New Society, 26*, 344–345.

Billig, M. (1998). *Banal nationalism.* London: Sage.

Blatchford, P., & Baines, E. (2006). *A follow up national survey of break times in primary and secondary schools.* London: Nuffield Foundation.

Bodrova, E. (2008). Make-believe play versus academic skills: A Vygotskian approach to today's dilemma of early childhood education. *Journal of Russian and East European Psychology, 16*, 357–369.

Bodrova, E., & Leong, D. J. (2003). Learning and development of preschool children from a Vygotskian perspective. In A. Kozulin (Ed.), *Vygotsky's educational theory in cultural context* (156–176). Cambridge: Cambridge University Press.

Bolin, A. (2011). Shifting subordination: Co-located interprofessional collaboration between teachers and social workers. Ph.D. thesis. Gothenburg: Gothenburg University.

 (2015). Children's agency in interprofessional collaboration. *Nordic Social Work Research, 5*(1), 50–66.

Bøttcher, L. (2012). Culture and the learning and cognitive development of children with severe disabilities: Continuities and discontinuities with children without disabilities. *Mind, Culture, and Activity*, 19(2), 89–106, https://doi.org/10.1080/10749039.2011.632050

 (2019). The cultural nature of the zone of proximal development: Young people with severe disabilities and their development of independence. In A. Edwards, M. Fleer, & L. Bøttcher (Eds.), *Cultural–historical approaches to studying learning and development* (69–83). Singapore: Springer.

 (2021). Supporting unusual development through moral imagination. *Learning, Culture and Social Interaction, 30*, 100384.

Bowlby, J. (1969). *Attachment and loss: Vol. 1. Attachment.* New York: Basic Books.

Bozhovich, L. I. (1969). The personality of school children and problems of education. In M. Cole, & I. Maltzman (Eds.), *A handbook of contemporary Soviet psychology* (209–248). New York: Basic Books.

(2009). The social situation of child development. *Journal of Russian and East European Psychology*, 47(4), 59–86.
Brandom, R. (1994). *Making it explicit: Reasoning, representing, and discursive commitment*. Cambridge, MA: Harvard University Press.
Brevik, L. M. (2019). Gamers, surfers, social media users: Unpacking the role of interest in English. *Journal of Computer Assisted Learning*, 35(5), 595–606.
Brevik, L. M., & Hellekjaer, G. O. (2018). Outliers: Upper secondary students who read better in the L2 than L1. *International Journal of Educational Research*, 89, 80–91.
Brevik, L. M., & Holm, T. (2022). Rethinking L2 teaching: Connecting informal and formal language use. *ELT Journal*, 76.
Bronfenbrenner, U. (1970). *Two worlds of childhood: U.S. and U.S.S.R.* New York: Russell Sage.
  (1979). *The ecology of human development*. Cambridge, MA: Harvard University Press.
Brown, A. L., Collins, A., & Duguid, P. (1989a). Situated cognition and the culture of learning. *Educational Researcher*, 18(1), 32–42.
Brown, J. S., Colins, A., & Duguid, P. (1989b). Debating the situation: A rejoinder to Paliscar & Wineburg's response. *Educational Researcher*, 18(4), 10–12+62.
Brown, G. T., & Harris, L. R. (2014). The future of self-assessment in classroom practice: Reframing self-assessment as a core competency. *Frontline Learning Research*, 2(1), 22–30.
Bruner, J. S. (1966a). On cognitive growth. In J. S. Bruner, R. R. Oliver, & P. M. Greenfield (Eds.), *Studies in cognitive growth* (1–67). New York: John Wiley & Sons.
  (1966b). *Toward a theory of instruction*. Cambridge, MA: Harvard University Press.
  (1968). Processes of cognitive growth: Infancy. *Heinz Werner Lectures*, 20, 1–75. https://commons.clarku.edu/heinz-werner-lectures/20
  (1970). *Man, a course of study*. Cambridge, MA: Educational Development Center.
  (1972). Nature and uses of immaturity. *American Psychologist*, 27(8), 687–708. https://doi.org/10.1037/h0033144
  (1986). *Actual minds, possible worlds*. Cambridge, MA: Harvard University Press.
  (1990). *Acts of meaning*. Cambridge, MA: Harvard University Press.
  (1996). *The culture of education*. Cambridge, MA: Harvard University Press.
Bruner, J. S., Jolly, A., & Sylva, K. (Eds.) (1976). *Play: Its role in development and evolution*. Harmondsworth: Penguin.
Callanan, M., Kinsella, R., Graham, J., Turczuk, O., Finch, S. (2009). Pupils with declining attainment at Key Stages 3 and 4: Profiles, experiences and impacts of underachievement and disengagement. Department for Children, Schools and Families Research Report DCSF-RR086.

Carr, M., & Claxton, G. (2002). Tracking the development of learning dispositions. *Assessment in Education*, 9(1), 9–37.
Caudill, W., & Weinstein, H. (1969). Maternal care and infant behavior in Japan and America. *Psychiatry*, 32(1), 12–43.
Cavada-Hrepich, P. (2019). Am I doing right? Normative performativity in the emergence of learning as a leading activity. In A. Edwards, M. Fleer, & L. Bøttcher (Eds.), *Cultural-historical approaches to studying learning and development. Societal, institutional and personal perspectives* (169–184). Singapore: Springer.
Chaiklin, S. (2003). The zone of proximal development in Vygotsky's analysis of learning and instruction. In S. Kozulin, B. Gindis, V. S Ageyev, & S. Miller (Eds.), *Vygotsky's educational theory in cultural context* (39–64). Cambridge: Cambridge University Press.
(2019a). Units and wholes in the cultural-historical theory of child development. In A. Edwards, M. Fleer, & L. Bøttcher (Eds.), *Cultural-historical Approaches to Studying Learning and Development* (263–277). Singapore: Springer.
(2019b). Age as a historical materialist concept in cultural-historical theory of human development. *Obutchénie. Revista de Didáctica e Psicologia Pedagógica*, 3(3), 1–27. https://doi.org/10.14393/OBv3n3.a2019-51707
(2022 (in press)). Developing science education through developmental teaching: Theoretical thinking, personality development, and radical-local teaching and learning. In K. Plakitsi, & S. Barma (Eds.), *Sociocultural approaches to STEM education*. Cham, Switzerland: Springer.
Chaiklin, S., & Hedegaard, M. (2009). Radical-local teaching and learning: A cultural–historical perspective on education and children's development. In M. Fleer, M. Hedegaard, & J. Tudge (Eds.), *Childhood studies and the impact of globalization: Policies at global and local levels* (182–201). *World yearbook of education*, 2009. New York: Taylor & Francis.
Chaiklin, S., Hedegaard, M., Navarro, K., & Pedraza, P. (1990). The horse before the cart: A theory-based approach to computers in education. *Theory into Practice*, 29(4), 270–275.
Chen, J. L., Leader, G., & Sung, C. et al. (2015). Trends in employment for individuals with autism spectrum disorder: A review of the research literature. *Review Journal of Autism and Developmental Disorders*, 2(2), 115–127.
Claxton, G. (2007). Expanding young people's capacity to learn. *British Journal of Educational Studies*, 55(2) 115–134.
Cole, M. (1996). *Cultural psychology: A once and future discipline*. Cambridge, MA: Harvard University Press
Collins, A., Brown, J. S. & Newman, S. E. (1989). Cognitive apprenticeship: teaching the crafts of reading writing and mathematics. In L. B. Resnick (Ed.), *Knowing, learning and instruction: Essays in honor of Robert Glaser*. Hillsdale, NJ: Lawrence Erlbaum.
Connolly K., & Bruner, J. S. (Eds.) (1974). *The growth of competence*. London: Academic Press.

## References

Cuschieri, E. (2018). Play therapy: An introduction to theory and practice. In P. K. Smith, & J. L. Roopnarine (Eds. (Chapter 35). Cambridge: Cambridge University Press.

Dafermos, M. (2018). *Rethinking cultural-historical theory: A dialectical perspective to Vygotsky*. Singapore: Springer

Damasio, A. (1999). *The Feeling of What Happens*. San Diego, CA: Harcourt Brace & Company.

Daniels, H., & Edwards, A. (2012). *Leading for Learning: How the intelligent leader builds capacity*. Nottingham: NCSL.

Davis, E. K., & Chaiklin, S. (2015). A radical-local approach to bringing cultural practices into mathematics teaching in Ghanaian primary schools, exemplified in the case of measurement. *African Journal of Educational Studies in Mathematics and Sciences, 11*, 1–16.

Davydov, V. V. (1977/1990). *Arten der Verallgemeinerung im unterricht*. Berlin: Volk und Wissen.

(1982). *Ausbildung der Lerntätigkeit*. In V. V. Davydov, J. Lompscher, & A. K. Markova (Eds.), *Ausbildung der Lerntätigkeit bei Schülern* (14–27). Berlin: Volk und Wissen.

(1988–1989). Problems of developmental teaching. *Soviet Education, 30*(8-9-10) 1–77.

(1990). *Types of generalization in instruction: Logical and psychological problems in the structuring of school curricula*. Reston, VA: National Council of Teachers of Mathematics.

(1999.)What is real learning activity? In M. Hedegaard, & J. Lompscher (Eds.), *Learning activity and development* (123–138). Aarhus University Press.

(2008). *Problems of developmental instruction: A theoretical and experimental psychological study*. Hauppauge, NY: Nova Science. (Original work published 1986).

Davydov, V. V., & Kurdriavtsev, V. T. (1998). Developmental education: The theoretical foundation of continuity between the preschool and primary school stages. *Russian Education and Society, 40*(7), 37–64. https://doi.org/10.2753/RES1060-9393400737

Davydov, V. V., & Markova, A. K. (1983). A concept of educational activity for schoolchildren. *Soviet Psychology, 21*, 50–76.

Delafield-Butt J., & Trevarthen, C. B. (2015). The ontogenesis of narrative: From moving to meaning. *Frontiers in Psychology, 6*, 1157. https://doi.org/10.3389/fpsyg.2015.01157

Demuth, C., & Keller, H. (2011). Mealtime as "cultural sites for socialization": Evidence from a longitudinal study in southern Germany. Paper presented at the Fourth Congress of the International Society for Cultural and Activity Research, August 2011.

Derry, J. (2008). Abstract rationality in education: From Vygotsky to Brandom. *Studies in the Philosophy of Education, 27*, 49–62.

(2013). Can inferentialism contribute to social epistemology? *Journal of the Philosophy of Education, 47*(2), 222–235.

Dunne, J. (1993). *Back to the rough ground: 'Phronesis' and 'techne' in modern philosophy and in Aristotle.* London: University of Notre Dame Press.

Edwards, A. (1984). The development of self in the pre-school child. Unpublished Ph.D. thesis. University of Wales.

(1988). Power games in early education. *Early Child Development and Care, 34*, 143–149.

(2005). Relational agency: Learning to be a resourceful practitioner. *International Journal of Educational Research, 43*(3), 168–182.

(2007). Working collaboratively to build resilience: A CHAT approach. *Social Policy and Society, 6*(2), 255–264.

(2009). *The social work remodeling project: Early indications of the implications of inter-professional work.* Leeds: CWDC.

(2010). *Being an expert professional practitioner: The relational turn in expertise.* Dordrecht: Springer.

(2011). Building common knowledge at the boundaries between professional practices: Relational agency and relational expertise in systems of distributed expertise. *International Journal of Educational Research, 50*(1), 33–39.

(2012). The role of common knowledge in achieving collaboration across practices. *Learning, Culture and Social Interaction, 1*(1), 22–32.

(2014). Designing tasks which engage learners with knowledge. In I. Thompson (Ed.), *Task design, subject pedagogy and student engagement.* (13–27). London: Routledge.

(Ed.) (2017). *Working relationally in and across practices: A cultural-historical approach to collaboration.* Cambridge University Press.

(in press). A Relational View of a Future-oriented Pedagogy: Sustaining the agency of learners and teachers. In N. Hopwood, & A. Sannino (Eds.), *Agency and transformation: Motives, mediation and motion.* New York: Cambridge University Press.

Edwards, A., & Apostolov, A. (2007). A cultural-historical interpretation of resilience: The implications for practice. *Outlines. Critical Practice Studies, 9*(1), 70–84.

Edwards, A., & Downes, P. (2013). Alliances for inclusion: Cross-sector policy synergies and inter-professional collaboration in and around schools. NESET/European Commission.

Edwards, A., & Evangelou, M. (2017). Easing transitions into school for children from socially excluded 'hard to reach' families: From risk and resilience to agency and demand. In M. Hedegaard, & A. Edwards (Eds.), *Supporting Difficult Transitions* (115–130). London: Bloomsbury.

Edwards, A., & Fay, Y. (2019). Supporting the transitions to work of autistic young people: Building and using common knowledge. In M. Hedegaard, & A. Edwards (Eds.), *Supporting difficult transitions: Children, young people and their carers* (262–278). London: Bloomsbury.

Edwards, A., & Mackenzie L. (2005). Steps towards participation: The social support of learning trajectories. *International Journal of Lifelong Education, 24*(4), 287–302.

Edwards, D., & Mercer, N. (2013). *Common knowledge (Routledge Revivals): The development of understanding in the classroom.* London: Routledge.

Edwards, A., & Montecinos, C. (2017). Working relationally on complex problems: Building the capacity for joint agency in new forms of work. In M. Goller, & S. Paloniemi (Eds.), *Agency at work* (229–247). Dordrecht: Springer.

Edwards, A., & Warin, J. (1999). Parental involvement in raising pupils' achievement in primary schools: Why bother? *Oxford Review of Education, 25*(3), 325–341.

Edwards, A., Chan, J., & Tan, D. (2019). Motive orientation and the exercise of agency: Responding to recurrent demands in practices. In A. Edwards, M. Fleer, & L. Bøttcher (Eds.), *Cultural-historical approaches to studying learning and development: Social, institutional and personal perspectives* (201–214). Singapore: Springer.

Edwards, A, Barnes, M., Plewis, I., & Morris, K. (2006). Working to prevent the social exclusion of children and young people: Final lessons from the National Evaluation of the Children's Fund. Research Report 734. London: DfES.

Edwards, A., Daniels, H., Gallagher, T., Leadbetter, J., & Warmington, P. (2009). *Improving inter-professional collaborations: Multi-agency working for children's wellbeing.* London, Routledge.

Eikset, A. S. B., & Ødegaard, E. E. (2020). Historical roots of exploration: Through a Fröbelian third space. In M. Hedegaard, & E. E. Ødegaard (Eds.), *Children's exploration and cultural formation.* Cham, Switzerland: Springer Open.

Elder, G. H. (1997). The life course of human development. In R. Damon, & M. Learner (Eds.), *Handbook of child psychology.* (939–991). New York: Wiley.

El'konin, D. B. (1987). Epilogue. In R. W. Reiber (Ed.). *The collected work of L.S. Vygotsky. Vol 5 child psychology* (297–317). New York: Plenum.

(1988). *Legens psykologi.* Copenhagen: Sputnik.

(1972/1999). Toward the problem of stages in the mental development of children. *Journal of Russian and East European Psychology, 37*(6), 11–30.

(2005). The psychology of play. *Journal of Russian and East European Psychology, 43*, 11–21.

Engeness, I. (2020). The study on the development of human mental activity Lecture 10: The development of mental actions and the orienting basis of actions. *Learning Culture and Social Interaction. 27,* 1000430. https://doi.org/10.1016/j.lcsi.2020.100430

Engeness, I., & Edwards, A. (2017). The complexity of learning: Exploring the interplay of different mediational means in group learning with digital tools. *Scandinavian Journal of Educational Research, 61*(6), 650–667.

Engeness, I., & Lund, A. (2020). Learning for the future: Insights from the contributions of Piotr Galperin to cultural-historical theory. *Learning Culture and Social Interaction. 27,* 1000476. https://doi.org/10.1016/j.lcsi.2018.11.004

Engeness, I., & Mørch, A. (2016). Developing writing skills in English using content-specific computer-generated feedback with EssayCritic. *Nordic Journal of Digital Literacy*, *11*(2), 118–135.

Erikson, E. H. (1950). *Childhood and society*. New York: Norton.

Erstad, O., & Silseth, K. (2019). Future-making and digital engagement: From everyday interests to educational trajectories. *Mind Culture and Activity*, *26* (4), 309–322.

Erstad, O, Gilje, Ø, Sefton-Green, J., & Arnseth, H. C. (2016). *Learning identities, education and communities: Young lives in the cosmopolitan city*. Cambridge, Cambridge University Press.

Evangelou, M., Sylva, K., Edwards, A., & Smith, T. (2008). Supporting parents in promoting early learning. London: DCSF Research Report 039

Evans, R., Pinnock, K, Beirens, H., & Edwards, A. (2006). Developing Preventative Practices: The experiences of children, young people and their families in the Children's Fund. London, DfES Research Report 735.

Faver, J. A. M. (1999). Activity setting analyses: A model for examining the role of culture in development. In A. Göncu (Ed.), *Children's engagement in the world: Sociocultural perspectives* (99–127). Cambridge: Cambridge University Press.

Fisher, R. (2011). Failing to learn or learning to fail? The case of young writers. In H. Daniels, & M. Hedegaard (Eds.), *Vygotsky and special needs education: Rethinking support for children and schools* (48–64). London: Continuum.

Fleer, M. (2013). Collective imagination in play. In I. Schousboe, & D. Winther-Lindqvist (Eds.), *Children's play and development: Cultural-historical perspectives* (73–88). Dordrecht: Springer.

(2014). *Theorising play in the early years*. Cambridge: Cambridge University Press.

(2017). Digital role-play: The changing conditions of children's play in pre-school settings. *Mind, Culture, and Activity* *24*(1), 3–17. https://doi.org/10.1080/10749039.2016.1247456

(2018). Conceptual playworlds: The role of imagination in play and learning. *Early Years*, *13*, 353–364. https://doi.org/10.1080/09575146.2018.1549024

(2020a). A tapestry of playworlds: A study into the reach of Lindqvist's legacy in testing times. *Mind, Culture, and Activity*, *27*(1), 36–49. https://doi.org/10.1080/10749039.2019.1663215

(2020b). Studying the relations between motives and motivation – How young children develop a motive orientation for collective engineering play, *Learning, Culture and Social Interaction*, *24*, 100355. https://doi.org/10.1016/j.lcsi.2019.100355

(2022). How an educational experiment creates motivating conditions for children to role-play a child-initiated PlayWorld. *Oxford Review of Education*, *48* (3), 364–379. https://doi.org/10.1080/03054985.2021.1988911

Fleer, M, Duhn, I., & Harrison, L. (2017). The relational agency framework as a tool for supporting the establishment, maintenance and development of multidisciplinary networks of professionals. In A. Edwards (Ed.), *Working

# References

*relationally in and across practices* (209–226). New York: Cambridge University Press.

Fleer, M., Hedegaard, M., & Tudge, J. (Eds.) (2009). *Word Yearbook of Education 2009: Childhood studies and the impact on globalization. Policies and practices at the global and local level*. London: Routledge.

Flórez, M. T., & Sammons, P. (2013). *Assessment for learning: Effects and impact*. London: CfBT Education Trust.

Friedman, J. (1996). *Cultural identity and global processes*. London: Sage.

Friedrich, J. (2021). Emergence and *perezhivanie*: The double face of the concept of development. *Mind, Culture, and Activity, 28*(4), 307–322.

Galperin, P. (2002). *Lectures in Psychology*. Moscow: Knizhnyy Dom. University.

Galperin, P. Y. (1969). Stages in the development of mental acts. In M. Cole, & I. Maltzman (Eds.), *A handbook of contemporary Soviet psychology* (249–273). New York: Basic Books.

Garvey, C. (1977). *Play*. Cambridge, MA: Harvard University Press.

Gee, J. P. (2017). *Teaching, learning, and literacy in our high-risk high-tech world: A framework for becoming human*. New York: Teachers College Press.

Giddens, A (1991). *Modernity and self-identity: Self and society in the late modern age*. Stanford, CA: Stanford University Press.

Göncü, A. (1999). Children's play as cultural activity. In A. Göncü (Ed.), *Children's engagement in the world: Sociocultural perspectives* (148–170). Cambridge: Cambridge University Press.

Göncü, A., & Gaskins, S. (2011). Comparing and extending Piaget's and Vygotsky's understandings of play: Symbolic play as individual, sociocultural, and educational interpretation. In A. D. Pellegrini (Ed.), *The Oxford handbook of developmental play* (48–57). New York: Oxford University Press.

Göncü, A., & Vadeboncoeur, J. A. (2017). Expanding the definitional criteria for imaginative play: Contributions of sociocultural perspectives. *Learning and Behavior, 45*, 422–431. https://doi.org/10.3758/s13420–017-0292-z

Gottzén, L. (2018). Money talks: Children's consumption and becoming in the family. In M. Hedegaard, K. Aronsson, C. Højholt & O. S. Ulvik (Eds.), *Children, childhood and everyday life* (75–90, 2nd ed.). Charlotte, NC: Information Age Publishing.

Gould, S. (1992). *Ever since Darwin: Reflections in natural history*. Harmondsworth: Penguin.

Grindheim, L. T. (2020). Conflict analyses: A methodology for exploring children's cultural formation in early childhood education. In M. Hedegaard & E. E. Ødegaard (Eds.), *Children's exploration and cultural formation*. Cham, Switzerland: Springer Open.

Grieshaber, S. (2004). *Rethinking parent and child conflict*. New York: Routledge.

Grieshaber, S., & McArdle, F. (2010). *The trouble with play*. Open University Press, McGraw Hill.

(2014). Social justice, risk and imaginaries. In M. N. Bloch, B. B. Swadener, & S. Canella (Eds.), *Reconceptualising early childhood care & education* (89–99). New York: Peter Lang.

Grigorenko, E. L., & Sternberg, R. J. (2001). Arguing for the concept of developmental niche. In E. L. Grigorenko, & R. J. Sternberg (Eds.). *Family environment and intellectual functioning: A life-span perspective* (23–48). Hillsdale, NJ: Erlbaum.

Gutierrez, K. (2008). Developing a sociocritical literacy in the third space. *Reading Research Quarterly, 43*(2), 148–164.

(2011). Designing resilient ecologies: Social design experiments and a new social imagination. *Educational Researcher, 45*(3), 187–196.

Gutierrez, K., Rymes, B., & Larson, J. (1995). Script, counterscript and underlife in the classroom: James Brown, versus Brown v. Board of Education. *Harvard Educational Review, 65*(3), 445–471.

Hakkarainen, P. (2010). Cultural-historical methodology of the study of human development in transitions. *Cultural-Historical Psychology, 4*, 75–89.

Hardman, J. & Teschmacher, N. (2019). Vygotsky's developmental pedagogy recontextualized as Hedegaard's double move: Science teaching in Grades 1 and 2 in a disadvantaged school in South Africa. In A. Edwards, M. Fleer & L. Bøttcher (Eds.), *Cultural-historical approaches to studying learning and development* (pp. 135–150). Singapore: Springer.

Hasse, C. (2017). Research as relational agency. In A. Edwards (Ed.), *Working relationally in and across practices* (229–246). New York: Cambridge University Press.

Hedegaard, M. (1984). Den Interaktionsbaserede beskrivelse af småbørn og børnehavebørn i deres dagligdag (The interactive observation approach for describing young children in everyday life). *Aarhus Universitet: Psykologisk skriftserie, 9*(4), 75.

(1988). *Skolebørns personlighedsudvikling – set gennem orienteringsfagene (The formation of children's personality development seen through the social science subjects)*. Aarhus: Aarhus University Press.

(1990). The zone of proximal development as basis for instruction. In L. Moll (Ed.), *Vygotsky and education* (349–371). New York: Cambridge University Press.

(1990/2013). *Beskrivelse af småbørn (Studying young children)*. Aarhus: Aarhus University Press.

(1995). Qualitative analyses of a child's development of theoretical knowledge and thinking in history teaching. In L. Martin; K. Nielsen & E. Toback (Eds.), *Cultural Psychology and Activity Theory*. Cambridge: Cambridge University Press.

(1996). How instruction influences children's concepts of evolution. *Mind, Culture, and Activity: An International Journal, 3*, 11–24.

(1999a). The influence of societal knowledge traditions on children's thinking and conceptual development. In M. Hedegaard, J. Lompscher (Eds.), *Learning activity and development* (22–50). Aarhus: Aarhus University Press.

(1999b). Institutional practice, cultural positions, and personal motives: Immigrant Turkish parents' conception about their children's school life.

In S. Chaiklin, M. Hedegaard, & U. J. Jensen (Eds.), *Activity theory and social practice*. Aarhus: Aarhus University Press.

(2002). *Learning and child development: A cultural-historical study*. Aarhus: Aarhus University Press.

(2003a). *At blive fremmed i Danmark*. Aarhus: Klim.

(2003b). Cultural Minority Children's Learning within culturally sensitive classroom teaching. 'Curriculum and Cultural Knowledge', Special Issue of *Pedagogy Culture & Society*, *11*(1), 133–152.

(2005). Strategies for dealing with conflicts in value position between home and school: Influences of ethnic minority students' development of motives and identity. *Culture & Psychology*, *11*(2), 187–2005.

(2008a). A cultural-historical theory of children's development. In M. Hedegaard, & M. Fleer (Eds.), *Studying children: A cultural-historical approach* (10–29). New York: Open University Press.

(2008b). Developing a dialectic approach to researching children's development. In M. Hedegaard, & M. Fleer (Eds.), *Studying children: A cultural-historical approach* (30–45). New York: Open University Press

(2008c). Principles for interpreting research protocols. In M. Hedegaard, & M. Fleer (Eds.), *Studying children: A cultural-historical approach.* (46–64). New York: McGraw Hill, Open University Press.

(2009). Children's development from a cultural-historical approach: Children's activity in everyday local settings as foundation for their development. *Mind Culture, and Activity*, *16*(1), 64–81.

(2012a). The dynamic aspects in children's learning and development. In M. Hedegaard, A. Edwards, & M. Fleer (Eds.), *Children's development of motives: A cultural-historical approach* (9–27). Cambridge: Cambridge University Press.

(2012b). Analyzing children's learning and development in everyday settings from a cultural-historical wholeness approach. *Mind, Culture, and Activity*, *19*, 1–12.

(2012c). Children's creative modelling of conflict resolutions in everyday life as central in their learning and development in families. In M. Hedegaard, K. Aronsson, C. Højholt, & O. S. Ulvik (Eds.), *Children, childhood and everyday life: Children's perspectives* (55–74). Charlotte: Information Age Publishing.

(2014). The significance of demands and motives across practices in children's learning and development: An analysis of learning in home and school. *Learning, Social Interaction and Culture*, *3*, 188–194.

(2016). Imagination and emotion in children's play: A cultural-historical approach. *International Research in Early Childhood Education*, *7*(2), 57–72.

(2017), When daycare professional's values from transition to school do not align with educational demands from society and school: A practice developing research project for daycare professionals support for children's transition to school. In A. Edwards, (Ed.), *Working relationally in and across practices* (247–264). New York: Cambridge University press.

(2018). Children's cultural learning in everyday family life exemplified at the dinner setting. In M. Fleer, & B. van Oers (Eds.), *International handbook of early childhood education* (1525–1540). Dordrecht: Springer.

(2019a). Child-based practice development for children in areas of concern: A model for enabling both the child's and the teacher's perspectives. In M. Hedegaard, & A. Edwards (Eds.), *Supporting difficult transitions* (21–42). London: Bloomsbury.

(2019b). Children's perspectives and institutional practices as keys in a wholeness approach to children's social situation of development. In A. Edwards, M. Fleer, & L. Bøttcher (Eds.), *Cultural-historical approaches to studying learning and development* (185–199). Singapore: Springer.

(2020). Ascending from the abstract to the concrete in school teaching – the double move between theoretical concepts and children's concepts. *Psychological Science and Education*, 25(5), 44–57. https://doi.org/10.17759/pse.2020250503

Hedegaard, M., & Chaiklin, S. (2005). *Radical-local teaching and learning.* Aarhus: Aarhus University Press.

(2011). Supporting children and school: A development and practice-centered approach for professional practice and research. In H. Daniels, & M. Hedegaard (Eds.), *Vygotsky and special needs education: Rethinking support for children and school* (86–1007). London: Continuum.

Hedegaard M., & Fleer M. (2008). *Studying children: A cultural-historical approach.* New York: McGraw Hill, Open University Press.

(2013). *Play, learning and children's development: Everyday life in families and transition to school.* New York: Cambridge University Press.

Hedegaard, M., Hansen, E., Engeström, Y. & Juul Jensen, U. (1985). Fagundervisning og udvikling af teoretisk tænkning. *Psykologisk Skriftserie Aarhus*, 10 (1).

Hedegaard, M., & Lyberth, N. (2019). Radical-local screening of preschool children's social situations of development: From abilities to activities. In M. Hedegaard, & A. Edwards (Eds.), *Supporting difficult transitions* (91–112). London: Bloomsbury.

(2022). Ideas for a radical-local approach to care and support for children's playful exploration in preschool and transition to school. In M. Fleer, M. Hedegaard, E. E. Ødegaard, & H. V. Sørensen (Eds.), *Qualitative studies in exploration in childhood education*. London: Bloomsbury.

Hedegaard, M., & Munk, K. (2019). Play and life competences as core in transition from kindergarten to school: Tension between values in early childhood education. In M. Hedegaard, & M. Fleer (Eds.), *Children's transitions in everyday life and institutions* (21–46). London: Bloomsbury.

Hedegaard, M., & Ødegaard, E. E. (Eds.) (2020). *Children's exploration and cultural formation.* Springer Nature. E. E. https://library.oapen.org/bitstream/handle/20.500.12657/39547/2020_Book_ChildrenSExploration

Hedegaard, M. Bang, J., & Egelund, N. (2007). *Elevens alsidige personlige udvikling – et dialogredskab* (Pupils' well-rounded development – a tool for creating dialogues). København: Dansk Psykologisk Forlag.

Hedegaard, M., Frost, S., & Larsen, I. (2004). *Krigsramte børn I exil (Children from war in exile)*. Aarhus: Aarhus University Press.

Hermansen, H., & Nerland, M. (2014). Reworking practice through an AfL project: An analysis of teachers' collaborative engagement with new assessment guidelines. *British Educational Research Journal, 40*(1), 187–206.

Hochschild, A. R. (1983). *The managed heart: Commercialization of human feeling*. Berkeley CA: University of California Press.

Holland, D., & Lave, J. (2001). *History in person: Enduring struggles, contentious practice, intimate identities*. Oxford: James Currey.

Holland, D., Lachicotte Jr, W., Skinner, D., & Cain, C. (2001). *Identity and agency in cultural worlds*. Cambridge, MA: Harvard University Press.

Holm, I. (2001). Family meals. In U. Kjaernes (Ed.), *Eating patterns: A day in the lives of Nordic people* (199–212). Lysaker: SIFO – National Institute for Consumer Research. Report No. 7.

Holodynski, M. (2013). The internalization theory of emotions: A cultural historical approach to the development of emotions. *Mind, Culture, and Activity, 20*(1), 4–38. https://doi.org/10.1080/10749039.2012.745571

Honess, T. (1989). A longitudinal study of school leavers' employment experiences, time structuring and self-attributions as a function of local opportunity structure. *British Journal of Psychology, 80*(1), 45–77.

Honess, T., & Edwards, A. (1986). Self-other appreciation and the adolescent parent relationship. *Bulletin of the British Psychological Society*, 39, 20.

(1990). Selves-in-relation: School leavers' accommodation to different interpersonal and situational demands. In H. A. Bosma, & A. E. S. Jackson (Eds.), *Coping and self-concept in adolescence* (69–86). Berlin: Springer.

Hopwood, N. (2010). A sociocultural view of doctoral students' relationships and agency. *Studies in Continuing Education, 32*(2), 103–117.

Hopwood, N., & Edwards, A. (2017). How common knowledge is constructed and why it matters in collaboration between professionals and clients. *International Journal of Educational Research, 83*, 107–119.

Howard, S., Dryden, J., & Johnson, B. (1999). Childhood resilience: Review and critique of the literature. *Oxford Review of Education, 25*(3): 307–323.

Hundeide, K. (2005). Socio-cultural tracks of development, opportunity, situations and access skills. *Culture & Psychology, 11*(2), 241–261. https://doi.org/10.1177%2F1354067X05052353

Hviid, P. (2018). "Remaining the same" and children's experience of development. In M. Hedegaard, K. Aronsson, C. Højholt, & O. S. Ulvik (Eds.), *Children, childhood, and everyday life* (241–257). Charlotte, NC: Information Age Publishing.

Iljenkov, E. V. (1982). *The dialects of the abstract and concrete in Marx's capital*. Moscow: Progress.

Jack, G. (2006). The area and community components of children's well-being. *Children and Society*. (20)5, 334–347.

James, W., Burkhardt, F., Bowers, F., & Skrupskelis, I. K. (1890). *The principles of psychology* (Vol. 1, No. 2). London: Macmillan.

Japiassu, R. O. V. (2008). Pretend play and preschoolers. In B. van Oers, W. Wardekker, E. Elbers, & R. van der Veer (Eds.), *Transformation of learning: Advances in cultural-historical activity theory* (380–397). Cambridge: Cambridge University Press.

Jensen, J. U. (1986). *Practice and progress: A theory of modern health-care systems.* London: Blackwell Scientific Publications.

Jensen, J. U., & Harré, R. (1981). *The philosophy of evolution.* London: St. Martin's Press.

Johansson, E. (2017). Toddlers' relationships: A matter of sharing worlds. In L. Li, G. Quiñones, & A. Ridgway (Eds.), *Studying babies and toddlers: Relationship in cultural contexts* (13–28). Singapore: Springer.

  (2018). The heart of values education in early childhood. In Johansson, E, Emilson, A., & Puroila, A-M. (Eds.), *Values in early childhood education* (33–54). Cham, Switzerland: Springer.

Joppe, S. R., Conner, R. E., & Umansky, W. (1986). The Cattell Infant Intelligence Scale: A review of literature. *Developmental Review, 6*, 146–164.

Kagan, 1973. *Change and continuity in infancy.* New York: Wiley.

Kajamma, A., & Kumpulainen, K. (2019). Agency in the making: Analyzing students' transformative agency in a school-based makerspace. *Mind, Culture, and Social Interaction, 26*(3), 266–281.

Kohl, H. (1991). *"I won't learn from you" and other thoughts of creative maladjustment.* New York: The New Press.

Kokkinaki, T. S., Vasdekis, V. G, S., Koufaki, Z. E., & Trevarthen, C. B. (2017). Coordination of emotions in mother–infant dialogues. *Infant and Child Development, 26*, e1973. https://doi.org/10.1002/icd.1973

Kragh-Müller, G. (2017). The key characteristic of Danish/Nordic child care culture. In G. Kragh-Müller, & C. Ringmose (Eds.), *Nordic social pedagogical approach to early years* (3–24). Switzerland: Springer.

Kravtsova, E, & Kravtsov, G. (2012). The connection between the motive and will in the development of the personality. In Hedegaard, A. Edwards, & M. Fleer (Eds.), *Motives in children's development* (115–132). Cambridge: Cambridge University Press.

Kudryavtsev, V. (2017). Play and the development of children's imagination from the perspective of cultural-historical psychology. *Journal of Russian & East European Psychology, 54*(4–5), 361–382. https://doi.org/10.1080/10610405.2017.1423843

Kumpulainen, K., Kajamaa, A., & Rajala, A. (2019). Motive-demand dynamics creating a social context for students' learning experiences in a making and design environment. In A. Edwards, M. Fleer, & L. Bøttcher (Eds.), *Cultural-historical approaches to studying learning and development* (185–199). Singapore: Springer.

Laurillard, D. (2013). *Teaching as a design science: Building pedagogical patterns for learning and technology.* London: Routledge.

Lave, J. (1988). *Cognition and practice: Mind mathematics and culture in everyday life.* Cambridge: Cambridge University Press.

Lave, J., & Wenger, J. (1992). *Situated learning: Legitimate peripheral participation*. Cambridge: Cambridge University Press.
Leo, E., & Galloway, D. (1996). Conceptual links between cognitive acceleration through science education and motivational style: A critique of Adey and Shayer. *International Journal of Science Education, 18*(1), 35–49. https://doi.org/10.1080/0950069960180103
Leont'ev, A. N. (1978). *Activity, consciousness, and personality*. Englewood Cliffs, NJ: Prentice-Hall.
  (1981). *Problems in the development of the mind*. Moscow: Progress.
  (2005). Study of the environment in the pedagogical works of L.S. Vygotsky. *Journal of Russian and East European Psychology, 43*, 8–28.
Lewin, K. (1946). Behavior and development as a function of the total situation. In L. Carmichael (Ed.), *Manual of child psychology* (791–844). New York: Wiley.
Lewis, A., & Norwich, B. (2005). *Special teaching for special children? Pedagogies for inclusion*. Buckingham: Open University Press.
Li, L., Ridgway, A., & Quiñones, G. (2021). Moral imagination: Creating affective values through toddlers' joint play. *Learning, Culture and Social Interaction, 30*, 100435. https://doi.org/10.1016/j.lcsi.2020.100435
Libaneo J. C., & Freitas da Madeira R. A. M. (2019). Mariane Hedegaard's contribution to developmental didactics and to pedagogical research in a Brazilian context. In A. Edwards, M. Fleer, & L Bøttcher (Eds.), *Cultural* (323–335). Singapore: Springer.
Lindqvist, G. (1995). *The aesthetics of play: A didactic study of play and culture in preschools*. Ph.D. thesis. Uppsala University.
  (2003). The dramatic and narrative patterns of play. *European Early Childhood Education Research Journal, 11*(1), 69–78.,
Lisina, M. S. (1985). *Child-adults-peers: Patterns of communication*. Moscow: Progress.
Lompscher, J. (1999). Learning activity and its formation: Ascending from the abstract to the concrete. In M. Hedegaard, & J. Lompscher (Eds.), *Learning activity and development* (139–168). Aarhus: Aarhus University Press.
Lowenfeld, M. (1935/2008). *Play in childhood*. Brighton: Sussex Academic Press.
Luthar, S. (1993). Annotation: Methodological and conceptual issues in research on childhood resilience. *Journal of Child Psychology and Psychiatry, 34*(4), 441–454.
Margolis, A. A. (2020). Zone of proximal development, scaffolding and teaching practice. *Cultural-Historical Psychology, 16*(3), 15–26.
Markova A. K. (1978–1979). The teaching and mastery of language. *Soviet Education, XXI*(2-3-4).
Marsh, J., Arnseth, H. C., & Kumpulainen, K. (2018). Maker literacies and maker citizenship in the MakEY (Makerspaces in the Early Years) project. *Multimodal Technologies and Interaction, 2*(3), 50. https://doi.org/10.3390/mti2030050
Masten, A., & Coatsworth, J. D. (1998). The development of competence in favorable and unfavorable environments: Lessons from research on successful children. *American Psychologist, 53*, 205–220.

Mayr, E. (1976). *Evolution and the diversity of life*. Cambridge, MA: Harvard University Press.

(1980). Prologue: Some thoughts on the history of evolutionary synthesis. In E. Mayr, & W. B. Provine (Eds.), *The evolutionary synthesis* (1–48). Cambridge, MA: Harvard University Press. https://doi.org/10.4159/harvard.9780674865389.c2

McDermott, R., & Varenne, H. (1995). Culture as disability. *Anthropology & Education Quarterly, 26*(3), 324–348.

Meireles Santos da Costa, N. M., & de Souza Amorim (2021). Babies in motion within daycare transition: (co)construction of locomotor exploration in a Brazilian case study. In M. Fleer, M. Hedegaard, E. E. Ødegaard, & H. V. Sørensen (Eds.), *Qualitative studies of exploration in childhood education: Cultures of play and learning in transition* (147–162). London: Bloomsbury

Meltzoff, A. N., & Moore, M. K. (1983). Newborn infants imitate adult facial gestures. *Child Development, 54*, 702–709.

Mercer, N. (1995). *The guided construction of knowledge: Talk amongst teachers and learners*. Clevedon: Multilingual Matters.

Mercer, N., & Littleton, K. (2007). *Dialogue and the development of children's thinking: A socio-cultural approach*. London: Routledge.

Mercer, N., Wegerif, R., & Dawes, L. (1999). Children's talk and the development of reasoning in the classroom. *British Educational Research Journal, 25*(1), 95–111.

Merleau-Ponty, M. (1962). *Phenomenology of perception*. London: Routledge and Kegan Paul.

Mjelve, L. H., Nyborg, G., Edwards, A., & Crozier, R. (2019). Teachers' understandings of shyness: Psychosocial differentiation for student inclusion. *British Educational Research Journal, 45*(6), 1295–1311.

Moll, L. C., & Diaz, S. (1993). Change as the goal of educational research. In E. Jacob, & C. Jordan (Eds.), *Minority education: Anthropological perspectives* (67–79). Norwood, NJ: Ablex.

Moll, L. C., & Greenberg, J. B. (1990). Creating zones of possibilities: Combining social contexts for instruction. In L. C. Moll (Ed.), *Vygotsky and education: Instructional implications and applications of sociohistorical psychology* (319–348). Cambridge: Cambridge University Press.

Moll, L. C., Amanti, C., Neff, D., & Gonzalez, N. (1992). Funds of knowledge for teaching: Using a qualitative approach to connect homes and classrooms. *Anthropology and Education Quarterly, 23*, 132–141.

Mook, B. (1994). Therapeutic play: From interpretation to intervention. In J. R. van der Kooij, B. Sutton-Smith, & J. Hellendoorn (Eds.), *Play and intervention* (39–52). Albany: State University of New York.

Nairn, A. (2011). *Children's well-being in UK, Sweden and Spain, The role of inequality and materialism. A qualitative study*. Bath, UK: Report from Ipsos Mori.

Newmann, F. M., & Associates. (1996). *Authentic achievement: Restructuring schools for intellectual quality*. San Francisco, CA: Jossey-Bass.

Nicholls, J. G. (2017). Conceptions of ability and achievement motivation: A theory and its implications for education. In S. G. Paris, G. M. Olson, & H. W. Stevenson (Eds.), *Learning and motivation in the classroom* (211–238). London: Routledge.

Nilsson, M. E. (2010). Creative pedagogy of play: The work of Gunilla Lindqvist. *Mind, Culture, and Activity, 17,* 14–22.

Nind, M., & Wearmouth, J. (2006). Including children with special educational needs in mainstream classrooms: Implications for pedagogy from a systematic review. *Journal of Research in Special Educational Needs, 6*(3), 116–124. https://doi.org/10.1111/J.1471-3802.2006.00069.x

Nisbet, J., & Shucksmith, J. (1986). *Learning strategies.* London: Routledge & Kegan Paul.

Noddings, N. (2013). *Caring: A relational approach to ethics and moral education.* University of California Press.

Nyborg, G., Mjelve, H., Edwards, A., & Crozier, R. (2020). Teachers' strategies for enhancing shy children's engagement in oral activities: Necessary but insufficient? *International Journal of Inclusive Education, 26*(7), 1–16. https://doi.org/10.1080/13603116.2020.1711538

Nyborg, G., Mjelve, L. H., Edwards, A., Crozier, R., & Coplan, R. (2022). Working relationally with shy students: Pedagogical insights from teachers and students. *Learning, Culture and Social Interaction, 33,* 100610. https://doi.org/10.1016/j.lcsi.2022.100610

Omland, M., & Rødnes, K. A. (2020). Building agency through technology-aided dialogic teaching. *Learning, Culture and Social Interaction, 26,* 100406 https://doi.org/10.1016/j.lcsi.2020.100406

Palinscar, A. S. (1989). Response to Brown, Collins and Duguid's 'Situated cognition and the culture of learning': Less chartered waters. *Educational Researcher, 18*(4), 5–7.

Pedersen, S. (2022).*Developmental dynamics and transitions in high school.* London: Bloomsbury.

Pekrun, R. (2009). Emotions at school. In *Handbook of motivation at school* (589–618). London: Routledge.

Piaget, J. (1923/2005). *Language and thought of the child: Selected works, Vol 5.* London: Routledge.

(1955). *The construction of reality in the child.* London: Routledge & Kegan Paul.

(1952). *Play, dreams and imitation in childhood.* London: Routledge & Kegan Paul.

Podolskij, A. (2020). The system of planned stage by stage formation of mental actions (PSFMA) as a creative design of the psychological conditions for instruction. *Learning, Culture and Social Interaction, 27,* 1000474. https://doi.org/10.1016/j.lcsi.2020.100474

Poliavanova K. N. (2015). The psychology of age-related crises. *Journal of Russian & East European Psychology, 52*(2), 59–68. https://doi.org/10.1080/10610405.2015.1064730

Pontecorvo, C. Fausolo, A., & Sterponi, L. (2001). Mutual apprentices: Making of parenthood and childhood in family dinner conversations. *Human Development*, *44*, 340–361.

Queensland Department of Education (2001). *The Queensland school reform longitudinal study* (Vol. 1). Brisbane: State of Queensland.

Quiñones, G., Li, L., & Ridgway. A. (2017). Transitory moments as "affective moments of action" in toddler play. In G. Quiñones, L., Li, & A. Ridgway (Eds.), *Studying babies and toddlers* (175–102). Singapore: Springer.

Rai, P. C. (2013). Building common knowledge: A cultural-historical analysis of pedagogical practices at a rural primary school in Rajasthan, India. DPhil, University of Oxford. https://ora.ox.ac.uk/objects/uuid:22402128-d2ca-4de5-8255-c15e4b4699dd

  (2017). Building and using common knowledge for developing school-community links. In A. Edwards (Ed.), *Working relationally in and across practices* (96–112). New York: Cambridge University Press.

  (2019). Building and using common knowledge as a tool for pedagogic action: A dialectical interactive approach for researching teaching. In A. Edwards, M. Fleer, & L. Bøttcher (Eds.), *Cultural-historical approaches to studying learning and development* (151–167). Singapore: Springer.

Rajala, A., Hilppö, J., & Lipponen, L. (2012). The emergence of inclusive exploratory talk in primary students' peer interaction. *International Journal of Educational Research*, *53*, 55–67.

Ramirez, F. O. & Boli, J. (1987). The political construction of mass schooling: European and worldwide institutionalisation. *Sociology of Education*, *60*, 2–17.

  (1992). Compulsory schooling in the Western cultural context. In R. Arnove, P. G. Altbach, & G. P. Kelly (Eds.), *Emergent issues in education comparative perspectives* (24–38). Albany: State University of New York Press.

Reichert, F., Lam, P., Loh, E. K. Y., & Law, N. (2020). *Hong Kong students' digital citizenship development: Initial findings*. Hong Kong: The University of Hong Kong.

Rickinson, M., & Edwards, A. (2021). The relational features of evidence use. *Cambridge Journal of Education*, *51*(4), 509–526.

Riegel, K. (1975). Toward a dialectical theory of development. *Human Development*, *18*, 50–64.

Ringsmose, C., & Kragh-Müller, G. (Eds.) (2017). *Nordic social pedagogical approach to early years*. Springer.

Rogoff, B. (1981). Adults and peers as agents of socialization: A highland Guatemalan profile. *Ethos*, *9*, 18–36. https://doi.org/10.1525/eth.1981.9.1.02a00030

  (2003). *The cultural nature of human development*. New York: Oxford University Press.

Rogoff, B., & Chavajay. P. (1995). What's become of research on the cultural basis of cognitive development? *American Psychologist*, *50*(10), 859.

Room, G. (1995). Conclusions. In G. Room (Ed.), *Beyond the threshold: The measurement and analysis of social exclusion* (233–247). Bristol: Policy Press.

Roth, W-M., & Walshaw, M. (2015). Rethinking affect in education from a societal-historical perspective: The case of mathematics anxiety. *Mind, Culture and Activity*, 22(3) 217–232.

Sameroff, A. (2009). The transactional model. In A Sameroff (Ed.), *The transactional model of development: How children and contexts shape each other* (3–21). Washington, DC: American Psychological Association.

Sannino, A. (2015). The emergence of transformative agency and double stimulation: Activity-based studies in the Vygotskian tradition. *Learning, Culture and Social Interaction*, 4, 1–3.

Scardamalia, M., & Bereiter, C. (1993–1994). Computer support for knowledge-building communities. *Journal of the Learning Sciences*, 3(3), 265–283.

Scardamalia, M., Bereiter, C., Brett, C, et al. (1992). Educational applications of a networked communal database. *Interactive Learning Environments*, 2(1), 45–71.

Schaffer, R. (1990). *Making decisions about children*. London: Blackwell.

(1992). Joint involvement episodes as contexts for cognitive development. In H. McGurk (Ed.), *Childhood and social development: Contemporary perspectives*. (99–129). Hove: Lawrence Erlbaum.

Scheiffelin, B., & Ochs, E. (1991). A cultural perspective on the transition from pre-linguistic to linguistic communication. In M. Woodhead, R. Carr, & P. Light (Eds.), *Becoming a Person* (211–229). London: Routledge

Schleicher, A. (2019). *Pisa 2018: Insights and interpretations*. Paris: OECD.

Schousboe, I. (2013). The structure of fantasy play and its implication for good and evil games. In I. Schousboe, & D. Winther-Lindqvist (Eds.), *Play and playfulness* (13–28). Dordrecht: Springer.

Schutz. A. (1972). *Collected works, Vol. 1: The problem of social reality*. Dordrecht: Springer.

(1976). *Collected papers II: Studies in social theory* (Vol. 15). Springer Science & Business Media.

Schweinhart, L. J., & Weikart, D. P. (1993). Success by empowerment: The High/Scope Perry Preschool Study through age 27. *Young Children*, 49(1), 54–58.

Scrimshaw, P. (1997). Computers and the teacher's role. In B. Somekh, & Davis, N. (Eds.), *Using information technology effectively in teaching and learning* (99–112). London: Routledge.

Sfard, A. (1998). On two metaphors for learning and the danger of choosing just one. *Educational Researcher*, 27(2) 4–13.

Shayer, M., & Adey, P. S. (1993). Accelerating the development of formal thinking in middle and high school students IV: Three years after a two-year intervention. *Journal of Research in Science Teaching*, 30(4), 351–366.

Shepherd, J. (2015). Experiences of transition from special school to mainstream college for young people with autism. Ph.D. thesis. University of Sussex.

Shires, L., & Hunter, M. (2020). *Enabler of leading teaching in secondary schools: Practical curriculum development through the use of theory.* London: BERA.

Shotter, J. (1993). *Cultural politics of everyday life: Social constructionism, rhetoric and knowing of the third kind.* Buckingham: Open University Press.

Skovbjerg, H. M., & Sand A.-L. (2021). Play in school – Toward an ecosystemic understanding and perspective. *Frontiers in Psychology, 12*, 780681. https://doi.org/10.3389/fpsyg.2021.780681

Solberg, S., Edwards, A., & Nyborg, G. (2020a). Leading for school inclusion: How school leadership teams support shy students. *Scandinavian Journal of Educational Research, 65*(7), 1–14. https://doi.org/10.1080/00313831.2020.1788156

Solberg, S., Edwards, A., Mjelve, L. H., & Nyborg, G. (2020b). Working relationally with networks of support within schools: Supporting teachers in their work with shy students. *Journal of Education for Children Placed at Risk, 26*(4), 279–301. https://doi.org/10.1080/10824669.2020.1854760

Spitz, R. A. (1945). Hospitalism: An inquiry into the genesis of psychiatric conditions in early childhood. *The Psychoanalytic Study of the Child, 1*(1), 53–74.

Spradley, J. P. (1980). *Participant observation.* New York: Wadsworth.

Stenild, K., & Iversen, O. S. (2012). Motives matters: A cultural-historical approach to IT mediated subject-matter teaching. In M. Hedegaard, A. Edwards, & M. Fleer (Eds.), *Motives in children's development: Cultural-historical approaches* (133–152). Cambridge: Cambridge University Press.

Stern, D. (1985/1998). *The interpersonal world of the infant.* New York: Basic Books.

Stetsenko, A. (2017). *The transformative mind: Expanding Vygotsky's approach to development and education.* New York: Cambridge University Press.

(2018). Nature culture in a transformative worldview: Moving beyond the "interactionist consensus". In G. Jovanović, L. Allolio-Näcke, & C. Ratner (Eds.), *The challenges of cultural psychology* (37–56). London: Routledge.

(2019). Cultural-historical activity theory meets developmental systems perspective: Transformative activist stance and nature culture. In A. Edwards, M. Fleer, & L. Bøttcher (Eds.), *Cultural-historical approaches to studying learning and development* (249–262). Singapore: Springer.

Stetsenko, A., & Arievitch, I. (2002). Teaching, learning and development: A post-Vygotskian perspective. In G. Wells, & G. Claxton (Eds.), *Learning for life in the twenty-first century: Sociocultural perspectives on the future of education* (84–87). London: Blackwell.

Stæhr, H., & Hedegaard, M. (2019a). Psykologens konsultative arbejde med observationer I PPR – med focus på opbygning af fælles succesmål. *Pædagogisk Psykologisk Tidsskrift, 57*(2), 106–120.

(2019b). Barnets perspektiv på tværfaglige møder – observation som konsultativ samarbejdsform. *Pædagogisk Psykologisk Tidsskrift, 57*(2), 121–135.

Stevenson-Hinde, J. (2011). Cultural and socioemotional development with a focus on fearfulness and attachment. *Socioemotional Development in a Cultural Context, 3*, 11–28.

Stones, E. (1984). *Psychology of education: A pedagogical approach.* London: Routledge.
Super, C. M., & Harkness, S. (1986). The developmental niche: A conceptualization at the interface of child and culture. *International Journal of Behavioral Development, 9*(4), 545–569
Sylva, K., Roy, C., & Painter, M. (1980). *Child watching at playgroup and nursery school.* London: Grant McIntyre.
Tan, D. (2017). *Student teachers learning to use assessment for learning in schools.* D.Phil. thesis. Oxford: University of Oxford.
Taylor, C. (1977). What is human agency? In T. Mischel (Ed.), *The self* (103–135). London: Basil Blackwell.
 (1989). *Sources of the self.* Cambridge: Cambridge University Press.
 (1991). *The ethics of authenticity.* Cambridge MA: Harvard University Press.
Tharp, R. G., & Gallimore, R. (1988). *Rousing minds to life.* Cambridge: Cambridge University Press.
Tharp, R. G., Estrada, P. Dalton, S. S., & Yamauchi, I. A. (2000). *Teaching transformed: Receiving excellence, fairness, inclusion and harmony.* Boulder, CA: Westview Press.
Treasury and DfES (2007). Policy review for children and young people: A discussion paper. London: Home Office.
Trevarthen, C. (1980). The foundation of intersubjectivity: Understandings in infants. In D. R. Olson (Ed.), *Developmental psychology and society* (46–95). London: Macmillan.
 (1993). The function of emotion in early infant communication and development. In J. Nadel, & L. Camaioni (Eds.), *New perspectives on early communication development.* London: Routledge.
 (2005). Action and emotion in development of the human self, its sociability and cultural intelligence: Why infants have feelings like ours. In J. Nadeland, & D. Muir (Eds.), *Emotional development* (61–91). Oxford: Oxford University Press.
 (2011a). What young children give to their learning making education work to sustain a community and its culture. *European Early Childhood, Education Research Journal, 19*(2), 173–193. https://doi.org/10.1080/1350293X.2011.574405
 (2011b). What is it like to be a person who knows nothing? Defining the active intersubjective mind of a newborn human being. *Infant and Child Development, 20*(4), 119–135.
Tudge, J. (2008). *The everyday life of young children: Culture, class and child rearing in diverse societies.* Cambridge: Cambridge University Press.
Ullstadius, E (1998). Exploring early imitation: Disputats. Göteborg: Department of Psychology, Göteborg University.
Undervisningsministeriet (1978). U-90 Samlet undervisningsplanlægning frem til 90'erne. Copenhagen: Ministry of Education.
Vadeboncoeur, J. A., & Vellos, R. E. (2016). Recreating social futures: The role of moral imagination in student-teachers' relationships in alternative education. *International Journal of Child, Youth and Family Studies, 7*(2), 307–323.

Vadeboncoeur, J., Panina-Bears, N., & Vellos, R. (2021). Moral imagining in student–teacher relationships in alternative programs: Elaborating a theoretical framework. *Learning, Culture and Social Interaction*, 30 Part B, 100470.

van Oers, B. (1999). Teaching opportunities in play. In M. Hedegaard, & J. Lompscher (Eds.), *Learning activity and development* (268–289). Aarhus: Aarhus University Press.

(2013). Is it play? Towards a reconceptualisation of role play from an activity theory perspective. *European Early Childhood Education Research Journal*, Special Issue: *Promoting play for a better future*, 21(2), 185–198.

Varenne, H., & McDermott, R. (1998). *Successful failure: The school America builds*. Boulder, Colorado: Westview Press.

Vogt, L. A. Jordan, C., & Tharp, R. G. (1993). Explaining school failure, producing school success: Two cases. In E. Jacob, & C. Jordan (Eds.), *Minority education: Anthropological perspectives* (53–65). Norwood, NJ: Ablex.

Vygotsky, L. S. (1967). Play and its role in the mental development of the child. *Soviet Psychology*, 5(3), 6–18. https://doi.org/10.2753/RPO1061-040505036.

Vygotsky, L. (1925/1971). *The psychology of art*. Cambridge: MIT Press.

Vygotsky, L. S. (1982). Legen og dens rolle In Vygotsky m. fl. Om barnets psykiske udvikling. In *Om barnets psykiske udvikling (About the child's psychic development)* (50–71). Copenhagen: Nyt Nordisk Forlag.

(1926/1997). *Educational psychology*. Boca Raton FL: St Lucie Press.

(1989). *The collected works of L. S. Vygotsky. Vol. 1. Problems of general psychology*. New York: Plenum Press.

(1991). The environment. In R. van der Veer, & J. Valsiner (Eds.), *Understanding Vygotsky: A quest for synthesis* (338–354). London: Blackwell Publishing.

(1993). *The collected works of L. S. Vygotsky: Vol. 2. The Fundamentals of defectology*. New York: Plenum Press.

(1994). The problem of the environment. In J. Valsiner, & R. van der Veer (Eds.), *The Vygotsky reader* (347–348). Oxford, UK: Blackwell.

(1997a). *The collected works of L. S. Vygotsky: Vol. 3. Problems of the theory and history of psychology*. New York: Plenum Press.

(1997b). *The collected works of L. S. Vygotsky: Vol. 4. The history of development of higher psychic functions*. New York: Plenum Press.

(1998). *The collected works of L. S. Vygotsky: Vol. 5. Child psychology*. New York: Plenum Press.

(1999). *The collected works of L. S. Vygotsky: Vol. 6. Scientific legacy*. New York: Plenum Press.

(2004). Imagination and creativity in childhood. *Journal of Russian and East European Psychology*, 42(1), 7–97.

(2019). Foundations and pedology. In D. Kellogg, & N. Veresov (Eds.), *Vygotsky's pedological works: Vol. 1*. Singapore: Springer Nature.

(2021). The problem of age. In D. Kellogg, & N. Veresov (Eds.), *L.S. Vygotsky's pedological works: Vol. 2*. Singapore: Springer.

Wartofsky, M. (1979). *Models: Representations and the scientific understanding*. Dordrecht and Boston: D. Reidel.

(1983). The child's construction of the world and the world's construction of the child: From historical epistemology to historical psychology. In F. S. Kessel, & A. W. Siegel (Eds.), *The child and other cultural inventions* (188–215). New York: Praeger.

Wegerif, R. (2010). Dialogue and teaching thinking with technology: Opening, expanding and deepening the 'inter-face'. In K. Littleton, & C. Howe (Eds.), *Educational dialogues* (316–334). London: Routledge.

(2013). *Dialogic: Education for the internet age*. London: Routledge.

Wegerif, R., & Scrimshaw, P. (Eds.) (1997). *Computers and talk in the primary classroom*. Bristol: Multilingual Matters.

Wegerif, R., Mercer, N., & Dawes, L. (1999). From social interaction to individual reasoning: An empirical investigation of a possible sociocultural model of cognitive development. *Learning and Instruction, 9*(6), 493–516. https://doi.org/10.1016/S0959-4752(99)00013-4

(2013). *Dialogic: Education for the internet age*. London: Routledge.

Weiner, B. (1972). Attribution theory, achievement motivation, and the educational process. *Review of Educational Research, 42*(2), 203–215.

Wertsch, J. V. (1998). *Mind as action*. New York: Oxford University Press.

Westbury, I., &. Wilkof, N. J. (Eds.) (1978). *Science, curriculum, and liberal education: Selected essays*. Chicago, IL: University of Chicago Press.

White, G., & Sharp, C. (2007). 'It is different…because you are getting older and growing up': How children make sense of the transition to year 1. *European Early Childhood Education Research Journal, 15*, 87–102.

Willis, P. E. (1977). *Learning to labor: How working class kids get working class jobs*. Aldershot: Gower.

Wineburg, S. S. (1989). Response to Brown, Collins and Duguid's 'Situated cognition and the culture of learning': Remembrance of theories past. *Educational Researcher, 18*(4), 7–10.

Winnicott, D. W. (1977). Leg, en teoretisk fremstilling, Chapter 3. *Leg og virkelighed* (73–92), København: Reitzels Forlag.

Winther-Lindqvist, D. (2012). Developing social identities and motives in school transition. In M. Hedegaard, A. Edwards, & M. Fleer (Eds.), *Motives in children's development* (115–132).Cambridge: Cambridge University Press.

Winther-Lindqvist, D. A. (2017). The role of play in Danish child care. In C. Ringsmose, & G. Kragh-Müller (Eds.), *Nordic social pedagogical approach to early years: International perspectives on early childhood education and development*. Cham: Springer. https://doi.org/10.1007/978-3-319-42557-3_6

Winther-Lindqvist, D. (2018). Social identity in transition: Two boys' stories when changing school. In M. Hedegaard, K. Aronsson, C. Højholt, & O. S. Ulvik. *Children, childhood, and everyday life* (221–240). Charlotte, NC: Information age publishing.

(2019). Becoming a schoolchild: A positive developmental crises. In M. Hedegaard, & M. Fleer (Eds.), *Children's transitions in everyday life and institutions* (47–70). London: Bloomsbury.

(2021). Caring well for children in ECEC from a wholeness approach: The role of moral imagination. *Learning, Culture and Social Interaction, 30*, Part B, 100452. https://doi.org/10.1016/j.lcsi.2020.100452

Wittemeyer, K., Charman, T., Cusack., Guldberg, K., Hastings, P. R., Howlin, P., McNab, N., Parsons, S., Pellicano, E., & Slonims, V. (2011). *Educational provision and outcomes for people on the autism spectrum*. London: Autism Education Trust.

Woodrow, C., & Staples, K. (2019). Relational approaches to supporting transitions into school: Families and early childhood educators working together in Regional Chile. In M. Hedegaard, & A. Edwards (Eds.), *Supporting difficult transitions* (131–152). London: Bloomsbury.

Yates, T., Egeland, B., & Sroufe, A. (2003). Rethinking resilience: A developmental process perspective. In S. Luthar (Ed.), *Resilience and vulnerability: Adaptation in the context of childhood adversities* (242–266). New York: Cambridge University Press.

Zanelato, E., & Urt, S. D. C. (2021). The pedagogical activity for adolescents: Contributions of historical-cultural psychology. *Psychology in Study, 26*. https://doi.org/10.4025/psicolestud.v26i0.45690

Zaporozhets, A. V. (2002). Toward the question of the genesis, function, and structure of emotional processes in the Child. *Journal of Russian & East European Psychology, 40*(3), 45–66. https://doi.org/10.2753/RPO1061-0405400345

Zimmerman, B. J. (2001). Theories of self-regulated learning and academic achievement: An overview and analysis. In B. J. Zimmerman, & D. H. Schunk (Eds.), *Self-regulated learning and academic achievement: Theoretical perspectives* (1–36, 2nd ed.). Mahwah, NJ: Lawrence Erlbaum Associates.

Zuckerman, G. A. (2011). Developmental education. A genetic modelling experiment. *Journal of Russian and East European Psychology*, 49(6), 45–63.

# *Index*

activity setting, 5, 8–10, 19–20, 22–23, 25, 28, 42, 44–47, 84, 86, 120, 127–128, 131, 141, 204, 242, 262–263
adolescence, 33, 36, 43, 137, 179, 236, 238, 240, 249, 256, 258
affect, 2, 34, 70, 81, 94, 140, 148
agency, 2, 4, 6, 9, 12, 14, 19–20, 24, 40, 46, 63, 65, 68, 74, 77, 79, 82, 95, 97, 99–100, 102, 122, 125, 149, 151, 158, 160–161, 163, 166, 168, 173, 176, 178, 180, 182, 184, 187, 191, 193, 195–196, 199, 201, 242, 249, 254, 256–258, 260, 262, 265, 268–269
agentic learner, 14, 94, 147, 166, 170, 183, 265
agentive relation, 71
age periods, 1, 4, 17, 19, 24, 29, 32, 35, 40, 42–43, 47, 106, 136, 149, 213, 264
assessment, 44–45, 63, 86–87, 118–122, 124, 184, 230, 246
assessment for learning, 187–188, 255
assessment material, 120
assessment tools, 120
assessments of a child's social situation, 119

care, 6, 23, 25, 38, 40, 68, 70, 75, 83, 93, 95, 101, 103, 117, 125, 148, 150, 164, 262–263, 265, 268–269
carers, 30, 48–49, 150, 201, 256
child development, 17, 19, 30–31, 33, 43, 46, 65, 83, 86, 95, 269
children's perspectives, 100, 158, 167, 182
collaboration, 5, 13–14, 17, 48–50, 53, 55, 58, 62–63, 65, 67, 123, 151, 154, 188–189, 194–195, 212, 266, 268
common knowledge, 13, 50, 55, 57, 95, 152–153, 157, 163, 165, 173, 181, 193, 248, 259, 262–263
communication, 27, 32–33, 36, 42, 70–72, 74–76, 78–79, 82–83, 87, 93, 100, 102, 119, 122, 125, 135, 190, 199, 234, 253

concept formation, 126, 135, 143–145, 202, 239
conceptual technique, 146
conceptual thinking, 238, 240
conscious relation to the world, 31, 68, 104, 125, 130, 177
core models, 224, 226, 230
core relations, 210–211, 227, 234–235
crises, 5, 7, 30, 34–35, 39, 47, 82, 175, 239
cultural practice, 161, 208, 244
Culturally Sensitive Teaching, 224

Davydov, 130, 146, 161, 186, 202, 208–209
demands, 3, 34, 82, 87, 90, 92, 119, 127–128, 132, 152, 170–171, 175, 180, 187, 244, 256
developmental teaching, 161, 202, 210, 233, 235
dialectical logic, 146
digital literacy, 193, 195
digital resources/tools, 196, 200, 254
double move, 162, 185, 192, 202, 212, 214, 221, 223–224, 231, 234, 251, 265–266
double perspective, 68, 84, 100

education, 46, 55, 75, 101, 130, 144, 149, 157, 159, 161, 164, 179, 230, 248, 250, 257, 266
El'konin, 29, 32, 35, 108, 161, 241
emotional communication, 43
emotional crises, 34
emotional engagement, 2, 185, 202, 252, 262, 264
emotional experience, 4, 9, 31, 35, 111, 142, 146, 204, 237, 239, 242
emotional imagination, 210
emotional orientation, 9, 100
emotional tension, 108, 114, 116
emotions, 126, 128, 138, 140, 148, 167, 204, 236
empirical knowledge, 204, 234
everyday concepts, 103, 126, 131, 133, 135, 137, 142–143, 234, 251, 265
evolution of species, 211–212

# Index

experience, 1, 4, 9, 21, 31, 84, 98, 104, 126, 134, 204–205, 248

families, 1, 14, 23, 28, 48, 54, 59, 98, 119, 163, 171, 197, 199, 224, 244, 250, 267
family practice, 24, 55, 98
forward (moving/looking), 1–2, 5–6, 16–17, 25, 31, 40, 45–46, 49, 60, 73–74, 76, 78, 83, 94, 97–98, 101, 121, 132, 140–142, 145–147, 149, 160–161, 163–164, 169, 173, 175, 177, 179, 183, 185, 188, 190, 197, 208, 211, 231, 234, 236, 242, 256, 258, 263, 265, 268–269
future-making, 238, 241, 243, 248

Galperin, 159, 168, 180, 195, 209, 254–255
germ cell, 186, 210, 215, 222
goal-result board, 185, 221, 227
goals, 29, 33, 69, 101, 142, 180, 184, 199, 266

higher psychic function, 22, 30, 34, 68, 125, 213, 235, 239
higher psychological functions, 30, 68–69

identity, 176, 197, 237, 242, 244, 255
imagination, 9, 68, 79, 102, 104, 107, 109–111, 117, 125, 130, 135, 137–138, 213, 236, 243
imitation, 42–43, 79, 103
infant, 6, 29, 69–70, 72–73, 75–76, 79, 95
institutional practice, 1, 3, 8, 20, 23, 28–29, 33, 45–46, 203, 225, 264
intentional orientation, 70–71, 73, 75–76
intentions, 1, 6, 44, 69, 81, 86, 101, 179, 204
interactive observation, 15, 84–85, 87, 90
interprofessional, 49, 66, 266
intersubjective, 72, 81, 96–97

knowledge forms, 145, 202–204

leader/leadership, 56, 63–64, 267
learning, 5, 27, 32, 39–40, 58, 97, 103–104, 117, 127, 130, 133, 142, 147, 153–154, 173, 183, 186, 208, 222, 233, 253
lifeworlds, 114, 126, 162, 202, 266

manipulative activity, 77
middle school, 170, 195, 256
modelling, 43, 82, 104, 161, 193, 227
motive orientation, 2, 5, 10, 13, 19, 23, 36, 44, 46, 50, 61, 69, 108, 138, 149, 152, 165, 172, 191, 196, 234

narrative knowledge, 204, 234
needs, 4, 22, 28, 31, 47, 75, 142, 164, 258, 261
neoformation, 30, 68, 71, 75, 77, 79, 82, 183, 239, 262

pedagogy, 1, 6, 12, 16, 23, 147, 149, 151, 162, 165, 176, 180, 188, 191, 193, 223, 263–264
personal knowledge, 202–203, 208, 210
play, 7, 27, 33, 38, 42, 79, 83–84, 88, 92, 101–108, 110–111, 115–116, 118, 124–125, 129–130, 137–138, 140, 176–177, 242, 254, 263
play world, 115–116, 126
policy, 149, 189, 198, 200, 231, 250, 262, 266–267
practitioner, 14, 51, 56, 59, 65, 104, 122–123, 199, 247
prevention, 62–63, 198
primary school, 170, 174–176, 190, 192, 200
professional, 13–14, 48–51, 58–59, 63, 65, 67, 85, 148, 150–151, 154, 164, 188, 198, 223, 262, 264–265, 267

Radical Local, 162, 164, 185–186, 190, 194, 197, 203, 224, 226, 230, 235, 266
relational agency, 13, 48, 51, 57, 64, 66, 70, 95, 97–98, 100, 124, 154, 157–158, 165, 173, 248, 258, 262
relational approach, 46, 69–71, 96, 148, 150, 163, 167, 173, 180, 234, 261
relational expertise, 13, 50, 52, 55, 57, 66, 95, 98, 153, 158, 165, 180, 256, 258, 262
Relational Agency Framework – RAF, 65
relational pedagogy, 23, 57, 150–151, 165, 168, 193, 263, 265, 269
resilience, 17, 49, 197–200

school inclusion, 16, 62, 164, 167, 197, 200, 246, 267
scientific concepts, 126, 176, 178–179
self-assessment, 158, 184, 189–190
social inclusion, 15–17, 62, 128, 131, 197–198
social situation of development, 3–4, 10, 15, 24, 30, 32, 40, 44–46, 68, 70, 76, 84, 87, 90, 107, 118, 120–122, 149, 175, 182–183, 196, 200, 263
societal conditions, 33, 70, 224, 236
space of reasons, 57–60, 64, 66, 157, 164
subject matter knowledge, 128, 131–132, 142–143, 149, 152–153, 157, 162, 168, 185–186, 190, 192, 201, 208, 234, 239, 251, 263

## Index

teaching, 3, 17, 28, 62, 65, 126–127, 130, 133–134, 143–144, 147, 151, 153–155, 158–162, 164, 168, 178, 182, 184–185, 187–189, 192, 196, 202–204, 208, 210–212, 214–215, 218, 221, 223–224, 226, 230, 233, 239, 251–252, 265
toddler, 6, 73
traditions, 20, 23–24, 36, 46, 61, 72, 83, 94, 103, 105–106, 120, 224, 229, 263
transition, 10, 30, 34–37, 117, 126, 128, 130, 134, 141–142, 147, 151, 171, 176, 196, 237, 239, 256, 258, 260

values, 4, 7, 12, 16, 22–23, 28, 35, 46, 51, 58, 64, 67, 109, 163, 174, 180, 189, 201, 208, 224, 226, 230–231, 238, 244, 246, 251, 266–267, 269

Wholeness Approach, 9, 19, 21–22, 24, 46, 65, 118, 242, 265
word meanings, 133, 136–137, 143

zone of concern, 54, 59, 180, 182